Jesus
and the
CHURCH

Jesus and the CHURCH

One, Holy, Catholic, Apostolic

AVE MARIA PRESS AVE Notre Dame, Indiana

The Subcommittee on the Catechism, United States Conference of Catholic Bishops, has found that this catechetical high school text, copyright 2014, is in conformity with the *Catechism of the Catholic Church* and that it fulfills the requirements of Core Course IV of the *Doctrinal Elements of a Curriculum Framework for the Development of Catechetical Materials for Young People of High School Age.*

Nhil Obstat: Reverend Monsignor Michael Heintz, PhD
Censor Librorum

Imprimatur: Most Reverend Kevin C. Rhoades
Bishop of Fort Wayne–South Bend

Given at Fort Wayne, Indiana on 17 September 2013.

The *Nihil Obstat* and *Imprimatur* are official declarations that a book or pamphlet is free of doctrinal or moral error. No implication is contained therein that those who have granted the *Nihil Obstat* or *Imprimatur* agree with its contents, opinions, or statements expressed.

Author Consultant:
Richard Gaillardetz, PhD
The Joseph McCarthy Professor of Catholic Systematic Theology
Boston College

Catechetical Consultant:
Michael Horan, PhD
Professor, Department of Theological Studies
Director, Theological Studies Graduate Program
Loyola Marymount University

Pedagogical Consultant:
Michael J. Boyle, PhD
Assistant Director, Center for Catholic School Effectiveness
Assistant Professor-Research and Psychology in the Schools
Loyola University, Chicago

Scripture texts in this work are taken from the *New American Bible with Revised New Testament and Revised Psalms* © 1991, 1986, 1970 Confraternity of Christian Doctrine, Washington, DC, and are used by permission of the copyright owner. All Rights Reserved. No part of the *New American Bible* may be reproduced without permission in writing from the copyright owner.

English translation of the *Catechism of the Catholic Church* for the United States of America copyright © 1994, United States Catholic Conference, Inc.—Libreria Editrice Vaticana. English translation of the *Catechism of the Catholic Church: Modifications from the Editio Typica* copyright © 1997, United States Catholic Conference, Inc.—Libreria Editrice Vaticana.

Founded in 1865, Ave Maria Press is a ministry of the United States Province of Holy Cross.

Engaging Minds, Hearts, and Hands for Faith® is a trademark of Ave Maria Press, Inc.

www.avemariapress.com

Paperback: ISBN-13 978-1-59471-212-8

E-book: ISBN-13 978-1-59471-538-9

Project Editor: Michael Amodei, Executive Editor, Adolescent Catechesis.

Cover images © W.P. Wittman Photography / superstock.com / NET Ministries, Inc.

Cover and text design by Andy Wagoner.

Printed and bound in the United States of America.

ENGAGING MINDS, HEARTS, AND HANDS FOR FAITH

An education that is complete is the one in which hands and heart are engaged as much as the mind. We want to let our students try their learning in the world and so make prayers of their education.

Bl. Basil Moreau
Founder of the Congregation of Holy Cross

In this text you will:

 learn the four characteristics or marks of the Church—one, holy, catholic, apostolic—and how they are linked together.

 realize that only through Faith can we recognize that the Church possesses these marks as gifts of God.

 be encouraged to draw on the marks of the Church to help fulfill the Church's mission of witnessing to the Gospel of Jesus Christ.

CONTENTS

1

WHY
WE NEED THE
CHURCH

"I'm Spiritual BUT NOT RELIGIOUS"

A recent survey of eighteen- to twenty-nine-year-olds noted that they described themselves as "more spiritual than religious." One respondent explained: "I don't need to define myself to any community by putting myself in a box labeled Baptist, or Catholic, or Muslim. When I die, I believe all my accounting will be done to God, and that when I enter the eternal realm, I will not walk through a door with a label on it."

Others said they are "spiritual but not religious" because organized religion denigrates itself with power struggles that often involve ego and money. Religion, they said, was associated with church attendance and commitment to orthodox beliefs.

Father James Martin, S.J., said the term "SBNR"(spiritual but not religious) may also be associated with something else: egotism.

"Being spiritual but not religious can lead to complacency and self-centeredness," Martin said. "If it's just you and God in your room, and a religious community makes no demands on you, why help the poor?"

FOCUS QUESTION

Why do people **NEED TO** BELONG to the Catholic Church?

We Are Meant to Be Together

MAIN IDEA
The Church calls and gathers people together to support them in achieving their fullest sense of identity.

Three childhood friends, now college freshmen, Nick, Terry and Mike, took advantage of their mutual spring break to go backpacking together at Big Bend National Park. The park is located along the Rio Grande River, which serves as the border between Mexico and Texas.

They had a hard time explaining the attraction of Big Bend to their other friends. It was the stark beauty of the place that convinced them to fill their week with an arduous hike rather than party with some other college kids at a beach resort. At the end of their first day, the group made it to the top of the south rim of the Chisos before sunset. From there they gazed out for miles toward Mexico. They walked to the very edge of the rim, peered down to a drop of thousands of feet, while also watching the sun disappear on the horizon, creating an exploding backdrop of purplish red hues.

They were all silent for several moments, before Terry tried to put it all into words. "You want to talk to me about God? There's God," he said pointing to the majestic sunset. "*This* is my church."

Terry's remark elicited familiar groans and rolled eyes from his friends. They had heard him make comments like this before. Nick and Mike were both practicing Catholics, and Terry once was. All three friends went to Catholic grade school together. But Terry had stopped going to Mass and practicing his faith after that. From time to time he would also bring up "issues" he had with the Church on some of the core Catholic beliefs. And, he would always fall back on similar words as he expressed on the south rim of the Chisos: "I am a spiritual person. I don't need to go to church to be with God." Pointing to his heart, Terry would often say, "My religion is right here."

NOTE TAKING

Collating Examples. As you read the section, create a chart like this to help you list positive and negative examples of individualism and consumerism. Use examples from the text and from your own experience.

	Positive Examples	Negative Examples
Individualism		
Consumerism		

You may wonder about the sighs and concern coming from Nick and Mike. What was wrong with Terry's perspective? Certainly a tenet of Catholicism is that God is Creator of the universe and he can be experienced in the beauty of his handiwork. And, at the center of Catholicism is God's incarnate Son, Jesus Christ, who calls each person to a personal, heartfelt relationship with him. Aren't all Catholics called to be "spiritual people"?

What bothered Nick and Mike was not Terry's desire to be spiritual. Rather, they took Terry's words and actions to mean that he didn't feel a need any longer to be a member of the Catholic Church, or any church, for that matter. Nick and Mike understood that being part of the Church is essential for an authentic relationship with God that leads to a Christian life. Because, as Pope Francis tweeted in September 2013, "We do not become Christians by ourselves. Faith is above all a gift from God which is given to us in and through the Church."

Yet Terry's attitude is a common one today. Various surveys reveal that a majority of people in developed nations like the United States believe in God, but fewer than half of them attend a place of worship on a regular basis. More and more people, including those in the eighteen- to twenty-nine-year-old category now, like Terry, describe themselves as "spiritual but not religious." This group includes those who hold to maintaining only a "private relationship with God" or who may blend writings, beliefs, and practices from several religions together to form their own strand of faith and practice.

In order to understand more about how this "SBNR" phenomenon arose in recent times, it's helpful to look at two forces in modern life: *individualism* and *consumerism*.

Individualism and Religion

There is nothing wrong with promoting and celebrating your individuality. God created you uniquely in his own divine image. God knows and loves each person as *distinct* and *unique*. Being made in God's image, you possess "the dignity of a person, who is not just something, but someone" (*CCC*, 357). The Book of Psalms recognizes how God values the individual:

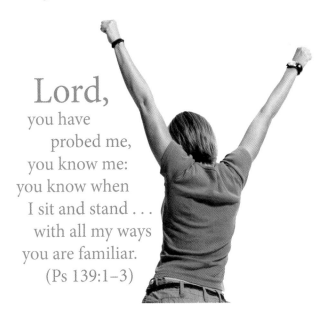

Lord, you have probed me, you know me: you know when I sit and stand . . . with all my ways you are familiar. (Ps 139:1–3)

Jesus, too, reminds us of the personal interest God takes in each of us:

Are not five sparrows sold for two small coins? Yet not one of them has escaped the notice of God. Even the hairs of your head have all been counted. Do not be afraid. You are worth more than many sparrows. (Lk 12:6–7)

Individualism only becomes a problem when it drives people apart from one another. When this happens, the individual creates his or her own definition of self and of the world. The person may not be willing to listen or dialogue with others. Perpetuating the value of "going it alone," modern media and culture have sometimes celebrated the more romantic types of individualism. Think about the "heroic loner" you have seen in film or on television who ignores people in authority and institutions, and plays by his own rules.

In fact, people in modern society today prize personal freedom and will fight for individual rights (e.g., the right to a free education, the right to own property). However, they may be slower to embrace common commitments (e.g., voting, paying taxes, assisting the poor). Put it this way: many people believe they have a right to a trial by jury, yet don't want to serve on one!

This individualist philosophy translates to the experience many people have of religion and Church. They may feel compelled to join with others who believe in God to worship, pray, socialize, and serve, but when they find themselves disagreeing with an aspect of the faith, they may retreat back to their autonomous world. Or, alternatively, they may simply grow tired or bored with the effort it takes to join in with the others. The bottom line is that many people do not feel that belonging to a church is vital to their maintaining a relationship with God.

Consumerism and Religion

Along with individualism, consider the far-reaching impact of how consumerism (the practice of an ever-increasing acquisition and consumption of goods) factors into how people participate in religion.

God created a good world to sustain us. Consumerism turns the goodness that God has provided into "packaged products" or material goods for personal enjoyment, with little or no reminder of the generosity of God or the effect on others. Consumerism also fosters an "upgrading mentality." To understand, just think of the frequent cell phone upgrades many people seem to require.

What does consumerism have to do with religion? Put simply, from a consumer's perspective it is easy to think of religion and religious experience as a kind of product to be consumed with little thought of its connectedness to its tradition and doctrine or to faith. The upgrading mentality comes into play, too.

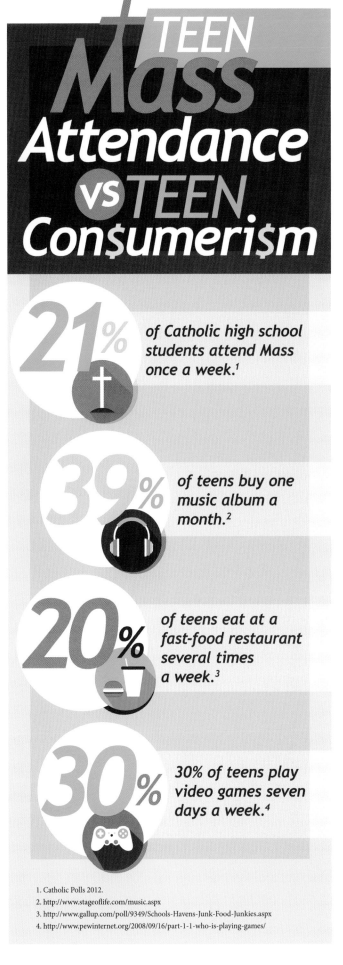

TEEN Mass Attendance vs TEEN Consumerism

21% of Catholic high school students attend Mass once a week.[1]

39% of teens buy one music album a month.[2]

20% of teens eat at a fast-food restaurant several times a week.[3]

30% 30% of teens play video games seven days a week.[4]

1. Catholic Polls 2012.
2. http://www.stageoflife.com/music.aspx
3. http://www.gallup.com/poll/9349/Schools-Havens-Junk-Food-Junkies.aspx
4. http://www.pewinternet.org/2008/09/16/part-1-1-who-is-playing-games/

Some people search out a church with better music or a more glitzy media presentation or a pastor who preaches a message more to their liking. The upgrading mentality also leads others to cobble together a personal spirituality that may combine the Christian story with myths, symbols, and rituals drawn from other religious traditions. Such a person might attend a contemporary retreat that includes participation in a Native American "sweat lodge" ritual. The person's prayer might begin with a meditation on a Buddhist koan, followed by some spiritual reading from a poem of the Sufi sage, Rumi. It's easy to see how this type of religious consumerism coupled with individualism could lead a person to describe himself or herself as more "spiritual than religious."

Another problem with viewing religion from a consumer perspective is that worship, prayer, and community can be subtly transformed into a religious product to be consumed and not a communal religious practice and system of beliefs that bind people together with others in a common commitment to God and neighbor.

Called to Church

In the First Letter to the Corinthians. St. Paul describes the Church as the "Body of Christ":

As a body is one though it has many parts, and all parts of the body, though many, are one body, so also Christ. (1 Cor 12:12)

St. Paul explained that just as the various parts of a human body (arms, legs, eyes, ears, etc.) rely on one another to function as a human body, so the members of the Church must rely on one another if they are to live as God intended. St. Paul's understanding of the Church stands in stark contrast to the notion of people coming together for a short time to fill up and satisfy their needs, only to return to their solitary lives unchanged. Such a sense of Church would have made no sense to St. Paul, who did not believe that individuals define the Church; but that the Church is what gives individuals their fullest sense of identity. In other words, St. Paul believed that individuals participate in the life of the Church because, at the very core of our being, everyone *needs* the Church.

In fact, the very term *church* points out the individual's need to be together with others. The word *church* means a convocation or assembly. The English word for Church translates to the Latin *ecclesia* and from the Greek *ek-ka-lein*, meaning to "call out of." People are literally called from their isolation to togetherness. As the *Catechism of the Catholic Church* teaches, "[in] the Church, God is 'calling together' his people from all the ends of the earth" (*CCC*, 751).

SECTION ASSESSMENT

NOTE TAKING

Use some of the examples in your completed chart to help you answer the following questions.

1. What are some positive reasons people may attempt to remain autonomous in their faith life?

2. What does consumerism have to do with religion?

COMPREHENSION

3. What did St. Paul teach about the oneness of the members of the Church?

4. What is the meaning of the word *church*?

CRITICAL THINKING

5. Provide examples of how the individualistic mentality is present in the life of your peer group.

6. Describe an occasion when you encountered religion as a product rather than a way of life.

SECTION 1
The Origins
of the Church

The Catholic Church has more than 1.2 billion members worldwide. This makes the Church one of the largest institutions in the world. Indeed, when people think of the Catholic Church, they may be as likely to think in terms of her institutional structure, and her visible dimension, such as the hierarchy (pope, bishops, priests), schools, or parish churches, as with the sacraments, Scripture, Mary and the saints, and Jesus himself. Although the Church has a human and visible structure to support her spiritual dimension, to understand the Church, one must look past what is visible and look to her origin in the Blessed Trinity.

To understand the origins of the Church, you can meditate on the Church "in the Holy Trinity's plan and her progressive realization in history" (*CCC*, 758). What does this mean? Simply, the creation of humankind was always a part of God's eternal plan. This plan continues to be carried out in history.

God created the world with people in mind, intending that everyone live in loving relationship with him and one another. When sin entered the world, God did not abandon humankind. Rather, he gradually formed humans into the family of God, believers in his Son, Jesus Christ, and the Church. This was done so that all people might be saved. Second-century theologian Clement of Alexandria (d. 215) wrote:

NOTE TAKING

Sequencing Events. As you read this section, create a chart like this one to help you label the following events in chronological order for founding of the Church: Sinai covenant, New Covenant, covenant with Abraham, Babylonian Exile, Protoevangelium, Prophets, and monarchy. Write brief notes to explain each event's significance.

Events	Notes
1.	
2.	
3.	
4.	
5.	
6.	
7.	

Just as God's will is creation and is called "the world," so his intention is the salvation of men, and it is called "the Church."

The Second Vatican Council reemphasized the important truth that the Church was foreshadowed or "already present in figure at the beginning of the world" (*Lumen Gentium*, 2), echoing the words of an ancient Christian writer that "the world was created for the sake of the Church." It is the Church that makes your communion with God possible.

Preparation for the Church in the Old Testament

The teaching of the creation accounts in the Book of Genesis is that God created the first humans in his own image, and endowed them with both *intellect* (an ability to ask questions, to wonder, and to learn) and *free will* (the power to make choices with the possibility that they could love God and one another). God made himself known to Adam and Eve from the time of creation, offering his intimate communion with them and clothing them "with resplendent grace and justice" (*CCC*, 54).

When the serpent tempted the woman to eat the fruit of the forbidden tree in the garden, it was with the promise that "your eyes will be opened and you will be like gods who know what is good and what is bad" (Gn 3:5). Instead of living lives of harmonious relationship with God and with one another, the first man and first woman sinned by believing they might find fulfillment in possessing perfect autonomy and control over the world, that is, that they could be "like gods." Adam and Eve's sin, which is called **Original Sin**, damaged their relationship with God and with one another. It also would affect these same relationships for all the human family.

Yet, from the chaos created by sin, God began to gather together the Church. After speaking to Adam and Eve, he said to the serpent:

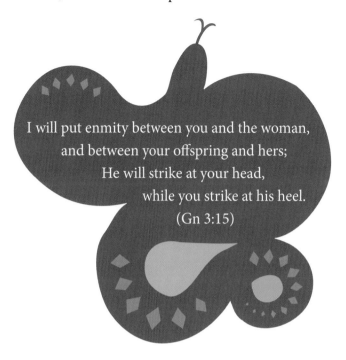

I will put enmity between you and the woman,
and between your offspring and hers;
He will strike at your head,
while you strike at his heel.
(Gn 3:15)

This passage in Genesis is called the **Protoevangelium**, or first Gospel. It was the first announcement that God would send a Messiah and a Redeemer, who is a descendent of Eve. From then on, God began to gather those who feared him and did what was right and acceptable in his eyes (see Acts 10:35).

Preparing with a Covenant

The *remote* preparation of the Church began when God called Abraham, a nomadic farmer, and promised that he would be "father of a host of nations" (Gn 17:5). Although Abraham and his wife, Sarah, were advanced

> **Original Sin** The sin of disobedience committed by Adam and Eve that resulted in their loss of original holiness and justice and their becoming subject to sin and death. Original Sin also describes the fallen state of human nature into which all generations of people are born. Jesus Christ came to save all people from Original Sin (and all sin).
>
> **Protoevangelium** A term that means "the first gospel," which is found in Genesis 3:15, when God revealed he would send a Savior to redeem the world.

God said: "I will make your descendants as numerous as the stars in the sky" (Gn 26:4).

in years, God promised them a son. They and their descendants were invited to enter with God into a mutually binding **covenant**. God willingly bound himself forever to this group of people and gave them a unique and pivotal role in his plan for the world. Catholics today are counted among Abraham's descendants, whom God promised would be as numerous as the stars in the sky.

The Church's *immediate* preparation began with God's covenant with the Israelites at Mount Sinai. The origins of Israel's sense of itself as a community began not with any human act, but with God's initiative. The Israelites were *chosen* or *elected* by God and became his

> **Covenant** The open-ended contract of love between God and human beings. Jesus' Death and Resurrection sealed God's New Covenant of love for all time.

Chosen People bound by a covenant. He told Moses that they were to be a priestly or consecrated People:

> Therefore, if you hearken to my voice and keep my covenant, you shall be my special possession, dearer to me than all other people. (Ex 19:5)

The Hebrew word used to describe the special relationship God had with Israel is *hesed*, which means "steadfast love." This steady, permanent, and faithful love of God for his people provided the basis for the Israelite's sense of community. This love was experienced concretely by the Law, which Moses received from God on Mount Sinai.

From the Law, the Israelites learned not only of a proper relationship they were to forge with God, but how they were to treat one another. For example, they were to show special concern for widows, orphans, and strangers:

> You shall not oppress an alien; you know well how it feels to be an alien, since you were once aliens yourselves in the land of Egypt. (Ex 23:9)

While other ancient religions affirmed an obligation to care for the poor and powerless (e.g., the ancient Babylonian Code of Hammurabi demanded that the kind show concern for the poor), Israel was unique in its conviction that the responsibility for the well-being of the vulnerable in the community be shared by all people, and not just those in leadership.

Israel's history did not proceed without division and sinfulness. After a time of unification under one king, political disputes led to the division of the Chosen People into two kingdoms, Israel and Judah. The ensuing years were marked by infidelity to God and ignorance of the needs of the poor. As a result, both the Southern Kingdom (Judah) and the Northern Kingdom (Israel) were plunged into periods of exile where the people were removed from their holy homeland and taken captive by foreign nations.

The MYSTERY of the Church

The Church is a mystery because her nature can never be grasped by the power of reason alone. The Church is a visible, tangible, historical reality, but she also embodies spirit of the invisible, intangible God.

Chapter I of the Second Vatican Council document *Lumen Gentium*, or the "Dogmatic Constitution on the Church," describes the mystery of the Church. Read the chapter. Outline the eight sections of the chapter using three concise sentences for each section. Two examples (for sections 1 and 5) are listed below.

SECTION 1
- Christ is the light of the nations and he is present in the Church.

SECTION 5
- Christ inaugurated the Church by preaching the Good News of the coming of the Kingdom of God.

Display your report as a graphic organizer.

In response to these abuses, God sent prophets to both warn the people of their sinfulness and to announce a *new and eternal covenant*. In practice, such rededication first translated to a restoration of the "survivors of Israel" in order to make them "a light to the nations, that my salvation may reach to the ends of the earth" (Is 49:6).

This special vision of Israel's place among nations had another effect on its understanding of community. In the period after the Babylonian Exile, Israel began to separate itself from its neighbors due to the belief that the Chosen People had been punished for previously intermingling with Gentile nations. Yet, this was not the only understanding or practice.

The Book of Jonah imparts that after the prophet Jonah was charged with bringing judgment on a sinful, pagan people, the Ninevites, he was surprised to find his announcement met with their communal penance for their sins. Accepting the repentance of this pagan people, God relented and did not carry out the evil that he had threatened to do to them (see Jonah 3:10). The message of this story is that God's compassion is not limited to Israel; it extends to all who are open to the call of repentance. Israel was to be a model of what God intended for *all* people.

In the Old Testament, God acts over and over to form a people who are chosen not because of merit, but simply because of his compassion and love for them. Though as a people, the Israelites (later called "Jews") frequently abandoned the demands of a loving relationship with God, he refused to abandon them. They were a people bound by a promise, a covenant that was not of their making.

In fact, in spite of their ongoing sinfulness, God announced through the prophets this new and eternal covenant. He was committed to the Jewish people as the faith community from which his own Son, Jesus, would be born. When the proper time came, God himself became a member of that community. The only

Son of God was entrusted not only to this Chosen People, but to humanity itself. In the Incarnation, the Second Person of the Trinity came down from Heaven and assumed human nature. It was through this great gift that Christ instituted the **New Covenant** specifically through his **Paschal Mystery**:

> he called a people together made up of Jews and Gentiles which would be one, not according to flesh, but in the Spirit, and it would be the new people of God. (*Lumen Gentium*, 9)

New Covenant The climax of Salvation History, the coming of Jesus Christ, the fullness of God's Revelation.

Paschal Mystery Christ's work of redemption, accomplished principally by his Passion Death, Resurrection, and glorious Ascension. This mystery is commemorated and made present through the sacraments, especially the Eucharist.

SECTION ASSESSMENT

NOTE TAKING

1. What event began the immediate preparation for the Church?
2. What was the new message from the Book of Jonah regarding the experience of God's compassion?

VOCABULARY

3. Define *Protoevangelium*.
4. Explain how Original Sin put into motion the beginning of the Church.

COMPREHENSION

5. Summarize the prophets' announcement on the nature of the People of God.

DISCUSSION AND REFLECTION

6. What can people do today to promote the message of justice found in the Book of Jonah?
7. Meet with a partner. Take turns brainstorming words associated with the Church. Write all of the suggestions. Circle three that are most prominent to you. Write about one of the words. What does it say about the meaning of the Church?

SECTION 2
The Church Is Instituted by Christ

MAIN IDEA
The Church was born from Christ's self-giving love that was expressed perfectly in the Paschal Mystery.

In a Catholic high school religion class, a student studying the differences in chronology and themes among the four Gospels commented to his teacher: "Jesus should have just written his own Gospel and saved us all of this trouble!" The teacher responded succinctly: "Jesus didn't write a Gospel because he was too busy founding a Church!"

The point is well taken. Jesus called, taught, and formed a group of **disciples** who would carry on his mission. In doing so, Jesus instituted the Church by ushering in the **Kingdom of God** on earth.

The Kingdom of God might be thought of as "the world as God would have it to be." Or, think of it this way: the Kingdom of God is in a state of "already, not yet." What this means is that in Jesus of Nazareth, the Kingdom of God is *already* present in a new and

disciples Followers of Christ. A disciple is someone who learns from and follows Jesus and who accepts a share of his ministry in the world.

Kingdom of God The reign or rule of God. The Kingdom of God has begun with the coming of Jesus Christ. It will exist in its perfect form at the end of time.

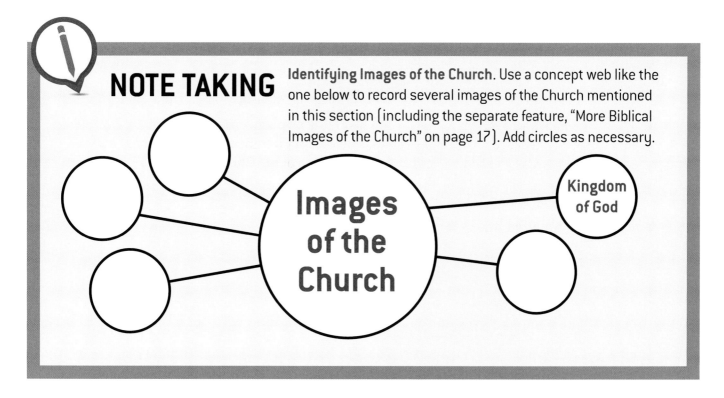

NOTE TAKING

Identifying Images of the Church. Use a concept web like the one below to record several images of the Church mentioned in this section (including the separate feature, "More Biblical Images of the Church" on page 17). Add circles as necessary.

Images of the Church

Kingdom of God

unprecedented way. At the same time, God's Kingdom has *not yet* transformed all creation; that will not take place until the end of all history. In the meantime, the Church is the "way to Salvation." This "already, but not yet" quality of the Church is evident in many of the parables Jesus told about the Kingdom. For example, in one parable Jesus said that the Kingdom of God

> is like a mustard seed that, when it is sown in the ground, is the smallest of all the seeds on the earth. But once it is sown, it springs up and becomes the largest of plants and puts forth large branches, so that the birds of the sky can dwell in its shade. (Mk 4:31–32)

It is also important to remember the Old Testament origins of the Kingdom and the Church. The Church's foundation is in the Chosen People and the Law of Mount Sinai of the Old Testament. Christ did not come to abolish the Law. But he did preach a radically new understanding of it. Jesus emphasized that in the faithful application of the 613 laws of the Torah, the command that expresses the inseparability of love of God and love of neighbor must guide all of the other laws. His preaching and ministry became a threat to many, both for political and religious reasons. The occupying Romans were doubtless concerned that Jesus of Nazareth would destabilize their hold in the region. Some of the Jewish leaders, particularly those associated with the Temple, saw Jesus' message as a threat to their own religious authority.

The Church Is Born on the Cross

Another ancient tradition affirms that the Church, in a certain sense, was born on the Cross. The concerns and actions of the Romans and some of the Jewish leaders led to the events of the Paschal Mystery. The

Catholics usually display (and wear) a crucifix with Christ present on the Cross rather than an empty Cross as a reminder of the saving act of his Death.

Second Vatican Council connected Christ's Death on the Cross with the founding of the Church:

> For it was from the side of Christ as he slept the sleep of death upon the cross that there came forth the "wondrous sacrament of the whole Church." (*Sacrosanctum Concilium*, 5)

The *Catechism of the Catholic Church* adds:

> As Eve was formed from the sleeping Adam's side, so the Church was born from the pierced heart of Christ hanging dead on the cross. (*CCC*, 766)

Jesus freely chose to go to the Cross. In so doing, he demonstrated the breadth and depth of the Father's love for his people. On the Cross, Jesus' complete gift is dramatically witnessed. Jesus' entire life was an act of complete self-giving love and it is this perfect expression of divine love of the Cross that brings about Salvation of humankind.

However, the full meaning of Christ's saving work does not *end* with the Cross. Jesus was crucified to atone for human sinfulness. A mystery of the Cross is that it finds its fulfillment in the Resurrection of Jesus. It is the Resurrection that reveals that the power of God's love, incarnate in Christ, triumphs over the power of death. In a world created good by God, sin, evil, and death cannot have the final word. The God of Abraham, Isaac, and Jacob is a God of the living, not of the dead (see Mark 12:26–27). What the Father accomplished in Jesus, he can accomplish in you through your participation in the life of the Church. Your own resurrection is one of the fruits of Christ's Death and Resurrection.

The love of God encountered in the Life, Death, and Resurrection of Jesus is now present in human history through the ministry of the Church. Catholics today share in both the struggles and graces of the Cross. They are Christ for the world.

Jesus Remains Present in the Church

Today, Jesus remains truly present in the Church, though not in flesh and bone. The Church is the Body of Christ in which Christ himself is the head. "Not only is she gathered *around him*; she is united *in him*, in his body" (*CCC*, 789). Christ is present in several ways in the Church but "most *especially in the Eucharistic species*" (*Sacrosanctum Concilium*, 7). In the Eucharist "the body and blood, together with the soul and divinity of our Lord Jesus Christ and, therefore, *the whole Christ is truly, really, and substantially* contained" (Council of Trent: DS 1651). This presence of Jesus is called the **Real Presence**.

Jesus' presence in the Church is a great blessing and privilege for all Catholics. The Church is where you are able to be with Jesus and, in turn, be sent out by him as his his follower.

Catholics sit and pray before the Blessed Sacrament. They bless God because he first blesses them. They adore his Real Presence in the Eucharist as a reminder that he is God and they are his creations. Blessing and adoration lead to praise.

> **Real Presence** The unique and true presence of Christ in the Eucharist under the species or appearance of bread and wine.

While there are certainly contemporary people who might imagine themselves as able to be Christian disciples apart from the Church, this really isn't possible. At some point most people realize that despite their best intentions and their many gifts and talents, there is a real limit to anything they can accomplish on their own. This is also the case in their search for God himself. When St. Augustine wrote in his *Confessions* that "our hearts are restless, Lord, until they rest in you," he had already found God *in the Church*.

Through Baptism, Catholics "are incorporated into Christ and integrated into the People of God" (*CCC*, 897). Jesus continues to invite all people into relationship with God the Father through the Church that he instituted. It is in the Church that people are able to continue to know and experience the healing and forgiving love of God. It is in the Church that you believe and witness to your faith in what Jesus revealed, that is:

- he came from God the Father
- he and the Father are one
- he has returned to the Father
- you will share in this love

This is the Good News of Jesus Christ, given to the Church in Faith. You respond to God's gift of Faith with free assent to what he has revealed in the Life, Death, and Resurrection of Jesus. Your response, guided and sustained by the Holy Spirit, is offered to God and shared with the world through the life of the Church.

The Kingdom of God is like...

Create a PowerPoint or video presentation on the Kingdom of God. Create your own metaphors and similes for the Kingdom that can be illustrated with back-to-back slides. For example:

Slide A

The Kingdom of God is like

Slide B

Intersperse other descriptions of the Kingdom of God from the Gospels into your presentation. See, for example:

- Matthew 13:31–32
- Matthew 13:33
- Matthew 18:1–5
- Matthew 18:23–35
- Mark 4:26–29
- Luke 7:18–23

Choose accompanying background music to intersperse with your presentation. Share the final results with your classmates and peers.

MORE BIBLICAL IMAGES OF
the Church

The Bible—both the Old and New Testaments—offers several other images of the Church. Each of these images helps us to understand more about our communion with other Catholics and our communion with God in the Persons of Father, Son, and Holy Spirit.

BODY OF CHRIST

The Church as the Body of Christ is the most complete image. The origin of this image comes from Jesus himself who taught that what we do to others we do to him (see Matthew 25:40). St. Paul highlighted this image further when he wrote: "Now you are Christ's body, and individually parts of it" (1 Cor 12:27).

To St. Paul, there was no such thing as a solitary Christian. Life with Christ is always a *shared life*. Though all the parts of the body share a common existence, they could not exist when severed from the whole. For example, a hand is only able to function as a hand when it is part of the rest of the body. He emphasized that Christians are bound together by Faith and Baptism. Paul also believed that the relationship to the Church established in Baptism was further nourished through the celebration of Eucharist.

You may have encountered some Christians who describe their faith in individual terms, such as an experience of being "born again" or of "accepting Jesus as my personal Savior." Although it is important to cherish the value of a personal relationship with Christ, this way of describing the relationship can miss an important point. Christian living is not about "inviting Christ into *my* life"; rather, it is about being drawn into *Christ's* life, principally through initiation into Christ's Body, the Church. French theologian Yves de Monthceuil explained: "It is not Christians who, in coming together, constitute the Church; it is the Church that makes us Christians."

VINE AND BRANCHES

Jesus used the image of a vine and branches to describe his relationship to each of us and to the Church:

> I am the vine, you are the branches. Whoever remains in me and I in him will bear much fruit, because without me you can do nothing. (Jn 15:5)

As with the image of the Body of Christ, the image of Church as a vine with branches teaches that all are members of the Lord's Body, each with individual talents and duties, but all united in the Holy Spirit to Jesus. The vine and branches image of Church emphasizes common goals, ideals, and intimate sharing. The Church forms a community with a life, tradition, and story of her own. The Church is responsible for continuing God's work of building up the community and serving others.

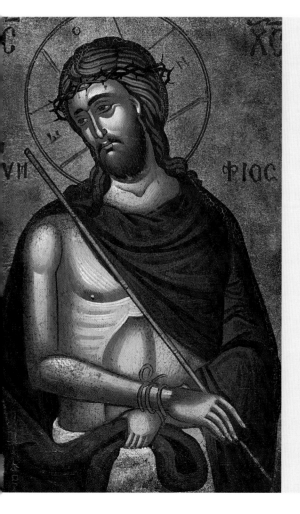

BRIDE OF CHRIST

The Old Testament established the image of Christ as the bridegroom and the Church as the bride. For example, the prophet Hosea in remaining faithful to his harlot wife, Gomer, represents God's covenantal fidelity to the spiritual philandering of Israel (see Hosea 2:21–25).

The bride of Christ image is likewise referred to in the New Testament. John the Baptist named Jesus as the Bridegroom, "the one who has the bride" (Jn 3:29). In Ephesians 5:21–32, St. Paul compared the relationship between Christ and the Church as a husband and wife being of one flesh (quoting Genesis 2:23).

In a covenantal marriage two people commit themselves to one another for the rest of their lives. For this reason, Christ instituted the Sacrament of Matrimony. A man and a woman become living symbols of God's love for his people.

Christ has entered a similar covenant with the Church, and has filled her with his grace. Headed by Christ, the bridegroom of the bride, the Church is the dwelling place of the Holy Spirit. The Church completes the mission of Christ and the Holy Spirit on earth.

SECTION ASSESSMENT

NOTE TAKING

1. What is your favorite image of the Church?

2. What do each of the images of the Church presented in this section have in common?

VOCABULARY

Fill in the blanks of each of the following definitions with a glossary term from this section.

3. _____ are those who learn from and follow Jesus and who accept a share of his ministry in the world.

4. God's saving love is most fully revealed in the _____.

5. The _____ will exist in its perfect form at the end of time.

COMPREHENSION

6. Explain the dimensions of the Kingdom of God as "already, not yet."

7. What was Jesus' understanding of the Law of Mount Sinai?

8. What does it mean to say that the Church was born on the Cross of Christ?

CRITICAL THINKING

9. How does the life and history of the Church model the Parable of the Mustard Seed?

SECTION 3
The Holy Spirit and the Church

MAIN IDEA
On Pentecost, Jesus fulfilled his promise to send the Holy Spirit to direct and guide the work of the Church.

After the Death of Jesus, the **Apostles** and other disciples were disoriented and confused. The One they had believed to be the Messiah had died a criminal's

Apostles Originally, the term referred to the Twelve whom Jesus chose to help him in his earthly ministry. The successors of the Twelve Apostles are the bishops. In the widest sense, the term refers to all of Christ's disciples whose mission is to preach his Gospel in word and deed. Apostles are those sent to be Christ's ambassadors to continue his work.

death. But then the Risen Christ began to appear to them and everything changed. They connected Jesus to their history as a Chosen People. They came to believe that Jesus was the Son of God, with power over sin and death. The four Gospels provide various accounts of what happened, but they agree that Jesus appeared to Mary Magdalene and a group of women, to Peter and James, to all the Apostles, and to two disciples on the road to Emmaus.

In the First Letter to the Corinthians, one of the earliest New Testament books, St. Paul wrote that Jesus "appeared to more than five hundred brothers at once, most of whom are still living, though some have fallen asleep" (1 Cor 15:6).

The Acts of the Apostles, a companion to the Gospel of Luke, chronicles the days after the Resurrection prior to Jesus' Ascension to Heaven. Some of the disciples, who perhaps had once imagined that the Messiah would be a political ruler who would restore self-rule to the Jews and remove the Roman oppression, asked the Risen Jesus: "Lord, are you at this time

NOTE TAKING

Reading Extension. When St. Peter's speech at Pentecost is referenced in this section (page 22), read the entire speech in the Acts of the Apostles (Acts 2:14–41). Answer the following questions.

1. What were Peter and the other Apostles accused of? (vs. 15)

2. Which prophet does he quote? (vss. 17–21)

3. How was Jesus different from King David? (vss. 29–35)

4. What did Peter say those who heard him must do? (vs. 38)

going to restore the kingdom to Israel?" (Acts 1:6). Jesus answered them:

> "It is not for you to know the times or seasons that the Father has established by his own authority. But you will receive power when the holy Spirit comes upon you, and you will be my witnesses in Jerusalem, throughout Judea and Samaria, and to the ends of the earth." (Acts 1:8)

Jesus' earthly life and ministry were over, but his work of Redemption would continue through his followers in the Church. Jesus' promise was to send the Holy Spirit to direct and guide their work. He fulfilled this promise on **Pentecost**.

> **Pentecost** The day when the Holy Spirit descended on the Apostles and gave them the power to preach with conviction the message that Jesus is risen and is Lord of the universe.

The Events of Pentecost

Pentecost was a traditional Jewish harvest feast that took place fifty days after Passover. The Acts of the Apostles records that the Apostles, Mary, Jesus' Mother, and some other disciples were gathered in prayer and waiting in an upper room in Jerusalem. This was the same place where Jesus had shared his Last Supper. The room filled with sounds like a violent wind. Acts describes how the Holy Spirit descended on those in the room in the form of "tongues of fire."

Immediately, being "filled with the Holy Spirit" (Act 2:4), the Apostles, and especially Peter, began speaking about Jesus to all the Jews who were in the city from many regions of the Roman Empire. Even though the pilgrims spoke in several different languages, they understood what the Apostles were saying. Peter recounted for them the entire story of Salvation from their Scripture (read Acts 2:14–41),

The Upper Room is the place in Jerusalem where Jesus held the Last Supper. Also known as the Cenacle (Latin for "upper room"), it was also the site of Pentecost. Since the fourth century the Upper Room has been a popular site for pilgrims. A niche on the site is traditionally held to be the burial place of King David.

explaining how Jesus Christ was the culmination of their history:

> You who are Israelites, hear these words. Jesus the Nazorean was a man commended to you by God with mighty deeds, wonders, and signs, which God worked through him in your midst, as you yourselves know. This man, delivered up by the set plan and foreknowledge of God, you killed, using lawless men to crucify him. But God raised him up, releasing him from the throes of death, because it was impossible for him to be held by it. . . . Therefore let the whole house of Israel know for certain that God has made him both Lord and Messiah, this Jesus whom you crucified. (Acts 2:22–25, 36)

Peter's powerful testimony moved his fellow Jews. When they asked him what they should do, Peter replied, "Repent and be baptized, every one of you, in the name of Jesus Christ for forgiveness of your sins; and you will receive the gift of the holy Spirit" (Acts 2:38). Acts also notes that about three thousand people who heard Peter were baptized that day.

With the coming of the Holy Spirit on the day of Pentecost, the Holy Trinity was fully revealed. Certainly the Holy Spirit had been at work in the world before this day. But on Pentecost, "the Church was openly displayed to the crowds and the spread of the Gospel among the nations, through preaching, was begun" (*Ad Gentes Divinitus*, 4). For this reason Pentecost has often been called the "birthday of the Church."

> **Magisterium** The official teaching authority of the Church. Jesus bestowed the right and power to teach in his name on Peter and the Apostles and their successors. The Magisterium is the bishops in communion with the successor of Peter, the bishop of Rome (pope).

The Holy Spirit Remains Present in the Church

The inspired preaching of St. Peter on Pentecost began a flurry of activity and growth in the early Church. Under the guidance of the Holy Spirit, he and the other Apostles set out to proclaim the *kerygma*, or essential teaching about Christ, that is:

- God loves the world and became incarnate.
- Jesus suffered for the sins of humankind, rose from the dead, and is alive.
- Jesus is Savior and Redeemer.

The Holy Spirit's presence continues to help the Church fulfill her mission. The human Church is filled with some good people trying their best to live the Good News passed on since the time of the Apostles. But even good people fail and sin. It is the divine energy of the Holy Spirit that empowers the Church to live as the Body of Christ. The Spirit continues to be present in

- Sacred Scripture;
- Sacred Tradition;
- the **Magisterium**, which he assists;
- the liturgy;
- prayer, wherein he intercedes,
- the gifts and ministries by which the Church is built up;
- the signs of apostolic and missionary life; and
- the witness of saints through whom he shows his holiness and continues the work of Salvation. (*CCC*, 688)

St. Augustine explained that "[w]hat the soul is to the human body, the Holy Spirit is to the Body of Christ, which is the Church" (*Sermo* 267). It is the Holy Spirit's role to help you share in the life of the Holy Trinity. Jesus made this his prayer:

The dove is a symbol of life. In the Old Testament, a dove released by Noah returned to the ark with an olive branch to show the floodwaters were receding. At Jesus' baptism, the Holy Spirit descended on him in the form of a dove. A dove also signifies gentleness, virtue, and peace—gifts those who are united with the Holy Spirit receive.

"I pray not only for them, but also for those who will believe in me through their word, so that they may all be one, as you, Father, are in me and I in you, that they also may be in us, that the world may believe that you have sent me." (Jn 17:20–21)

The image of the Church as the Body of Christ has been described previously (see page 17). Another image is that the Church is a Temple, home for the Holy Spirit (see *CCC*, 797–801). The Holy Spirit lives in the Church as if in a Temple. The Holy Spirit guides the Church and unites her in fellowship and ministry. Both of these images foretaste the Church's intimate connection to the Risen Lord. Jesus is the head of the Body. As St. Augustine taught, the Holy Spirit is the soul, giving the body life and sustaining it. The Church is to be united in Christ as a community of love, worship, and service.

Catholics believe that their eternal destiny has been accomplished through Jesus. But in order to accept this Good News, the Church must try to live the truth that Jesus came to teach. The Holy Spirit, dwelling in the Church, facilitates this task.

SECTION ASSESSMENT

NOTE TAKING

1. Write a one-sentence summary of St. Peter's speech at the first Pentecost.

COMPREHENSION

2. What were Jesus' disciples finally convinced of after his Resurrection?
3. Explain the origins of the feast of Pentecost.
4. What is the Holy Spirit's role in the Church today?
5. What was Jesus' Last Supper prayer for the Church?

REFLECTION

6. How do you think you would have felt if you had heard St. Peter's speech at Pentecost?

ANALYSIS

7. Think of a current event in the Church. How have you witnessed the Holy Spirit acting in the Church, either locally or universally?

SECTION 4
The Apostolic Foundation and Mission of the Church

The growth of the Church and her history through today is tied intimately to the Apostles.

Though Jesus had many disciples during the years of his public ministry (both men and women), he specifically called some men to follow. Early in his ministry, when he was walking along the Sea of Galilee, he asked two sets of brothers, all fishermen, to abandon their nets, boat, families, and former way of life to follow him. Jesus' promise to them was a share in his work: "Come after me, and I will make you fishers of men" (Mt 5:19). Brothers Simon (called Peter) and Andrew and brothers James and John (the sons of Zebedee) all accepted the invitation.

These four joined eight others with Jesus on a mountain, where he "summoned those whom he wanted and they came to him" (Mk 3:13). He commissioned the Twelve to be with him and to go out to preach. He also gave them authority, specifically to drive out demons. The Twelve are called the Apostles, from a Greek word *apostollein*, meaning "to send." After Jesus had risen, he said to them: "As the Father has sent me, so I send you" (Jn 20:21).

There is special meaning in the **Great Commissioning** taking place on a mountain and with Jesus' choice of exactly Twelve Apostles. Both in the Old Testament and the New Testament, mountains are associated with solemn events. It was on Mount Sinai that Moses received the Ten Commandments. Matthew's

Great Commissioning The instruction given to the Apostles by Jesus in Matthew 28:16–20 to spread the Gospel to the world and to baptize all nations in the name of the Father, and of the Son, and of the Holy Spirit.

NOTE TAKING

Recognize Main Ideas. Copy a design like the one here that depicts the Church being built on the foundation of the Apostles. In the upper floors, add decisions made by the Apostles and their successors (the bishops) that helped form the Church. Add as many "steps" as needed.

Instituted New Rituals and Worship

Apostolic Foundation

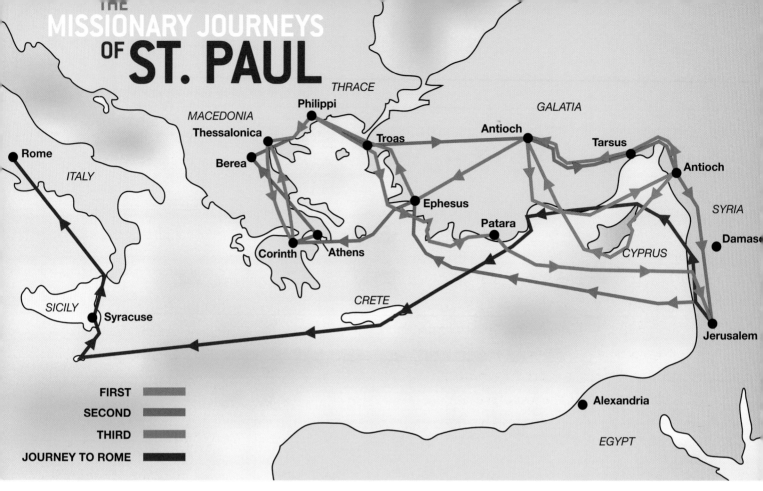

THE MISSIONARY JOURNEYS OF ST. PAUL

FIRST

SECOND

THIRD

JOURNEY TO ROME

Gospel records Jesus offering his most important teachings in the Sermon on the Mount. The number Twelve is significant because it represents the twelve tribes of Israel.

Clearly, Jesus gave Peter a special role of leadership among the Apostles. Peter's name is mentioned more than any other besides Jesus' in the Gospels. When Jesus asked his disciples how the crowds were identifying him they gave a variety of answers, none of which were correct. Then Jesus asked Peter, "But who do you say that I am?" Peter said in reply, "You are the Messiah, the Son of the living God" (Mt 16:15, 16). From this response, Jesus established a structure for the Church that will remain in place until the Kingdom is fully achieved:

> "And so I say to you, you are Peter, and upon this rock I will build my church, and the gates of the netherworld shall not prevail against it. I will give you the keys to the kingdom of heaven; and whatever you loose on earth shall be loosed in heaven." (Mt 16:18–19)

Peter's preaching on Pentecost began a flurry of growth in the early Church. Jesus commissioned his Apostles to spread his message. The Acts of the Apostles shows how the Apostles heeded this command. The first part of Acts (chapters 1–12) focuses on Peter's missionary career, which took place in and around Jerusalem. The later chapters focus on St. Paul, the "missionary to the Gentiles," and how he proclaimed the Gospel to the rest of the Roman Empire, including Rome itself.

Both Peter and Paul were **martyred** in Rome. But before their deaths, they contributed greatly to the growth of the early Church and in laying her foundation.

> **martyr** Someone who has been killed because of his or her faith. To be martyred is to be killed for one's faith.

Growth of the Church

The Greek word *koinonia* describes the life of the early Church. Led by the Holy Spirit, the early Christians lived as one community—working, celebrating, preaching, and worshiping together. The Acts of the Apostles offers this description:

> The community of believers was of one heart and mind, and no one claimed any of his possessions was his own, but they had everything in common. With great power the apostles bore witness to the resurrection of the Lord Jesus, and great favor was accorded them all. There was no needy person among them, for those who owned property or houses would sell them, bring the proceeds of the sale, and put them at the feet of the apostles, and they were distributed to each according to need. (Acts 4:32–35)

The early Church in Jerusalem was also active in service (*diakonia*). The community distributed food and other goods to poor widows who lived in the city. The Greek-speaking Jews complained that their widows were not getting their fair share. As a result, the Apostles appointed seven men of good reputation to look after the distribution of goods. These ministers were called *deacons.*

These first followers of Christ also thought of themselves as devout Jews. They continued to worship at the Temple and follow the Mosaic Law. They viewed themselves as fulfilling their Jewish faith, while at the same time belonging to the Church instituted by Christ. It was in the Church that they began to participate in new rituals that Jesus had also instituted in their presence. The first was a rite of initiation, Baptism. A second was the "breaking of the bread" and prayers in Jesus' name. Meeting in private homes, Jesus' disciples shared a common meal to commemorate the Last Supper and Jesus' Death on the Cross. They believed that when they shared the blessed bread and drank from the cup the Risen Lord was present in their midst. This was the Sacrament of Holy Eucharist.

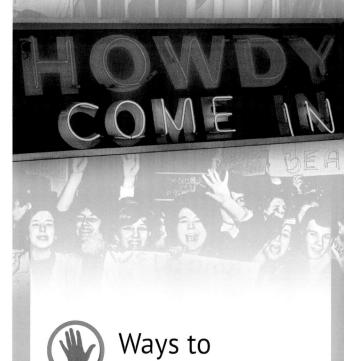

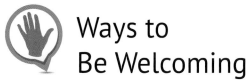

Ways to Be Welcoming

The community life of the Church—*kononia*—has always involved welcoming others to join with the Church in full membership. Help to be welcoming of others. Try one of the following ideas. Report on what you did.

- Go out to lunch with a peer or younger student who is in need of a friend.

- Form a welcoming committee for teenagers new to your parish or school. Parishes often make a point to welcome new families. Make the task of your committee to specifically address welcoming teenagers. This could mean inviting the new teen to a party you arrange or attending a game or movie with the new person along with some of your other peers.

- Provide free baby-sitting to a family new to your parish or neighborhood.

- If you are bilingual, volunteer to be a translator to a local agency that serves non-English-speaking people new to your area.

St. Stephen, the first Christian martyr, and Sr. Leonella Sgorbati, a Catholic nun killed by terrorists at a children's hospital in Mogadishu on September 17, 2006. Her final words were, "I forgive, I forgive."

Conflict and Persecutions in the Early Church

The preaching of the Gospel and the living out of the Faith resulted in conflict for the early Christians, both with Jewish and Roman authorities. Persecution, even to the point of martyrdom, was also often a result.

St. Stephen and St. James the Apostle were the first Christian martyrs. St. Stephen was condemned to death by Jewish authorities for preaching the Gospel. He was thrown out of the city and stoned to death (see Acts 6:8–7:60). Stephen's origins were that of Hellenistic Jews. This means he was not likely from Jerusalem and he may have only spoken Greek. From Acts, it is clear that Hellenistic Jews were punished more severely for practicing Christianity than non-Hellenistic Jews who practiced Christianity, known in the New Testament as Hebrews. The non-Hellenistic Jews insisted on maintaining the purity and customs of Judaism. The martyrdom of James at the hands of Herod Agrippa is recorded in Acts 12:1–2. Earlier in Acts, Apostles with Hebrew origins were flogged, ordered to stop preaching, and dismissed by the authorities for a so-called crime similar to Stephen's (see Acts 5:17–42). But they were not killed.

The Romans also persecuted the early Church. At first Rome tolerated Christianity as another Jewish sect. The government extended to Christians the same privileges granted to Jews throughout the Empire, such as exemption from serving in the military. As Christians began to move apart from Judaism, Rome began to behave differently, primarily because of what was seen as their lack of loyalty to Rome. Christians refused to worship the Roman emperor as a god. This led to the most severe persecutions of the first century under the emperor Domitian (AD 81–96). Christians who refused to worship the emperor were executed.

Nevertheless, during these years more and more disciples preached the Gospel outside of Jerusalem. For example, the Apostle Philip began to preach in Samaria. Peter traveled and preached throughout the Roman Empire. Under the guidance of the Holy Spirit, both Philip and Peter recognized the faith of God-fearing Gentiles and were inspired to baptize them. Following the martyrdom of Stephen, many Hellenist Christians fled to Antioch, Phoenicia, and Cyprus. They continued to preach in Jewish synagogues, but also began to share the Good News with Gentiles. It was in Antioch "that the disciples were first called Christians" (Acts 11:26). Antioch also served as center of the missionary activity to Gentiles and its most vigorous advocate, St. Paul.

The Church and the Gentiles

The greatest missionary to the Gentiles was a traveling merchant—a tentmaker—who had been raised a **Pharisee** and studied Jewish Law under a famous

> **Pharisee** A person who belonged to a religious party or sect in Jesus' day. *Pharisee* means "separated." The Pharisees thought of themselves as separated from others in Judaism because they strictly observed the Law to distinguish themselves from lukewarm religious practice and Gentile influence.

rabbi, Gamaliel, in Jerusalem. Once a persecutor of Christians, St. Paul of Tarsus experienced a dramatic conversion, which led to him taking several missionary trips throughout the Roman Empire. His second journey alone was nearly two thousand miles through the modern countries of Macedonia, Turkey, Greece, and Syria. Along the way he founded several local churches, in places such as Corinth, Galatia, Ephesus, Colossae, and Philippi. When he left those places he wrote letters of instruction and correction in the Faith to them. The letters addressed to them became part of the New Testament canon of the Christian Scripture.

By the time Paul was arrested in Jerusalem and charged with speaking out against Jewish Law and sent to trial in Rome (he was also a Roman citizen), his missionary trips had led to Christianity being preached and accepted throughout the Empire. Paul's travels throughout the Empire represented the "ends of the earth" that Jesus had spoken of before ascending to Heaven.

St. Paul preached throughout the Roman Empire.

However, the mission to allow Gentiles into the Church did not come without controversy and conflict. When God spoke to Peter in a vision (Acts 10:9–49), Peter became convinced that the offer of Salvation in Jesus Christ was available for Gentiles as well as Jews. But subsequent questions arose about what elements of Judaism were essential to Christianity. For example:

- What parts of Mosaic Law did the Gentile Christians need to follow?

- Did they have to follow Jewish dietary laws?

- Was it necessary for Gentile Christians to worship in the Jewish Temple?

- Did male Gentiles who converted to Christianity need to be circumcised? (Circumcision was the sign of the covenant between Abraham and his descendent.)

Peter himself began to have doubt. He stopped eating with Gentile Christians who did not follow Jewish dietary customs. The answers to these questions were not resolved until the first gathering of Church leadership at the Council of Jerusalem.

The Council of Jerusalem

The Council of Jerusalem met in AD 49 to solve those issues. Paul and Barnabas argued for freedom from the Law for Gentile Christians while the Apostle James, the leader of the Jerusalem Church, supported imposing Jewish Law on all converts. Upon hearing both arguments, Peter, who had recently stopped eating with Gentile Christians who did not follow Jewish dietary customs, reversed his position and sided with Paul. Gentiles no longer had to submit to the entirety of Jewish Law. This was consistent with the words of Jesus who taught that it is not unclean foods that defile a person, but rather "what comes out of a person, that is what defiles" (Mk 7:2).

The Council of Jerusalem determined that all Christians, both Gentile and Jew, were required to keep three basic laws:

- First, they should not eat meat that had been sacrificed to idols.

- Second, no Christian should eat the meat of strangled animals or eat blood. Because God had given this law to Noah, the Jewish Christians believed it should be binding on Gentiles as well. (God's covenant with Noah reestablished his communion with

Cardinal Andrea Cordero Lanza di Montezemolo, Archpriest of the Basilica of St. Paul Outside-the-Walls, shows a sarcophagus unearthed beneath the basilica. The sarcophagus is believed to contain the remains of the Apostle Paul and dates back to at least AD 390. It has been the subject of an extended excavation that began in 2002 and was completed in November 2006.

humankind and is another image of the Church prefigured.)

- Finally, the Council said that all Christians must avoid illicit sexual practices. Christians grew to understand and act on the teaching that sex was to only be reserved for marriage.

The Council of Jerusalem was the first opportunity to witness how the Apostles would be taught and guided, and the Church made holy by the Holy Spirit until Christ's return. But how was this apostolic leadership maintained when the Apostles began to die? Early Church writings speak of bishops (*episcopai*) who were to continue the mission of Christ commissioned to them by the Apostles. The Second Vatican Council

pointed out that the Apostles "designated such men and then made the ruling that likewise on their death other proven men should take over their ministry" (*Lumen Gentium*, 20).

Also, St. Peter's position of primacy was passed on to the bishop of Rome. Rome had the central place in the Church from the time Peter led the local church there. The bishop of Rome, or the pope, was respected and had authority over the universal Church in the same way Peter once did.

The Apostles and their successors also convened on other occasions besides the Council of Jerusalem in the first two centuries. Decisions like these were important for another reason: It made it clear that Christianity

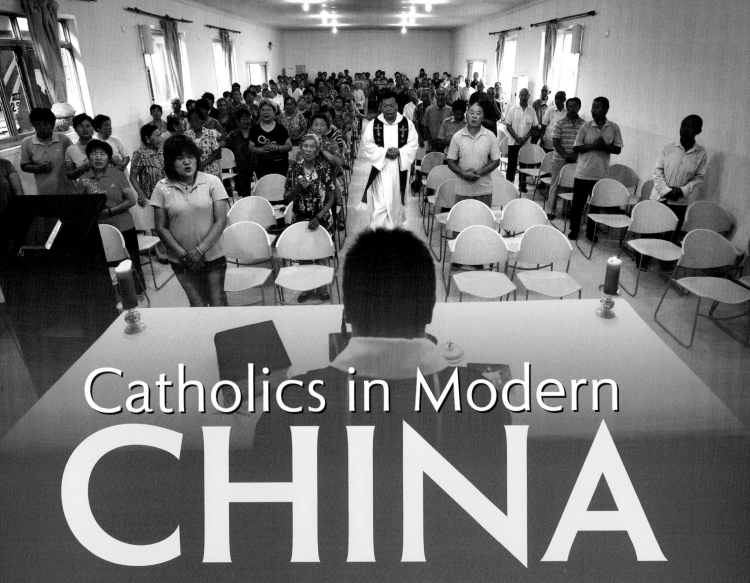

Catholics in Modern CHINA

When Mao Zedong ascended to power in China in 1949, the People's Republic of China was established as a communist nation. Though China had a very small percentage of Catholics, the government imprisoned or exiled foreign missionaries, killed professing Catholics, and forced others to go underground.

Today, there are between an estimated twelve to fifteen million Catholics in China, still a very small percentage of a population of 1.3 billion. Officially, Catholics are allowed to worship openly, but they must be part of a registered nationalized Catholic Church. In 2006, the Chinese national church ordained new bishops without the Vatican's approval, risking excommunication. Through the years, an underground Church loyal to Rome has also remained present in China and, in fact, outnumbered members of the registered national Church. In 2007, Pope Benedict XVI wrote a letter to Chinese Catholics that acknowledged all of the tensions while looking for a course of action in the future to create new relations between Chinese Catholics, the government of China, and the Vatican. The pope wrote:

> As all of you know, one of the most delicate problems in relations between the Holy See and the authorities of your country is the question of episcopal [bishop] appointments. On the one hand, it is understandable that governmental authorities are attentive to the choice of those who will carry out the important role of leading and shepherding the local Catholic

communities, given the social implications which—in China as in the rest of the world—this function has in the civil sphere as well as the spiritual. On the other hand, the Holy See follows the appointment of Bishops with special care since this touches the very heart of the life of the Church, inasmuch as the appointment of Bishops by the pope is the guarantee of the unity of the Church and of hierarchical communion.

Cardinal Joseph Zen takes part in a demonstration to demand religious freedom in China outside the China Liaison Office in Hong Kong.

Vatican-appointed Cardinal Joseph Zen Ze-kiun, who retired as bishop of Hong Kong in 2002, said in 2010 that the Church in China continues to face difficulties around this issue: "It is obvious that the situation is not for the good of the country because everyone knows that the Church is not really free."

The cardinal said that an ideal situation would be if the Vatican and the Chinese government could agree on the choice of bishops. But he, added, "Certainly it is not true that the Chinese government willingly accepts all the candidates of the Holy See."

The issue of evangelization in China remains at the forefront. How the Church addresses this situation in the coming years will have a great impact on its legitimacy in China and its ability to preach the Gospel and minister to Catholics there.

RESEARCH TOPICS

- Report on one or more Catholic missionaries who have witnessed to the Faith in China. Consider Matteo Ricci, S.J., and Michael Ruggieri, S.J., two of the first Jesuit missionaries to China, or St. Francis Xavier and his Jesuit companions.
- Name at least five key events in the life of the Catholic Church in China since 1949.
- Read and summarize Pope Benedict XVI's May 27, 2007, letter to Chinese Catholics. See: http://www.vatican.va/holy_father/benedict_xvi/letters/2007/documents/hf_ben-xvi_let_20070527_china_en.html.

was a religion of the body and not just the spirit. Christ had chosen the Apostles to be pastors. Inspired by the Holy Spirit, the Apostles and their successors were ordained to teach the true way of Christian living, both with respect to Faith and morals, under the inspiration of the Holy Spirit.

Jesus certainly did not dictate to the Apostles every specific feature of Church structure that is present today, but he clearly recognized the need for ordained leadership necessary for teaching the Faith, administering the sacraments, and preserving the unity of the Church. In summary, Jesus chose Apostles to ensure that the Church would remain faithful to his mission. Today, the Church remains the place where Christ is present and his mission is being fulfilled. If you desire a relationship with Christ, the Savior, the Church is the place to be!

Marks of the *Church:*

A Preview of Chapters 2 to 5

St. Paul

St. Irenaeus

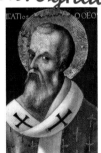

St. Ignatius

St. Paul wrote about the unity of members of the Church because of their membership in the Body of Christ. A few years after, St. Ignatius of Antioch added that there could be only one Church and that Church was known by her unbroken connection with the Apostles. St. Irenaeus of Lyons (d. 202) maintained that the role of the Church is to unite people with Christ.

The teachings of Sts. Paul, Ignatius, and Irenaeus were formalized in the Nicene Creed in the early fourth century. In 381 at the First Council of Constantinople, the words "I believe in one holy catholic and apostolic church" were officially added to the creed. These characteristics are known as the four **marks of the Church**. The Church does not possess them of herself, but

> **marks of the Church** The four essential marks or qualities of the Church: one, holy, catholic, and apostolic.

from Christ who is their source. The four marks of the Church—and how they are manifested throughout the history of the Church in different ways and in different cultures—form the heart of this textbook and course. They help to point out how the nature of the Church is an expression of Jesus Christ. Through the Holy Spirit, Christ makes the Church, one, holy, catholic, and apostolic.

SECTION ASSESSMENT

NOTE TAKING

Use your completed chart to answer the following questions.

1. What did Jesus charge his Apostles with in the Great Commissioning?

2. What were two ways the early Church differentiated herself from Judaism?

3. Who are the successors of the Apostles?

4. Why was St. Peter's position of primacy in the Church passed on to the bishop of Rome?

5. What are three messages of the Church's *kerygma*?

COMPREHENSION

6. Why might St. Stephen have been martyred while Peter and John were not for similar offenses?

7. Where were the disciples first called "Christians"?

8. What was the main issue surrounding the Council of Jerusalem?

9. What was the solution?

10. What did the results of the Council of Jerusalem reveal about the rights of apostolic leadership?

ANALYSIS

11. What are some ways Catholics today go against the mainstream of government and society?

CRITICAL THINKING

12. What challenges do you think the early Christians felt when they distanced themselves from their Jewish roots and practices?

Section Summaries

Focus Question

Why do people need to belong to the Catholic Church?

Complete one of the following:

 Look up and define the term *moral relativism*. Does this concept connect with the phenomenon of people believing themselves to be "spiritual but not religious"? How so?

 Research more information on the phenomenon of "SBNR." List five surprising statements you encounter in your research. Counteract the statements with your argument on how religion is necessary in each case.

 Based on your study of this chapter, list five reasons why it is important to belong to the Catholic Church. Rank the reasons from least (1) to most important (5).

INTRODUCTION (PAGES 3–7)

We Are Meant to Be Together

Individualism has often reinforced the idea of a private relationship with God and undermined the need for community. Life is not a solitary journey, but one that takes place with others and most fully through participation in the Catholic Church.

 Describe how being part of a group helped you to accomplish something you would not have been able to do on your own. How does the Church fulfill a similar role?

SECTION 1 (PAGES 8–12)

The Origins of the Church

To understand the Church, it is important to remember that God created the world with people in mind. God's plan for the Church unfolded over time. It was a plan that began the moment sin destroyed the unity between God and humanity. The founding of the Church reached its culmination at the time of the New Covenant in Jesus Christ.

 What does God's relenting in the punishment of the Ninevites from the Book of Jonah have to do with your own participation today in the Church?

SECTION 2 (PAGES 13–19)

The Church Is Instituted by Christ

The Church is the Kingdom of God already present in mystery. The Church is formed in the Blood of Christ. Jesus remains present in the Church today, especially through his Real Presence in the Eucharist. The task of a disciple is to ascent to the Good News and to share it with others.

 Why do people searching for God need the Catholic Church?

SECTION 3 (PAGES 20–24)

The Holy Spirit and the Church

Jesus fulfilled his promise to send the Holy Spirit to direct and guide the Church. The Spirit moved Peter and the early Church to continue Christ's mission. The Holy Spirit remains present in the Church today.

 Explain the meaning of St. Augustine's words: "What the soul is to the human body, the Holy Spirit is to the Body of Christ, which is the Church."

SECTION 4 (PAGES 25–34)

The Apostolic Foundation and Mission of the Church

Jesus commissioned Peter and the Apostles for leadership in the Church. The Apostles forged growth in the early Church and ruled on disputes, including the issue of how Gentiles would be welcomed into the Church. The pope and bishops are successors of the Apostles.

 What challenges do you think the early Christians experienced when they distanced themselves from their Jewish roots and practices?

Chapter Assignments

Choose and complete at least one of the following three assignments assessing your understanding of the material in this chapter.

1. Survey of Religious Beliefs

Research current information on religious beliefs and practices among the so-called "millennials." Focus your research on the following: (1) the religious affiliation of those in the survey and (2) their level of religious participation. Use information gleaned from The Pew Forum on Religion and Public Life and the Center for Applied Research on the Apostolate. Focus your research further by naming a question for which you would like data. For example: "How often do you pray?" "Who can be saved?" "What is your attitude about Faith?" Supplement these official findings with two other data elements: (1) an anecdotal story told by a millennial related to the main topic of your survey and (2) a sample survey using the same focus questions, but this time with data that you collect from the target age group. Display all results in an appropriate format. Write a summary of your study.

2. Essay: Reaching Out to the Spiritual But Not Religious

Cardinal Timothy Dolan of New York recently told a large group of high school students: "We are living in an era where people believe in Christ, but not his Church. They want the king, but not the kingdom; they want to believe without belonging; they want the faith but not the faithful. But for the committed Catholic, the answer to that is 'no can do: Jesus and the Church are one." Cardinal Dolan went on to suggest three things to address this problem:

1. Focus on the Church as a "spiritual family."

2. Discover a "non-combative apologetics" which can "credibly, convincingly, and compellingly articulate our Catholic Faith" both to those inside the Church and to those who are hostile to the Church.

3. Fess up to the sinful side of the Church.

Write an essay that focuses on how you can both individually and with your Catholic peers enact these three suggestions with the objective of encouraging those who have left the Catholic Church to return.

3. Role Play: Council of Jerusalem

The Council of Jerusalem (Acts 15:1–21) was convened to deal with a crucial issue in the early Church. The Council set historical precedent for dealing with conflict and controversy in the Church. It was the first in a long line of councils. Work with your classmates to develop a role play for the Council of Jerusalem. Choose a cast for the following roles:

Paul

Barnabas

Peter

James

a group of Jewish Christians

members of the Council

Work with the cast members to write a script for each part. Structure the drama as a debate, giving both sides an opportunity to speak before a verdict is given by Peter and the Council.

Optional: Choose a contemporary issue facing the Church today and hold a council meeting using the same format as above.

Faithful Disciple

St. Clement of Rome

St. Clement of Rome was pope in the first century. In most second-century lists of popes, he is named the third pope, behind St. Peter and St. Anacletus, also known as Cletus. However, according to the second-century defender of the faith Tertullian, and St. Jerome (347–420),Clement was Peter's immediate successor, and was consecrated by St. Peter himself.

Clement might have grown up as a slave in the household of the cousin of the Roman emperor Domitian. It is also possible that Clement was associated with Peter and the Apostles. In Philippians 4:3 a reference is made to a "Clement" who was Paul's "true yokemate" and who "struggled at my side promoting the gospel." These elements, like other parts of the life of St. Clement cannot be proven for sure.

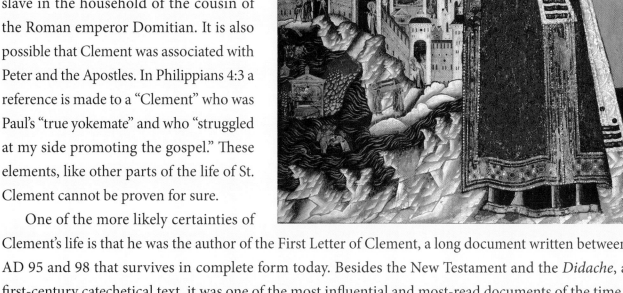

One of the more likely certainties of Clement's life is that he was the author of the First Letter of Clement, a long document written between AD 95 and 98 that survives in complete form today. Besides the New Testament and the *Didache*, a first-century catechetical text, it was one of the most influential and most-read documents of the time.

The First Letter of Clement was addressed to the church in Corinth. The main subject involves how presbyters, or priests, were being treated poorly there and were actually deposed from their positions. It doesn't appear that the Corinthian church explicitly sought out Clement's opinion on what was occurring, but as the bishop of Rome occupying the seat of St. Peter, he took the initiative to provide it. He wrote of both the authenticity of apostolic succession and of the injustice being done to priests in Corinth:

> Our Apostles, too, were given to understand by our Lord Jesus Christ that the office of the bishop would give rise to intrigues. For this reason, equipped as they were with perfect foreknowledge, they appointed the men mentioned before, and afterwards laid down a rule once for all to this effect: when these men die, other approved men shall succeed to their sacred ministry. Consequently, we deem it an injustice to eject from the sacred ministry the persons who were appointed either by them, or later, with the consent of the

whole Church, by other men in high repute and have ministered to the flock of Christ faultlessly, humbly, quietly and unselfishly, and have moreover, over a long period of time, earned the esteem of all. (*First Letter of Clement*, 44)

The First Letter of Clement was read frequently in the early Church.

A legend surrounding the end of Clement's life is that he was exiled to the Crimea, where he worked in the mines before eventually being killed by being thrown into the sea with an anchor around his neck. The legend also says that the angels made him a grave in the sea, which was discovered once the tides ran low.

St. Clement of Rome should accurately be remembered for his devotion to the Church, and his prayers for her leadership. The following is a prayer for bishops and attributed to him:

> Grant to them, Lord, health, peace, concord and stability, so that they may exercise without offence the sovereignty that you have given them. Master, heavenly King of the ages, you give glory, honor and power over the things of the earth to the sons of men. Direct, Lord, their counsel, following what is pleasing and acceptable in your sight, so that by exercising with devotion and in peace and gentleness the power that you have given to them, they may find favor with you.

 Reading Comprehension

1. What is one certainty about the life of St. Clement?

2. Who was the audience for the First Letter of St. Clement?

3. What was the main subject of the letter?

Writing Task

- Write and send a note (preferably a letter, not an e-mail) to a priest who you know commending him for something he does well.

Explaining the Faith

Why do we need organized religion?
Isn't it possible or even preferable to worship God in our own personal way?

Christian faith cannot be separated from a relationship with the Church, because where the Church is, God is.

The Catholic Faith is rooted in faith in God who became incarnate in history in the person of Jesus of Nazareth, the Second Divine Person of the Blessed Trinity, true God and true man. In Jesus, people were able to touch, listen to, and speak to God directly. In Jesus, people came to know God's healing and forgiveness in an immediate way. In Jesus, God's offer of Salvation and fullness of life became a tangible reality. Following Jesus' Passion, Death, Resurrection, and Ascension, Salvation and fullness of life became accessible to all people through the Church. Jesus breathed his Spirit into the Church so that the Church could become his Body on earth. Because of the gift of the Holy Spirit, the Church is able to be God's continuing presence in the world.

Why else do we need the Church? The *Catechism of the Catholic Church* teaches that we need the Church because:

- God wants to come to us as members of his family. The Church was made for that purpose. (*CCC*, 760)

- We have to hear the Good News from others. No one can preach the Gospel to himself or herself. (*CCC*, 875)

- Humans are social in nature. We need the encouragement of others that the Church provides. (*CCC*, 820)

- Worship of God is communal in nature. It is the whole Church who celebrates the liturgy on earth. Christ is present with the Church in worship, acting as the Head of his Mystical Body. (*CCC*, 1140–1141)

- By participating in the Eucharist, we unite ourselves with Christ's self-offering. (*CCC*, 1322–1324)

- As the Scripture teaches, Christ uses the Church's liturgy to prepare you to see him in one another and to love one another despite the differences of race, gender, and personality. (*CCC*, 1093–1097)

- The Church is structured and instituted by Christ to provide a means of grace through the Sacraments that guide us to our eternal destiny. (*CCC*, 871–879)

Finally, keep in mind the words of St. Joan of Arc: "About Jesus Christ and the Church, I simply know they're just one thing, and we shouldn't complicate the matter."

 Further Research

- Briefly define the Church's origin, foundation, and mission as reported in the *Catechism of the Catholic Church*, 758–769.

Prayer

For the Church

O glorious St. Michael,

guardian and defender of the Church of Jesus Christ,

come to the assistance of this Church,

against which the powers of hell are unchained,

guard with special care her august Head,

and obtain that for him and for us the hour of triumph may speedily arrive.

O glorious Archangel St. Michael, watch over us during life,

defend us against the assaults of the demon,

assist us especially at the hour of death;

obtain for us a favorable judgment,

and the happiness of beholding God face to face for endless ages.

Amen.

—Pope Leo XIII

THE CHURCH IS ONE

COME TOGETHER

Our Lady, Queen of Peace Catholic Church has been called a "destination parish." Located in Arlington, Virginia, it attracts membership from far reaches of the region, from Washington, DC, to Maryland. The walls of Our Lady, Queen of Peace can be seen as a symbol of the diversity of the parish, past and present. Some segments are made of stone, others brick; some are whitewashed while others are not.

Fr. Tim Hickey C.S.Sp., pastor of Our Lady, Queen of Peace, says he has often thought of the walls as a metaphor for the parish. "None of them are equal and some stick out further than others. [But] somehow it all forms the church and it works."

The parish has a long history of both diversity of membership and a spirit of welcome. Founded primarily as a parish for African Americans, its black parishioners immediately began to accept white families "at a time when that was not something that was considered all that acceptable," said Fr. Hickey.

Today, the parish continues to pride itself on being welcoming to all people—including those with mental and physical disabilities, people who struggle with alcoholism, and those with a homosexual orientation.

Fr. Hickey said that many kinds of people come to the parish because it feels like home to them. "Living out the Gospel is what inspires us as a community of faith to understand how important it is to welcome people into our community. As we do that, we also challenge the parishioners to pick up the Gospel and to bring it into their everyday life."

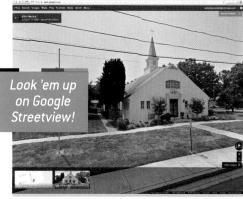

Look 'em up on Google Streetview!

Among its many projects, the parish sponsors a thrift store for the needy, which is located in its ministry center.

"We really challenge [parishoners]," said Katie Remedios, religious education director. "Once they get involved, they're here for everything—making pies, working in the food pantry, making scarves for the homeless. They travel a long distance, but it changes their lives."

The parish has six weekend liturgies, all of them well attended. "We're packed in like sardines, but we're all on the same page," Fr. Hickey said. "People aren't looking for a forty-five minute experience of Church. They come here and expect to participate in the Eucharist, and they do that with a strong sense of community."

Our Lady, Queen of Peace Catholic Church is located at 2700 South 19th Street, Arlington, Virginia. (Information from an article by Gretchen R. Crowe in *Arlington Catholic Herald*, http://www.catholicherald.com/opinions/detail.html?sub_id=16282.)

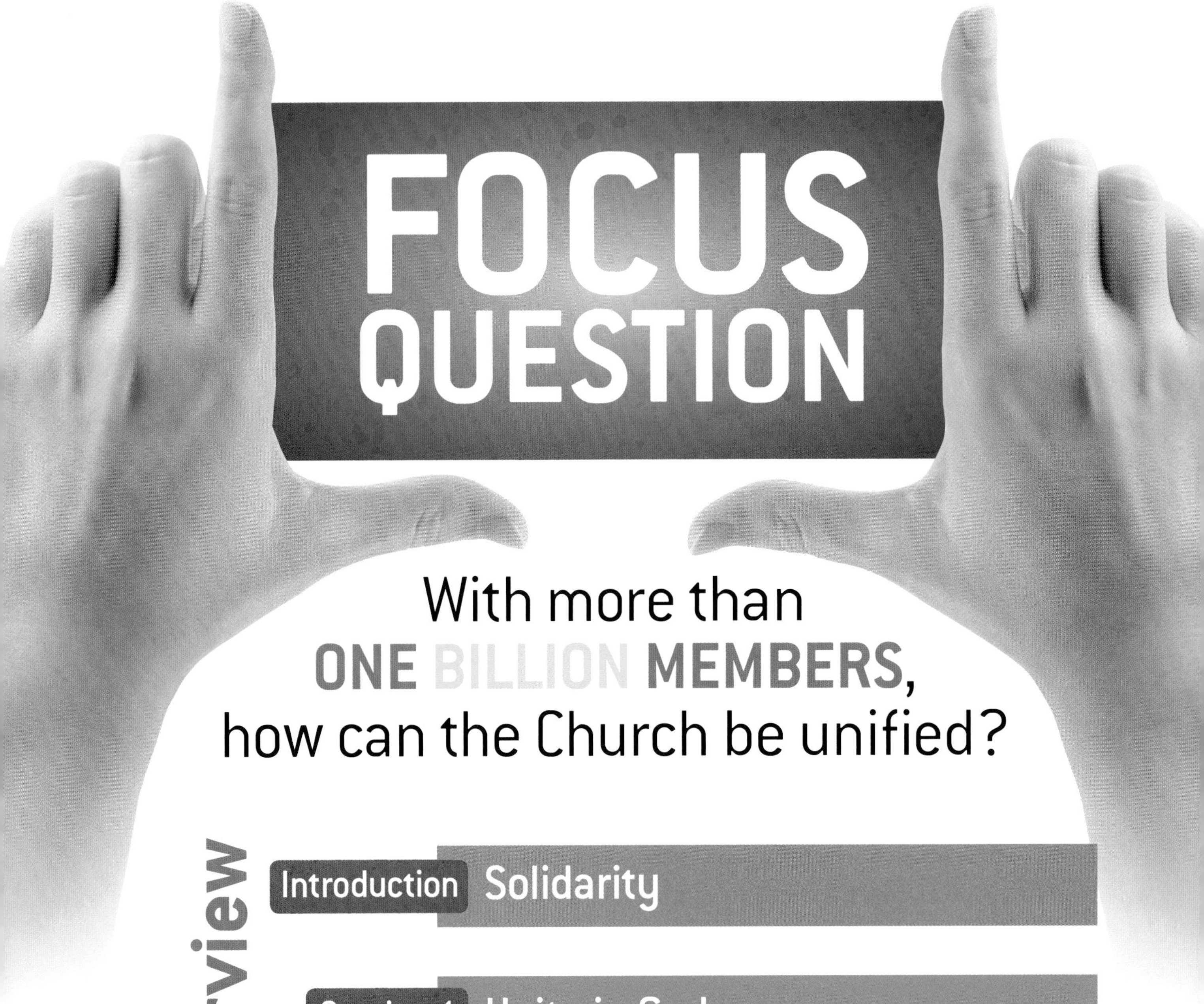

FOCUS QUESTION

With more than
ONE BILLION MEMBERS,
how can the Church be unified?

Chapter Overview

Introduction Solidarity

Section 1 Unity in God

Section 2 Unity of Belief

Section 3 Unity in Common Worship

Section 4 Unity with Apostolic Succession

INTRODUCTION
Solidarity

The unity amidst the diversity of people at Our Lady, Queen of Peace Catholic Church in Arlington, Virginia, is worth considering in greater detail. You may have experiences with friends and acquaintances of different genders and ages and from different locales coming together. Consider the conversations that take place on social networking sites. For example, you might post something on your social media site and then be amazed that it draws comments and discussion from your best friend, a high school student from South Africa you met as part of a class assignment, a family acquaintance who is your parents' age, and a college freshman you met last weekend when you were taking an aptitude test at a nearby college.

These online connections and conversations are amazing. But how well do you really *know* the people you interact with in these ways? The same might be asked of the parishioners of Our Lady, Queen of Peace Catholic Church. They socialize, serve, and worship together, but how deep is their connection with one another?

St. John Paul II called people to move beyond superficial conversations to a renewed sense of **solidarity**. For example, students at a Catholic high school in California recently shaved their heads in solidarity with a classmate undergoing cancer treatment. He used that term to refer to a sense of human interdependence and mutual responsibility. In his encyclical *Solicitudo Rei Socialis* ("On Social Concern") he wrote:

> Solidarity helps us to see the "other"—whether a person, people, or nation—not just as some kind of instrument, with a work capacity and physical strength to be exploited at low cost and then discarded when no longer useful, but as our "neighbor," a "helper" (cf. Gn 2:18–20), to be made a sharer on par with ourselves in the banquet of life to which all are equally invited by God. (39)

solidarity A Christian virtue of charity and friendship whereby members of the human family share material and spiritual goods.

NOTE TAKING **Recognize Main Ideas.** Write words or draw symbols like the ones below to help you remember four ways the Church's unity is guaranteed. Some examples are provided.

LOVE

PROFESSION OF ONE FAITH

SACRAMENTS

APOSTOLIC SUCCESSION

The practice of solidarity expresses a basic conviction about the unity of all humanity. Pope Benedict XVI wrote that "solidarity is first and foremost a sense of responsibility on the part of everyone with regard to everyone . . ." (*Caritas in Veritate*, 37). In many ways, the descriptions of solidarity by St. John Paul II and Pope Benedict XVI both describe the unity that is basic in the Church.

In fact, the Church is unified and one. This is not a unity that is casual, superficial, or unreal. Rather, it is a unity that is modeled on the perfect, intimate relationship of the Three Divine Persons of the **Blessed Trinity**.

THE CHURCH IS
UNIFIED
AND
ONE
BECAUSE OF

 her unity in the Trinity: God the Father, Son, and Holy Spirit

 her founder, Jesus Christ, who came to restore unity among all people and between people and God the Father. Christ is the principle of the Church's unity

 the Holy Spirit who brings about the communion of the faithful and unites them in Christ

Unity is one of the four marks of the Church. This chapter will focus on this mark of the Church. The other essential signs that mark the true

> **Blessed Trinity** The central mystery of the Christian faith. It teaches that there are Three Divine Persons in one God: Father, Son, and Holy Spirit.

Church—holiness, catholicity, and apostolicity—are the focus of the following chapters.

How Is the Unity of the Church Guaranteed?

Is the Church really unified? Sometimes you may wonder if this is so.

Certainly there is a dichotomy present whenever the Church's unity is described. Interestingly, one of the strengths of the Church's unity is her great *diversity*, "which comes from both the variety of God's gifts and the diversity of those who receive them" (*CCC*, 814). But does diversity support unity?

There are different gifts among Catholics who are gathered together in the Church. But from the different gifts, a unity arises in the Church. Think of how this occurs in your own family. You, your parents, siblings, and other relatives have things in common, but also have many differing talents, interests, and points of view. These do not prevent you from being a family. Fr. Hickey described a similar feeling at Our Lady, Queen of Peace: "The people are wonderful. It's a real strong sense of a family of faith. They want us here and we want them here, and we want to do this together."

Also, there are divisions in the Church and wounds to her unity, just as there are in any family. You may know of divisions within the membership of your own parish community. And you are certainly aware that there are different ecclesial or church communities—for example, Baptists, Methodists, Presbyterians, and more—that profess belief in Jesus Christ but that are not fully united with the Catholic Church. These divisions must be addressed through prayer and human effort while understanding the reconciliation of all

Christians to the Church transcends human powers and remains in the charge of God.

However, the mark of unity in the Church draws strength in the Church's diversity and transcends the divisions. The mark of unity is basic to the human experience because all people are children of God and created in the image of God. The very mission of the Church is oriented toward expressing this universal unity:

> The Church, in Christ, is a sacrament—a sign and instrument, that is, of communion with God and of the unity of the entire human race.... (*Lumen Gentium*, 1)

Put simply, this means that the Church offers the world a vision of the unity of the human race that God intends for all and also offers his grace that unites people to him and one another. In other words, if you want to understand how God intends for people to relate to one another, you should look to the Church. Primarily, the Church's unity is guaranteed by her charity, or love, which St. Paul described in the Letter to the Colossians as "the bond of perfection" (Col 3:14). In addition to charity, the Church's unity is guaranteed through her:

- profession of one faith, received from the Apostles;
- common celebration of divine worship, especially the Sacraments;
- apostolic succession through the Sacrament of Holy Orders.

The bonds of love, the profession of one faith, common worship, and apostolic succession ensure that the Church's unity will never be destroyed. These bonds are explored in greater detail in the sections that follow.

SECTION ASSESSMENT

NOTE TAKING

1. Use the symbols you made to answer the following question: How do the people of Our Lady, Queen of Peace parish seem to be connected?

COMPREHENSION

2. How is the nature of the Church united and one?

3. What are the four marks of the Church?

APPLICATION

4. Name two ways to practice solidarity through social networking.

5. What might be some of the reasons that Our Lady, Queen of Peace is successful in bringing people together?

SECTION 1
Unity in God

One way to understand *unity* is to remember how the thirteen American colonies banded together as *one* to declare their independence from Great Britain and then defended that decision as *one* by engaging the British in the Revolutionary War. The result was a united nation, the United States of America. Or, more currently, the word *unite* is often used to describe the common efforts of a smaller group that comes together, maybe in protest over an environmental issue or over abortions being performed at a local clinic. Notice that in each of these examples unity involves two or more "somethings" (colonies, people) joining together, even if only temporarily.

You may envision the unity of the Catholic Church in the same way: many different kinds of people united by common beliefs gathered together for worship. Many young Catholics who have attended a World Youth Day have experienced this kind of unity. However, as remarkable as it is to pray together with people from every continent on earth, even a World Youth Day event doesn't completely represent the Church's unity. Her unity goes even deeper. The Church's unity is in God's very being. The Church's unity is in love, for "God is love, and whoever remains in love remains in God and God in him" (1 Jn 4:16).

NOTE TAKING

Scripture Reading. Read the entire Scripture passages on love and unity introduced in this section and listed in the following table. Create and summarize the main idea of each passage in the second column.

Scripture Passage	Main Idea
1 John 4:13–21	
Mark 12:28–34	
John 10: 22–42	
Colossians 1:15–20	
Matthew 18:15–20	

A Relational God

The Second Vatican Council's document on **ecumenism**, *Unitatis Redintegratio* ("Separated Brethren"), teaches that The Church's highest source of unity is the Blessed Trinity. St. Cyprian of Carthage, writing in the third century, asserted that the Church is "a people made one with the unity of the Father, Son, and the Holy Spirit."

Nevertheless, it is challenging to first imagine God, and then to understand a God who is in Three Persons.

Many people are stuck at imagining God as a "superhero" with amazing powers that can do it all. In fact, God is *omnipotent*, meaning that he has supreme power and authority over all of creation. But there is error in thinking of God as a super *being* that can be lumped with all other beings in the universe. Rather God is as St. Thomas Aquinas described "pure being"—the very power and possibility of *all* being. God is not a member of any category of things you can imagine. Rather, God is the author and source of all that is.

How, then, *can* you imagine such a God? In one sense you can't. Part of the mystery of God is that he is incomprehensible. But this does not mean you cannot *know* God. While you can't figure God out like you might master a periodical table in chemistry class, you have the opportunity to know God in a deep and profound way. *The way to know God is to love.* In a commentary on Psalm 21, St. Augustine wrote:

> Are you contemplating what God is like? Everything you imagine, God is not. Everything you put in your thoughts, God is not. But if you wish to savor something of God, then know that God is love, the same love by which we love one another.

A Greek word used in the New Testament for this type of love is *agape*. This word for love does not describe a quality that someone *has* ("Jane is a loving person"). Neither does it refer to your fondness

Only by thinking of God in terms of perfect relationship between Father, Son, and Holy Spirit can you come to a closer understanding of God.

for some object ("Laura loves her dog" or "Eric loves pizza"). Agape is even more than romantic love, though the deep and loving relational aspect of love between a man and woman in marriage is closer to its meaning. In a marital relationship, love is directed toward the other. This is the same for an agapic love between God and humans. The relation between God and humans is made deeper, however, because it involves in a relationship between the Three Persons in one God who are already in a loving community with one another.

The New Testament definition that "God is love" means that God himself is a perfect loving relationship. When the Three Persons in one God are named—Father, Son, and Holy Spirit—three relationships within one God are also being named. So only by thinking of the Blessed Trinity in terms of a perfect relationship can you come closer to an intellectual understanding of God.

More help in understanding the loving relationship of community among the Blessed Trinity comes from St. Augustine, who described the Three Persons within the framework of the unifying love of God. According to Augustine, the Father is the *Lover*, the source of

> **ecumenism** The movement, inspired and led by the Holy Spirit, that seeks the union of all Christian religions and eventually the unity of all peoples throughout the world within the Catholic Church.

divine love. The Son, as the Beloved, returns that love back to the Father and this shared bond of love is the Holy Spirit. Note that the Three Persons are understood in terms of their perfect relationship with one another. Note also that the Trinity consists of Divine Persons, meaning that it is possible to know them.

Consider that distinguishing the individuality of people, you might list characteristics that differentiate one person from the next. However, getting to know the *person* is way more than separating out characteristics. To know another person you have to engage him or her in a relationship. It would not be enough to know facts about the person; you would have to actually have interaction or communion with him or her. The term *person* suggests relationship in a way that the term *individual* does not.

The Triune God who loved the world into its existence and whose very being is perfect love among the community of the Blessed Trinity, has created you in the divine image. He has made you for relationship:

> God created man in his image;
> in the divine image he created him;
> male and female he created them. (Gn 1:27)

It is love that unites the Three Persons of the Blessed Trinity. Love is God. God is love. When you love God you are united with him and able to know him and share his love with others.

Jesus' Lesson on Love

Jesus Christ, God's love Incarnate, taught a practical way for people to participate in the love of God. When asked about the first of the commandments, Jesus said:

> The first is this: "Hear, O Israel! The Lord our God is Lord alone! You shall love the Lord your god with all your heart, with all your soul, with all your mind, and with all your strength." The second is this: "You shall love your neighbor as

Andrei Rublev's Trinity, *created by the Russian artist in the thirteenth century. See page 87 for more information.*

yourself." There are no other commandments greater than these. (Mk 12:29–31)

Jesus' teaching is clear: love of God and love of neighbor are inseparable. You enter into the love of God when you love one another. The truth of this teaching was revealed in Jesus' very life in relationship—as the Second Person of the Blessed Trinity—to God the Father: "The Father and I are one" (Jn 10:30). Jesus' love for others is a natural expression of the love he shares with his Father. This is the reason for his teaching on the commandments: he knows that love of God and love of neighbor do not compete with one another; instead, they are intimately related.

This command of love is also represented in the way St. Paul described the relationship between Christ and the Church: "He is the head of the body, the church" (Col 1:18). When a person is baptized into the Church, he or she is baptized into Christ's Body and shares this unity with the Father. Unity with the Father in Christ and unity with one another do not compete, because in the Holy Spirit, they have the same source.

It isn't easy to surrender your life to Christ as an individual; it is even more difficult to do so as a member of a community in which the many individuals have different concepts of what it means to surrender. Nonetheless, you can be united in your faith with others. It is only in the context of unity in the Church that you can really come to know and understand the God who "is love." Jesus said: "Where two or three are gathered in my name, there I am in the midst of them" (Mt 18:20). Catholics are blessed with a personal relationship with God, and are even more deeply blessed in their relationship with God as part of the Church.

SECTION ASSESSMENT

NOTE TAKING

Use your completed chart for this section to help you to complete the following definitions:

1. Write a definition of *love* that uses the word *God*.
2. Write a definition of *God* that uses the word *love*.

VOCABULARY

3. How can your school or parish practice the spirit of *ecumenism* in a practical way?

COMPREHENSION

4. What did St. Thomas Aquinas mean when he described God as "pure being"?
5. What did Jesus teach about participating in the love of God?
6. How is Jesus' command of love represented in St. Paul's description of the relationship between Christ and the Church?

CRITICAL THINKING

7. How is the unity of the Church different from people or groups coming together, as for a special cause?
8. Explain how knowing someone as a person is different from distinguishing someone's individuality?

SECTION 2
Unity of Belief

MAIN IDEA
The Church is unified because she professes the same creeds, including one whose origin is with the Apostles.

Another sign of the Church's unity is that her members profess one faith as received from the Apostles. This faith is expressed in creeds, a term from the Latin *credo*, which means "I believe." You are probably familiar with two Church creeds. The Nicene Creed is

recited at Mass on Sundays and Holy Days. Also called the Nicene-Constantinopolitan Creed, the Nicene Creed dates to the Councils of Nicaea (325) and Constantinople (381). The Apostles' Creed is another faith summary that is professed at Baptism and recited while praying the Rosary. While there have been other creeds in Church history, the Nicene Creed and the Apostles' Creed are the most important.

The Apostles' Creed is the Church's oldest creed. It highlights the essential Christian doctrine of the Blessed Trinity (see *CCC*, 190). Part One of the *Catechism of the Catholic Church* expands on the teachings of the Apostles' Creed.

The Apostles' Creed is a great source of unity because those who recite it and those on whose behalf it is recited at Baptism gain entrance into the Church and communion with God: Father, Son, and Holy Spirit. St. Ambrose described the Apostles' Creed as "the spiritual seal, our heart's meditation and an ever present guardian."

All Are Called to the Church's Unity

Most Catholics by high school age can recite the Nicene Creed by memory, at least in the context of Sunday Mass. Reciting the creeds, especially in public worship, is a sign of your unity with Catholics both in

NOTE TAKING

Recognize Sequence. Create a timeline, like the one below, of the main occurrences of apostasy, heresy, schism, and martyrdom mentioned in this section. Also include on the timeline the Church Councils that responded to these occurrences. Look for dates and other clues for sequence in the text.

249
Decius Decree

2010
Baghdad Massacre

your local community and worldwide. To think that millions of people also professed the same faith on the same day is overwhelming to consider.

In a recent year, 42,000 new Catholics were initiated through the adult catechumenate, and 760,000 more were baptized as infants in the United States.

This unity among all people and between people and God was restored through the Life, Passion, Death, and Resurrection of Jesus Christ. This unity is present in the Church because the Holy Spirit brings people together and joins them in Christ. The one, true Church of Christ was formed so that it can function in the world, subsist, and live on in the Catholic Church. Jesus gave the Catholic Church this role in the world when he commissioned Peter and the Apostles to leadership.

The Catholic Church, however, is not an exclusive club. The Church extends an invitation to all people to participate in the unity of the new People of God.

> **apostasy** The denial of Christ and the repudiation of the Christian Faith by a baptized Christian.

At Baptism, the Church initiates her members by calling them to profess faith in

- the first Divine Person, God the Father, and the work of creation;
- the second Divine Person, God the Son, and his work of Redemption; and
- the third Divine Person, the Holy Spirit, who is the origin and source of holiness that comes to those who are baptized.

Unfortunately, professing and holding these creedal beliefs has not always been simple. There have been misunderstandings and even outright denials of these basic statements of faith. The role of the Apostles and their successors, the pope and bishops, also led to disputes.

Wounds to Unity

From the earliest time in her history, there have been divisions in the Church's unity. These divisions have led to apostasy, schism, and heresy. The Protestant Reformation occured. The effects of some of these divisions can still be felt today.

Apostasy

Apostasy is a total denial of Christ and a disavowal of the Church by a person who has been baptized. In the early Church, the sin of apostasy ranked as one of the most serious. Apostasy was common in the early centuries of the Church, before Christianity was legalized in the fourth century. For example, when the Roman emperor Decius (249–251) required all citizens to possess a certificate proving that they offered sacrifice to pagan gods of the Empire, many Christians

Our Lady of Salvation Cathedral in Baghdad, Iraq

On October 31, 2010, an Islamic militant group attacked Our Lady of Salvation Cathedral in Baghdad during Mass. Fifty-eight worshippers were killed and many more were injured. According to the local archbishop, Philip Najim, the victims could have saved their lives had they agreed to renounce their faith and say, "I will become a Muslim."

An *EWTN News* article reported that Archbishop Najim visited with survivors of the attack at a Baghdad hospital: "They are still proud to be Christian, to be faithful, to be part of the Church," he said. "I saw strength, I saw faith, I saw witness, testimony."

Heresies

The Church's creeds are prayers that recognize and express the faith of the Church. The Church's primary beliefs—beliefs shared with many other Christians—are expressed in the Apostles' Creed and Nicene Creed. Other essential beliefs are called **dogmas**, which have been specifically revealed by God and taught by the Magisterium. It is not possible to remain a member of the Church and reject any of the creedal statements or dogmas. A person who deliberately does commits **heresy**. A heretic is a baptized person who denies or stubbornly doubts a dogma of the Catholic faith. There were several early Church heresies (see pages 58–59). Most of these had to do with misunderstandings of the nature of Christ. The Church typically responded to these false teachings at an ecumenical council.

Schism

There have been a number of public disagreements within the Church that have also threatened her unity.

denied their faith rather than be put to death. Even after Christianity was legalized, apostasies continued, though to a lesser degree. A famous apostate was a later Roman emperor, Flavius Claudius Julianus, known as Julian the Apostate. Though educated as a Christian, as soon as Julian became emperor in 361 he took up a deliberate campaign to renounce Christianity; he promoted pagan worship, fired Church teachers, and ended subsidies for the Church. In fact, he did everything within his power to suppress the growth of the faith.

Throughout history, resisting the temptation to deny the faith has many times been a life and death choice. For those who do make the choice to proclaim their faith in Christ, martyrdom sometimes follows.

dogmas Central truths of the Catholic faith, defined by the Magisterium, that Catholics are obliged to believe.

heresy An obstinate denial after Baptism to believe a truth that must be believed with divine and Catholic faith, or an obstinate doubt about such truth.

Early **ecumenical councils** settled many of these disputes. However, in 1054 a major **schism** occurred in the Church. This Eastern Schism had its roots in differences in Church belief and practice in the Roman (Western) and Byzantine (Eastern) empires. For example, the Church in the East (based in Constantinople) was not as dependent on the authority of the pope as the Church in the West (based in Rome). In some cases, the Eastern Church looked to the Byzantine emperor to resolve Church issues instead of the pope.

Three main issues led to the schism.

1. The first conflict had to do with Pope Leo the Great's condemnation in the fifth century of the Council of Chalcedon's ruling that gave the Church of Constantinople the authority to make decisions for all the territories in the Byzantine Empire. The pope could not accept surrendering Church authority that was properly his as bishop of Rome.

2. A second dispute was known as *iconoclasm*. Byzantine Emperor Leo III (ca. 685–741) condemned the veneration of sacred images called icons as **idolatry**. The pope did not agree with this ruling.

3. The third issue was the ninth-century dispute over the Western Church's addition of the phrase *filioque* ("and from the Son") to the Holy Spirit section of the Nicene Creed without the approval of a Church council. The Eastern Church believed that the Holy Spirit descended *through* the Son, not *from* the Son. This controversy alone might have led to a split between the Western and Eastern Church, but that didn't happen until two centuries later. At that time, the head of the Church in the East, the Patriarch Michael Cerularius, closed all churches in his city that were loyal to Rome and excommunicated priests who said the Mass in Latin. He also opposed Western practices of clerical celibacy, the use of unleavened bread for the Eucharist, and the *filioque* clause in the Nicene Creed.

ecumenical councils Gatherings of all the Catholic bishops of the world. The word *ecumenical* pertains to a theological recognition of and willingness to learn from those different faith traditions. Ecumenical councils determine those things which all the local churches (dioceses) will hold in common.

schism A break in Christian unity that takes place when a group of Christians separates itself from the Church. This happens historically when the group breaks in union with the pope.

idolatry Worshiping something or someone other than the true God.

THE CHURCH RESPONDS (TO) EARLY HERESIES

HERESY GNOSTICISM (first developed in the second century)

FALSE BELIEFS VS. CHURCH'S RESPONSE

Claimed that secret knowledge (*gnosis*) of salvation was transmitted by Christ to the Apostles or selected followers.

St. Irenaeus, the Bishop of Lyons, argued against Gnosticism in his *Against Heresies*, highlighting the importance of **Sacred Tradition** for arriving at religious truth.

Denied the Resurrection of Christ and would not accept that the Son of God took on human flesh. Said material reality is evil.

Argued that God intended to join the physical nature of humans with his spiritual nature.

Denied the validity of Scripture and the authority of the pope and bishops to rule the Church.

The source of right teaching and belief resides with the Church because the Church was founded by Jesus and entrusted to St. Peter.

Sacred Tradition The living transmission of the Church's Gospel message found in the Church's teaching, life, and worship. It is faithfully preserved, handed on, and interpreted by the Church's Magisterium.

HERESY ARIANISM (first taught in the third century)

FALSE BELIEFS VS. CHURCH'S RESPONSE

Named for Arius, a priest from Alexandria who was influenced by Greek philosophy, Arianism denied Jesus' divinity.

The Council of Nicaea (325) condemned Arianism and expressed the Church's belief in the Nicene Creed.

Held that Jesus was God's greatest creature who was made before time, but a creature nonetheless.

Taught that Jesus is consubstantial with the Father, that is, Christ possesses the same nature as God the Father.

APOLLINARIANISM HERESY
(fourth century)

FALSE BELIEFS VS. CHURCH'S RESPONSE

Named for Apollinaris, a fourth-century bishop of Laodicea, this heresy claimed that although Jesus had a human body, he had no human soul.

In 381 the First Council of Constantinople labeled this belief a heresy and taught that Jesus was fully man and fully God.

NESTORIANISM HERESY
(fifth century)

FALSE BELIEFS VS. CHURCH'S RESPONSE

Nestorius, the patriarch of Constantinople, made a further distinction between Christ's humanity and divinity, teaching that some of Christ's traits were purely human and others were purely divine.

The Council of Ephesus responded in 431 stating clearly that Jesus is one Person with two natures. Everything Jesus experienced was with his whole Person. From the moment of his conception, Jesus was fully human and fully divine.

Nestorius declared that Mary was the Mother of only Jesus' human self and that she should not be called *Theotokos*, or Mother of God.

Mary can rightly be called the Mother of God. (Following the Council of Ephesus, churches that followed Nestorius returned to union with Rome.)

hypostatic union A Greek term employed to describe the union of the human and divine natures of Jesus Christ, the Son of God, in the one divine person (*hypostasis*). The First Council of Ephesus used and affirmed this teaching.

MONOPHYSITISM HERESY
(fifth century)

FALSE BELIEFS VS. CHURCH'S RESPONSE

Preached by Eastern monks and theologians, this heresy held that Christ possessed only a divine nature and that his human nature was absorbed into his divine nature like "a drop of honey into the water of the sea."

At the Council of Chalcedon in 451, the doctrine of **hypostatic union** was taught by Pope Leo I and endorsed by the Council with the resounding words: "Peter has spoken through Leo." It taught that Jesus is one Divine Person with two natures: a divine nature and a human nature. (Following the Council of Chalcedon, those who accepted monopohystism formed the Oriental Orthodox churches.)

The sixteenth-century Council of Trent was held in response to the challenges of the Protestant Reformation.

teachings of the first eight Church councils. They considered these councils *orthodox*, that is adhering to traditional and authentic standards. Hence, the Eastern churches adopted the name Orthodox. At first, it was likely that neither the East nor West thought that this division would last as long as it has. However, the sacking of Constantinople by **Crusaders** in 1204 delayed a possible restoration of relations for centuries.

The Second Vatican Council and the popes that followed have worked to restore unity with the Orthodox Church. In 1965, Pope Paul VI and the Patriarch Athenagoras I lifted the mutual excommunications imposed in 1054. In 2001, St. John Paul II apologized for the Roman Catholic involvement in the siege of Constantinople. In 2004, the pope returned the relics of St. John Chrysostom and St. Gregory Nazianzen to Istanbul, modern-day Constantinople. (Crusaders had taken the relics of St. John as war booty in 1204; Byzantine monks brought St. Gregory's bones to Rome in the eighth century during the iconoclast controversy.) Ecumenical dialogue between the Roman Catholic and Orthodox Churches has continued in the years since.

Protestant Reformation

During the **Protestant Reformation**, some Catholics embraced beliefs that were heretical and caused division in the Church. These beliefs were promoted in the early sixteenth century by a German Catholic monk, Martin Luther. Luther challenged Church teaching in several areas, including the role of Scripture in the Church. Luther taught a theology of *sola scriptura* ("the Bible alone") that rejected the authority of the Church's Tradition asserting that the Scriptures, especially the New Testament, were the only infallible source and rule of faith and practice. From this, he taught that the pope and bishops were not the only infallible interpreters of Scripture; individuals, according to Luther, could just as legitimately interpret Scripture.

These issues reached a climax when representatives of Pope Leo IX traveled in 1053 to Constantinople to try and persuade Cerularius to submit to the pope's authority on these key issues. When the patriarch refused, an uncompromising representative of the pope, Cardinal Humbert, excommunicated Cerularius on the spot. Cerularius then hastily called a council, and he excommunicated Pope Leo, who had already died!

Most Eastern churches sided with their patriarch. From then on, these churches only accepted the

Crusaders The name for participants in one of the nine armed expeditions by Christians beginning in 1095 and ending in 1291 that were intended to drive the Muslims out of the Holy Land and, in the process, reunite Christians of the East and West.

Protestant Reformation An effort to reform the Catholic Church in the sixteenth century, which led to the separation of large numbers of Christians from communion with Rome.

DIVISION & REFORM

Research the following people and terms. Explain what they have to do with the division of the Church at the time of the Protestant Reformation and the Church's response to the division that ensued.

People	Terms
Ulrich Zwingli	Indulgence
John Knox	Predestination
King Henry VIII	*Augsburg Confession*
St. John Fisher	*Book of Common Prayer*
St. Thomas More	Index to Forbidden Books
St. Ignatius Loyola	*Spiritual Exercises*

The Church teaches that Scripture cannot be separated from Tradition. It was the Church, guided by the Holy Spirit, that came to decide what was Scripture. In other words, the Church understands that God reveals himself through a single **Deposit of Faith**. Christ entrusted this Deposit to the Apostles to share through the Church by their writings and preaching until Christ comes again. This single Deposit of Faith is found in Sacred Scripture *and* in the Sacred Tradition of the Church.

Luther also argued for *sola gratia* ("grace alone"). He said that no person could possibly keep all of God's commandments and that everyone would be condemned if Salvation hinged upon human behavior. He and other Protestant reformers believed that the key to Salvation was found in a person's faith (*sola fide*) and not in his or her actions. The Council of Trent (1545–1563), held in the wake of the Protestant Reformation, agreed on one point with the reformers: people are saved because of the grace of God and the sacrifice of Jesus Christ, not their own merit. But the Council reemphasized the fact that one receives this saving grace first and foremost in the Sacrament of Baptism.

The Council agreed that a person could not be *justified* (reunited with God) without faith. However, the Council pointed out that Baptism, not personal faith, is the first step toward Salvation.

Other Protestant reformers, including Ulrich Zwingli and John Calvin, followed Luther. Zwingli set up reform Protestantism in Switzerland. Calvin, best known for the doctrine of **predestination**, also denied Catholic beliefs in the sacraments, papacy, monasticism, and clerical celibacy. The Protestant Reformation also came to England in the sixteenth century, not over a doctrinal dispute, but because the pope would not allow King Henry VIII to divorce his wife. Henry made himself the head of the Church of England.

Deposit of Faith "The heritage of faith contained in Sacred Scripture and Sacred Tradition, handed down in the Church from the time of the Apostles, from which the Magisterium draws all that it proposes for belief as being divinely revealed" (*Catechism of the Catholic Church*, Glossary).

predestination A false doctrine taught by John Calvin that God determines people for Salvation or damnation before they are born and that no human effort can merit Salvation or entrance into the elect.

Ecumenism

You may belong to an ecumenical family, that is, one in which one parent is Roman Catholic and the other belongs to another ecclesial community, for example Lutheran.

In such a case, even though both Catholic and Lutheran parents are Christians and share many common beliefs, the differences can be both enriching and taxing on family life. In Minneapolis, home to many Lutherans and Catholics, the leadership of the Catholic Archdiocese of Saint Paul and Minneapolis and the Saint Paul and Minneapolis Synods of the Evangelical Lutheran Church in America issued a joint statement offering teaching and suggestions on some of these issues. For example, one section of the document addressed four differences in the understanding of marriage and other elements of faith that can affect marriage:

1. Catholics define marriage as a sacrament. Lutherans understand marriage as covenant, but not a sacrament.

2. Following the understanding of marriage as a sacrament, Catholics hold that marriage is a permanent union that cannot be broken by civil divorce but can only be declared null through the annulment process. While Lutheran teaching recognizes the life long intent of marriage, it also acknowledges that the marriage covenant is sometimes broken and that divorce may be justified.

3. Catholic and Lutheran teaching on sexuality in marriage differ. Catholics teach the centrality of the unitive *and* procreative nature of sex, and safeguard this teaching by not accepting the use of artificial contraceptive methods that can act against *both* the procreative and unitive ends of sex in marriage. Lutherans affirm the right of couples to use a variety of contraceptive methods.

4. Mainly because of the absence of the Sacrament of Holy Orders in in the Lutheran church, Catholics and Lutherans have a different understanding of Eucharist. Also, Lutherans do not accept many other Catholic beliefs (e.g., the Communion of Saints, the authority of the pope). Therefore, a Catholic should not receive Communion in a Lutheran church and vice versa.

The practical pains of Christian division like those described above persist today and are real in many ecumenical families. Yet, there are many signs of hope. Christians are working together to repair these divisions. This effort is the work of ecumenism. At the heart of the Church's commitment to ecumenism is its fidelity to the prayer of Jesus, who sought unity among his disciples:

> And now I will no longer be in the world, but they are in the world, while I am coming to you. Holy Father, keep them in your name that you have given me, so that they may be one just as we are. (Jn 17:11)

Tracing Ecumenical Efforts

The Church's response to the Protestant Reformation began with the Council of Trent (1545–1563). This Council had a significant and lasting effect on the Church for the next four hundred years. Besides rejecting Luther's assertion of *sola scriptura*, *sola gratia*, and *sola fide*, the Council also emphasized the importance of the hierarchy in the administration of the sacraments. The Council of Trent outlined the way that Catholics must live and the faith they must profess. An image of the Church that emerged from the Council was as a "Mother"; that is, a Church that will feed, educate, and protect her people through her leaders.

The Council made it clear that those who disagreed with its pronouncements were separated from the Church.

The Council of TRENT

- formalized the Church's position on the number and nature of the Sacraments
- defined how the liturgy is celebrated and articulated the theology of Eucharist
- reemphasized the authority of the hierarchy
- explained the role of Mary and the saints
- reaffirmed the existence of free will in contrast to Calvin's teachings about predestination

Following the Council of Trent, divisions in Christianity persisted. However, in the twentieth century this began to change. Among the separated Protestant communities the commitment to work toward Christian unity began with the World Missionary Conference in Edinburgh, Scotland, in 1910, where a focus was, according to news reports, "to exchange views on the ways and means of executing the Gospel to the whole creation."

Pope Pius XI, however, forbade Catholics to attend the conference. Though he acknowledged that superficially the goals and efforts of the conference were worthy, he was concerned that those in attendance would fail to understand the mystical nature of the Catholic Church as the true Church of Christ. Instead, they might name a visible Church as only "a federation composed of various communities of Christians, even though they adhere to different doctrines that may even be incompatible with each other."

While the Catholic Church did not participate in the World Missionary Conference, many renewal events of the early twentieth century did pave the way for her full participation in the ecumenical movement. These events provided a continuation of the Church's

social justice teaching, new focus on biblical scholarship highlighted by Pope Pius XII's encyclical *Divino Afflante Spiritu*, and a recognition of the dangers of blending missionary work with colonialism. These and other efforts were precursors for the announcement in 1959 of St. John XXIII of the Church's twenty-first ecumenical council, the Second Vatican Council.

Teachings and Tasks of Ecumenism

The Church "must always pray and work to maintain, reinforce, and perfect the unity that Christ wills for her" (*CCC*, 820). To this effort, a major focus of the Second Vatican Council was forging efforts for greater Christian unity. The Council's Decree on Ecumenism, while reaffirming that the Catholic Church is entrusted with the fullness of the means of Salvation, committed the Church to the ecumenical movement and affirmed the many positive qualities in other religions. It taught that those who grow up in other Christian communities should not be treated as if they themselves caused the rift in Christianity. Rather, they,

> believing in Christ cannot be accused of the sin involved in the separation, and the Catholic Church embraces upon them with respect and affection. For [those] who believe in Christ and have been truly baptized are in communion with the Catholic Church even though this communion is imperfect. (*Unitatis Redintegrattio*, 3)

The Decree on Ecumenism was a landmark statement in many ways. First, the decree acknowledged that both sides shared in the blame of divisions that occurred in either the Eastern Schism between East and West or during the Protestant Reformation. Second, the decree focused more on what Catholics shared in common with other Christians—for example, in the areas of shared Scripture, celebration of at least some of the sacraments, work for justice and peace, and aspirations for holiness and discipleship in Christ—rather than on differences. In these separated Christian communities there are many elements of sanctification and truth that come from Christ. These elements are calls to Christian unity.

God calls the entire Church to participate in these efforts, first, by calling on individual Catholics to examine their own conscience, as suggested both by the "Decree on Ecumenism" and later by St. John Paul II in his encyclical, *Ut unum sint* ("That They May Be One"), mindful of the words from the First Letter of John: "If we say, 'We are without sin,' we deceive ourselves, and the truth is not in us" (1 Jn 1:8). St. John Paul II did this himself by meeting frequently with other religious leaders and by asking that they forgive the Roman Catholic Church throughout history for any harm done to the cuse of Christian unity.

Also, since the Second Vatican Council, the Church has engaged in formal dialogue with Lutherans, Anglicans, the Orthodox, Reformed churches, Pentecostals, Methodists, and Disciples of Christ, among others. Often, as a result of these formal dialogues, significant disagreements have been overcome. For example, in 1999, the Catholic Church and Lutheran World Federation agreed that each shared the same essential commitment to the saving work of Jesus Christ.

Pope Benedict XVI mentioned this common bond among Christians in the introduction to his first encyclical, *Deus Caritas Est* ("God Is Love"): "Being Christian is not the result of an ethical choice or a lofty idea, but the encounter with an event, a person, which gives life a new horizon and a decisive direction." It is primarily in the Person of Jesus Christ that Christians find unity.

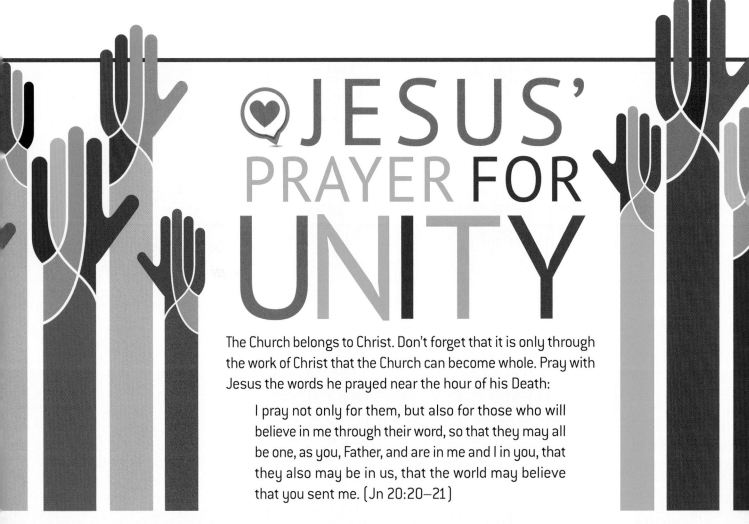

JESUS' PRAYER FOR UNITY

The Church belongs to Christ. Don't forget that it is only through the work of Christ that the Church can become whole. Pray with Jesus the words he prayed near the hour of his Death:

I pray not only for them, but also for those who will believe in me through their word, so that they may all be one, as you, Father, and are in me and I in you, that they also may be in us, that the world may believe that you sent me. (Jn 20:20–21)

WORKING TOWARD UNITY

Several times in his pontificate—most specifically in his encyclical *Ut Unum Sint* ("That they may be one")—St. John Paul II said the work toward Christian unity involved everyone, the faithful and clergy alike, while acknowledging that the reconciliation of all Christians into the Catholic Church remains the work of God. For this reason, the greatest ecumenical effort you can take is to pray along with Christ for the Church. The pope also named these other areas where all Christians can work to toward greater unity:

1. Renew and be faithful to your Christian vocation. Your vocation, given at Baptism, is to seek out the Kingdom of God and arrange your life to the Kingdom by following God's will.

2. Live a holier life according to the Gospel. Holiness is a perfection of love. You are called to "be perfect as your heavenly Father is perfect" (Mt 5:48).

3. Pray with and for separated Christians. You can pray both privately and in ecumenical prayer services for the unity of Christians. St. John Paul II regarded this as the "soul of the whole ecumenical movement" (*Unitatis redintegrattio*, 821).

4. Grow in knowledge of people in other ecclesial communities and their beliefs. Without abandoning your own convictions, you must recognize Christ's presence in these communities. St. John Paul II described this dialogue as an ecumenical "exchange of gifts" (*Unitatis Redintegrattio*, 28). This exchange often takes place through participation together in social and service activities.

5. Form yourself in the faith. This can take place by studying the Catholic faith so that you can comfortably share your knowledge of it with others. When a non-Catholic confronts you with the statement that "Catholics worship Mary," for example, you should have the correct understanding of Mary's role in your life and in the life of the Church. You should also pray for priests and seminarians and all who minister in the Church as they grow in their own knowledge of the faith.

6. Remain informed about the latest dialogue among theologians and meetings among different churches and communities.

7. Work together with other Christians in efforts of service to all people, especially the poor. Often common opportunities arise around the holidays. Examples include serving Thanksgiving meals to the homeless or providing Christmas gifts to families in need.

SECTION ASSESSMENT

NOTE TAKING

Use the timeline you developed to help you to rewrite each sentence to make it true.

1. Julian the Apostate became Roman emperor fifteen years after the emperor Decius's reign.

2. The Council of Nicaea condemned Apollinarianism in the third century.

3. The Council of Chalcedon endorsed Pope Leo's teaching on the hypostatic union with the resounding "Jesus has spoken through Leo."

VOCABULARY

4. Explain the difference between a dogma and a creed, a schism and a heresy, and iconoclasm and idolatry.

COMPREHENSION

5. Name the four issues that led to the Eastern Schism of 1054.

6. How did the *filioque* controversy end?

7. How did the Church respond to Luther's theology of *sola scriptura* ("the Bible alone"), *sola grátia* ("grace alone"), and *sola fide* ("faith alone")?

8. What makes the Second Vatican Council's document "The Decree on Ecumenism" a landmark on the ecumenical efforts?

APPLICATION

9. Choose two of St. John Paul II's suggestions for participating in the Church's ecumenical efforts that you can take part in, and provide examples of how you can do so.

SECTION 3
Unity in Common Worship

MAIN IDEA
The sacraments, especially the Eucharist, are a source of unity that strengthens the connection of those who pray and worship.

One of the great college football game day experiences occurs before home games at the University of Notre Dame. The players and coaches walk through the picturesque campus on the way to Notre Dame Stadium, with students, alumni, and fans crowded on both sides. Some of the players slap palms with the people on the way. Other players smile and nod. A few more already have their "game faces" on and continue the march straightaway.

The tradition brings about a great bond between those who will be on the field playing and coaching the game and those who will be in the bleachers rooting them on.

Actually, there is even more to the tradition than the walk to the stadium. For many years, the procession originated at Sacred Heart Basilica on campus where the team shared in a pre-game Mass. (Nowadays the team Mass is often held the night before the game.)

It has been a tradition for Notre Dame football players to attend Mass and receive Communion before a game from the time the school first fielded a team in 1887. The practice attracted little attention until 1921 when on the way to West Point, the team stopped in Albany, New York, for Mass. Fr. John F. O'Hara, C.S.C., the team chaplain, also arranged for the team to visit a replica of the Our Lady of Lourdes shrine before getting back on the train. He also tipped off the newspaper reporters on the train to these events.

The press really played up the story about "manly" football players who went to church. The story also told how the team's non-Catholic players also participated in "parts of the ceremony."

NOTE TAKING

Understand Effects. Create and fill in a chart like the one below explaining how the liturgy highlights effects of the Church's unity.

Parts of the Liturgy Where the Church's Unity Is Highlighted		
Eucharistic Prayer	Lord's Prayer	Communion
•	•	•
•	•	•

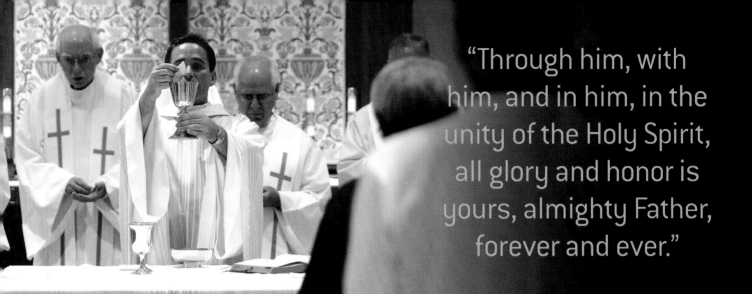

Today, there are usually more non-Catholic players on the Notre Dame team than Catholics. But *everyone* attends the pre-game Mass. In a recent year, quarterback Brady Quinn, an Episcopalian, said that Mass helped to center him before the game. Ryan Harris, an offensive tackle and a Muslim, said, "I feel very fortunate to be able to spend time with my teammates, especially time to relax and place God in my thoughts before a game."

Another date on the schedule with Army started another Notre Dame tradition. In 1923, the Cadets invited a famous actress, Elsie Janis, to take part in a ceremonial kickoff. When Fr. O'Hara heard of this stunt he said, "Elsie Janis will kick off for Army, Joan of Arc will kick off for Notre Dame." He then gave all the players religious medals of St. Joan of Arc. To this day, Notre Dame football players are given a religious medal, usually of a saint, before each game.

Finally, Notre Dame Stadium has to be among the few venues in the entire country where the public address announcer gives not only the other college football scores, but also the locations and starting times of the many Masses offered on campus for following the game!

The sacraments, especially the Eucharist, have always been a source of unity and have enhanced the connection between those who worship together—and in the case of the Notre Dame team, among Catholics and non-Catholics alike. In the concluding doxology to the Eucharistic prayer, the faithful are reminded that every celebration of the Eucharist also strengthens their unity with the Blessed Trinity. It is a "sacrifice of praise to the Father . . . offered *through* Christ and *with* him, to be accepted *in* him" (*CCC*, 1361). United with Christ, the faithful give glory and honor to the Trinity. Also, the gathering of people together as a Church to celebrate the sacraments fosters a unity between the Church of Heaven, Purgatory, and earth; that is, between the living and the dead. Some of these dimensions of unity are explored next.

Unity with Christ and One Another

A primary grace of participation at Mass is that "the Eucharistic sacrifice is wholly directed toward the intimate union of the faithful with Christ through communion" (*CCC*, 1382). The communicant's unity with Christ is the principal fruit or positive outcome of the Sacrament. The Risen Lord is present in his Word proclaimed at Mass and in the Liturgy of the Eucharist in his Body and Blood under the species of bread and wine.

Celebration of the sacraments also brings the members of the Church into communion with one another. In fact, the original meaning of the term *liturgy* refers to "public work" or "service done on behalf of people." The primary meaning of the term is participation of the Church in the "work of God." This has been true since the Church's earliest days. The first-century text of the *Didache* said that the Eucharist is a meal that forms the Church into the new People of God:

> Even as this broken bread was scattered over the hills, and was gathered together becoming one, so let your Church be gathered together from the ends of the earth into your kingdom.

In the early Church, no one came to the Eucharist without having resolved any disagreements that might prevent the Church from being truly united in the Lord. As Jesus taught:

> Therefore, if you bring your gift to the altar, and there recall that your brother has anything against you, leave your gift there at the altar, go first and be reconciled with your brother, and then come and offer your gift. (Mt 5:23–24)

There are many specific parts of the liturgy where the unity of the Church is highlighted. One of these is during the intercessions of the Eucharistic Prayer. The intercessions are prayed by the priest offering the Mass on behalf of the whole Church in Heaven and on earth, the living and the dead, for the pope, bishop, and all the clergy, for Catholics in need ("the prayer of the family you have gathered here before you") and for those who have died ("welcome into your kingdom our departed brothers and sisters, and all who have left this world in your friendship").

The Lord's Prayer also promotes unity with God. It acknowledges the identity of each person as God's adopted children and as brothers and sisters to one another: "When we pray to the Father, we are *in*

All Are WELCOME

Make sure that people you come in contact with know they are welcome in the Church. How so? Do one of the following or similar deeds to remind someone that the Catholic Church should feel like home.

Write a letter (not an e-mail) to a relative or friend who has been away from Church. You can tell this person that your letter is part of a school assignment if you wish. Be sure to share something about your life and the importance of your Catholic faith. Invite the person to attend Mass or a prayer service at your church with you.

Form a welcoming committee for teenagers new to your school or parish. Make the task of your committee to specifically focus on teens. This could mean inviting a new teen to a party you arrange or to attend a game or movie with a group of teens from your school or parish.

If you are not Catholic, arrange to attend a parish event with one of your classmates (e.g., Sunday liturgy, youth group, or bazaar). Write a short reflection on the experience and rate how welcome you felt.

THE LITURGY IS BOTH
UNIFIED AND DIVERSE

In the sixteenth century, the Council of Trent codified one uniform way for the celebration of the Mass in the Roman Catholic Church. This Mass is known as the *Tridentine Mass*. The name is connected to Trento, a city in Italy in the Adige River valley, the place where the Council took place.

The Tridentine Mass is sometimes known as the "Latin Mass" because Latin is the language of its text. There is often a misconception that the Council of Trent established the Latin Mass. Actually, Mass was being said in Latin throughout most of the Roman Empire by the mid third century, because Latin was the official language of the empire. The Council of Trent standardized the liturgy and made specific texts and actions mandatory.

THE *MISSAL OF PIUS V*

In 1570 the *Missal of Pius V* was printed and gradually put to use throughout the Roman Catholic Church as the standard text or canon for Mass. To maintain uniformity, Pope Alexander VII, in 1661, prohibited translation of the *Missal* to the vernacular (commonly spoken language). From this time until the Second Vatican Council, the celebration of the Mass remained virtually unchanged, no matter where in the world it took place.

THE *MISSAL OF PAUL VI*

In the past century, the Second Vatican Council document *Sacrosanctum Concilum* ("Constitution on the Sacred Liturgy") allowed for revision of the liturgy. The Council addressed the need for greater participation of the laity in the liturgy. The *Missal of Paul VI* (the ordinary form of the Mass) was released in 1969 and the Mass began to be celebrated in various local languages. This change did not diminish the "fundamental structure [of the Mass] which has been preserved throughout the centuries down to our day" (*CCC*, 1346). The structure is made up of the Liturgy of the Word (readings, homily, and General Intercessions); and the Liturgy of the Eucharist (presentation of the bread and wine, Consecration, Thanksgiving, and Communion).

With the translations into the vernacular languages, the pope and bishops exercised vigilance in assuring that there was fidelity to the Latin text. To that end, for example, the International Commission for English in the Liturgy worked for more than eight years on a new translation of the Roman Missal, attempting to find English wording that most accurately corresponds to the Latin. In 2010, Pope Benedict XVI approved the translation for use in all English-speaking areas. The pope wrote: "Through these sacred texts and the actions that accompany them, Christ will be made present and active in the midst of his people."

In 2007, Pope Benedict issued a ***motu propio*** allowing for the celebration of the Extraordinary Form of the Mass (the Latin

> ***motu propio*** A Latin term that means "of his own accord." It signifies words in papal documents that were decided by the pope personally.

Mass). The pope reminded Catholics that there "is no contradiction between the two editions of the *Roman Missal*."

NON-LATIN RITES

Interestingly, contrary to popular understanding, Catholic unity does not depend on a uniform religious ritual. There are non-Latin Church traditions that are in full communion with Rome. These twenty-one Eastern Catholic Churches, as the one Roman Catholic Church, are linked to the Apostles. Like the Orthodox churches (pages 56–60), the Eastern Catholic Churches trace their origins to the patriarchates, or communities with patriarchs at the head, in the East: Alexandria, Antioch, Jerusalem, and Constantinople. The difference between the Eastern Catholic Churches and the Orthodox churches is that the Eastern Catholic churches are in full communion with the pope while the Orthodox churches are not.

While all of these Eastern Catholic Churches accept the authority of the pope, they also have a great deal of autonomy in Church life. This is reflected in the fact that they are governed by a separate code, called the *Code of Canons of the Eastern Churches*. This separate code helps to preserve some of their traditions that differ from the Roman Catholic Church, including the ordination of married men to the priesthood and, in some instances, the election rather than appointment of bishops.

The separate code also affects the celebration of the liturgy. The Armenian, Byzantine, Coptic, Ethiopian, East Syrian (or Chaldean), West Syrian, and Maronite liturgical rites and certain other liturgical rites of local churches and religious orders have been recognized as authentic liturgical expressions within the Catholic Church. Within each of these rites the essence of the Sacraments is the same as it is in the Roman rite, but the form used in celebrating the sacraments is not exactly the same.

7 THINGS TO KNOW ABOUT Eastern Catholics

1. The East-West Schism happened in 1054.

2. Eastern churches no longer in union with Rome came to be known as Eastern Orthodox or simply "Orthodox Churches."

3. Eastern Churches that remained in union with Rome are called Eastern Catholic Churches, or often the "Eastern Church." Remember: If the name of the Eastern Church has "Orthodox" in its title, it is not in union with Rome.

4. Eastern Churches accept the pope as leader of the Church.

5. Eastern Churches are fully Catholic.

6. Eastern Churches worship with their own style of liturgy.

7. The three largest Eastern churches are the **Byzantine Ukranian Greek Catholic Church** (4.3 million members), the **Syro-Malabar Catholic Church** (3.9 million members), and the **Maronite Catholic Church** (3.29 million members). By comparison, the Roman Catholic Church has more than 1 billion members.

Roman Catholic Church

Byzantine Ukranian Greek Catholic Church

Syro-Malabar Catholic Church

Maronite Catholic Church

communion with him and with his Son, Jesus Christ" (*CCC*, 2781).

Finally, the reception of Holy Communion is so intimate that Christ becomes part of those who receive, and they of him. This bond of unity is the primary grace of the Sacrament. Jesus said: "Whoever eats my flesh and drinks my blood remains in me and I in him" (Jn 6:56). Assuming the person is properly disposed, the Church recommends that a Catholic receive Communion at every Mass. At the very least, Catholics are obliged by the Church to receive Communion at least once a year.

Unity with the Church of Heaven and Earth

It can be easy to forget that the Church is not solely made up of people living on earth in the present. The Church on earth is also united with pilgrims in Purgatory and with the saints in Heaven, and it is especially in the liturgy where this union is realized. These three states of the Church traditionally have gone by these names: the Militant Church on earth, the Suffering Church of Purgatory, and the Triumphant Church in Heaven. It is in the liturgy that

> We celebrate, rejoicing together, the praise of the divine majesty, and all who have been

The Militant and Triumphant Church is represented in this fourteenth-century fresco by Andrea Di Bonaiuto.

redeemed by the blood of Christ from every tribe and tongue and people and nation, gathered together into one church glorify, in one common song of praise, the one and triune God. (*Lumen Gentium*, 50)

The intercession by the saints in Heaven helps to strengthen the weakness of those on earth and bring everyone closer to Christ, who is the fountain of all grace. The relationship with the saints is not meant to be one-way. Those on earth should imitate the virtues of the saints.

From her earliest days, the Church has also remembered, honored, and prayed for those in Purgatory to reach Heaven, and vice versa.

This unity between the Church of Heaven, Purgatory, and earth represents the participation in one family of God. When you love others and join as the communion of the Church of Heaven and earth in praising the Holy Trinity, you are faithful to your deepest vocation in the hope that you will eventually share in the richness of Heaven.

SECTION ASSESSMENT

NOTE TAKING

Use your completed idea chart to help you to answer the following question.

1. How are the Militant Church, the Suffering Church, and the Triumphant Church each remembered in the Eucharistic Prayer at Mass?

COMPREHENSION

2. Why did the Church offer a new translation of the Roman Missal in 2010?

3. Why are the Eastern Churches united with the Roman Catholic Church while the Orthodox churches are not?

4. What is the principal fruit of the Sacrament of Eucharist?

5. What is the fundamental structure of the Mass that is the same throughout the world?

APPLICATION

6. Rate the unity of the parish where you worship. How is the unity strong? How can it be improved?

7. What tradition does your family have for remembering deceased relatives?

SECTION 4
Unity with Apostolic Succession

MAIN IDEA
The Sacrament of Holy Orders ensures that the Church's apostolic leadership and ministry instituted by Christ will be intact until the end of time.

Christ instituted the Catholic Church. Through his choice of the Twelve Apostles and his designation of Peter as their leader, he gave the Church a structure to succeed and to live on. The Sacrament of Holy Orders ensures that the mission entrusted by Jesus to his Apostles continues to be exercised by the Church, and will be so until the end of time. The Sacrament includes three degrees: episcopate (bishop), presbyterate (priest), and diaconate (deacon).

Apostolic succession involves the careful selection of new bishops to carry on the faith. Without a system for preserving Scripture and Tradition, the Church would be vulnerable to "the latest" interpretations of Scripture, a current popular leader, and intentionally or unintentionally incorporating ideas from other religious traditions. You may have recently witnessed some situations like this in other Christian ecclesial communities where divisions have sprung up between various local communities. You may have noticed that some of these communities are called "first" or "reformed." Often this is because a local leader had a disagreement with the original community and simply broke away.

NOTE TAKING

Organizing the Main Idea. Create drawings like the one below to represent each Church ministry. Write one or two words below each drawing to remind you how this ministry is (1) connected to the Apostles and (2) helps to preserve and share the faith today.

| Pope | Bishops | Priests | Deacons | Laity |

Apostolic succession protects the Church from divisions among local dioceses and parishes. This has been true since the early days of the Church, after the deaths of the Apostles. The word *episkopos* or its plural *episkopoi* appears five times in the New Testament (Acts 20:28; Phil 1:1; 1 Tm 3:2; 1 Pt 2:25). In English, the term is often translated as "overseer" although it is impossible to know the exact meaning as it was originally intended. What is known is that by the end of the second century, an individual bishop who succeeded in authority directly from the Apostles, led each regional church, called a diocese. Presbyters and deacons assisted the bishops.

YOU ARE CALLED TO SPREAD THE CATHOLIC FAITH

What does it mean for a Catholic teen to be an evangelist—that is someone charged with sharing the Good News of Jesus Christ and helping to make the Kingdom of God more visible on earth?

Does it mean going door-to-door for a year after graduation from high school (as many Mormon teens do) to tell the world about your faith? Does it mean engaging in clever arguments with non-believers or non-Catholics to try to "win them over" to Christianity or Catholicism? Does it mean signing up as a missionary to a foreign land?

The Catechism of the Catholic Church explains simply that evangelization is "the proclamation of Christ by word and the testimony of life" (*CCC*, 905).

What follows is that the first way you can evangelize is by word of mouth, by sharing your faith with those who are searching and questioning. Perhaps a classmate asks why you don't join in gossiping about another classmate. You can simply say that gossiping about others is not something that Jesus would do. Maybe another peer teases you for being diligent about going to Sunday Mass. You can explain that Mass provides you with a "spiritual recharging" because it helps you grow close to Jesus and others in the Church who are members of the Body of Christ. You can also ask this person to join you.

At your age, one of the best ways to evangelize is simply to keep learning about your faith so you can respond to questions and disagreements both intelligently and as a passionate believer. More important, you can share the faith through the testimony of your life—that is, by your good example and by striving to live a life disposed to the theological virtues of faith, hope, and love and in practice of the cardinal virtues: prudence, justice, fortitude, and temperance.

If you live a life motivated by love, people will take notice. They will ask you about your motivation. And then you can tell them about your faith in Christ and your participation in the Catholic Church.

The laity, too, has a role in sharing the faith and passing it to generations. This role often depends on the laity's ability to defend the faith, a skill described by the term **apologist**. Taking the lead from the pope and bishops and the long teaching Tradition of the Church, the laity are called to work hard to dispel false rumors about Christianity and to make Christianity appear both reasonable and acceptable to non-Christians. Hand in hand with defending the faith, all Catholics are called to evangelize. Some techniques for **evangelization** are offered on page 75 and more information on a current practice called "new evangelization" is included in Chapter 6.

The next sections focus on the role of the ordained leadership in serving and preserving the unity of the Church and also examine the special role of the successors to Peter, the pope.

Emerging Role of the Bishop

From the time of the early Church, bishops were recognized as men who had the presence of the Holy Spirit within them. After his election (often by the community as a whole), a bishop received imposition of hands from another bishop. St. Ignatius of Antioch decreed by the early second century that only a bishop or his designate could preside at Eucharist or baptize.

Most of the local churches in the first two centuries were small; in fact, they resembled modern-day parishes in size, though they were really the forerunner of modern dioceses. The bishop presided over the Sunday Eucharist. He also preached, baptized, and forgave sins. Because the Eucharist was the central act of Christian worship and a vital sign of Christian unity, it was natural for Christians to look to their bishops for inspiration, leadership, and direction in other areas, including on questions that might cause a rift in the unity of the Church. As the churches grew, several

outlying communities arose. Later these were called parishes. The bishop assigned a presbyter to take some of the consecrated hosts from the bishop's celebration of Eucharist to the people in the outlying communities.

Though Christianity was illegal in the first three centuries, the Church grew rapidly. Local churches were founded in nearly every region of the Roman Empire. Because of the role of the bishop, each local church was not viewed as an independent congregation, but as a church in spiritual communion with all other local churches. Also, because the various bishops were united with one another as descendants of the Apostles, their local churches were united as well.

This unity among the local churches was realized in many ways. For example, when Christians traveled in the Empire they often brought with them a letter of commendation from their own bishop and offered it to the bishop of the church where they were visiting. An authentic letter from a bishop signified that the visitor could participate at Eucharist. The acceptance of the letter also pointed out the communion between the bishops and the two local churches.

Also, from the earliest days, bishops preserved the unity of the local churches with the universal Church through gathering regionally in **episcopal synods**. At the synods, the bishops addressed questions of common concern. For example, in the late second century episcopal synods were called to respond to threats of a schismatic group known as Montanists,

apologist "Defender of the faith." A Catholic who works hard to dispel the false rumors about Catholicism and Christianity and who makes the faith appear both more reasonable and acceptable to non-Christians.

evangelization To bring the Good News of Jesus Christ to others.

episcopal synod A representative body of bishops assembled periodically by the pope to advise him on important Church concerns. It is not a legislative body.

St. IGNATIUS of ANTIOCH on Roles in the Church

"I exhort you to study to do all things with a divine harmony, while your bishop presides in the place of God, and your presbyters in the place of the assembly of the apostles, along with your deacons, who are most dear to me, and are entrusted with the ministry of Jesus Christ, who was with the Father before the beginning of time, and in the end was revealed. Do ye all then, imitating the same divine conduct, pay respect to one another, and let no one look upon his neighbor after the flesh, but do ye continually love each other in Jesus Christ."

who believed in Christ's imminent coming and who taught a rigorous form of asceticism, or self-denial. Likewise, in 190 AD a series of regional synods were called to address disagreements regarding the dating of Easter. This practice of calling and participating in synods recognized that the bishops of local churches bore responsibility for the universal Church as well.

In the fourth century, the role of the bishops expanded further though initially accompanied by participation of the state. With the legalization of Christianity in the *Edict of Milan*, the emperors in both the West and East became more involved in Church affairs. Often the emperors themselves called ecumenical councils, including the Council of Nicaea in 325 AD, the first of twenty-one ecumenical councils. Eight of the councils were held in the first millennium. Councils differ from synods as they are a legislative Church gathering, synods are not.

There were abuses to the ministry of the bishop beginning around the second millennium. At times, bishops were appointed by nobility, with some interested in the material benefits of the appointment. Often bishops would not even live in the dioceses where they were assigned. (This situation was corrected by the Council of Trent, which required bishops to reside in their home diocese.) Further, bishops began to lose their day-to-day interaction with the people as priests took on a more prominent role in the daily life of the parish.

The Second Vatican Council reemphasized the bishop's role as teacher and pastor confirmed through the fullness of the Sacrament of Holy Orders. This consecration ordains bishops for the highest priesthood, the summit of sacred ministry. The Council taught that the bishop was not a representative of the pope in a local place, but rather the vicar of Christ in his own diocese, mindful of the words of St. Ignatius of Antioch who taught that the "bishop presides in the place of God." Also, as in the past, bishops do not just minister in their own diocese. Each bishop is also a member of the entire body of bishops, called the "college of bishops." This teaching is underscored in the words of Pope Pius XII:

> Though each bishop is the lawful pastor only of the portion of the block entrusted to his care, as a legitimate successor of the apostles he is, by divine institution and precept, responsible with the other bishops for the apostolic mission of the Church. (*Fidei donum*: AAS 49)

The college of bishops exists for the purpose of preserving the unity of the universal Church. As such, the whole college shares with the pope authority over the whole Church. This is sometimes called the doctrine of **episcopal collegiality**.

> **episcopal collegiality** All the bishops of the Church with the pope as their head. This college together, but never without the pope, has supreme and full authority over the universal Church.

After the laying on of hands by the bishop, the brother priests of the newly ordained do the same.

Priests and Deacons Share in Apostolic Ministry

Priests also receive the Sacrament of Holy Orders. In the early Church, as today, the bishop ordained presbyters, or priests, and other presbyters joined in the laying on of hands at the rite of ordination. Priests share in the bishops' apostolic ministry by exercising oversight at each parish, always doing so in communion with and in obedience to the bishop. Priests can only exercise their ministry in dependence on the bishop and in communion with him. As the *Catechism* states:

> The promise of obedience they make to the bishop at the moment of ordination and the kiss of peace from him at the end of ordination mean that the bishop considers them his co-workers, his sons, his brothers and his friends, and that they in return owe him love and obedience. (*CCC*, 1567)

Priests share in the universal dimension of Christ's charge to the Apostles to preach the Gospel everywhere. The principal power of the presbyterate is to offer the Sacrifice of the Mass, in which the prayers of the people are united with the sacrifice of Christ, the Head of the Church.

A third level of Church hierarchy is the diaconate. Through ordination deacons share a special attachment to bishops in the carrying out of their ministry. The word *diakonoi* comes from the Greek word for "servant" or "waiter." The origins of the diaconate are described in the Acts of the Apostles (see 6:1–7), where seven men were chosen to look after the distribution of goods to the needy so that the Apostles could remain devoted to preaching the Gospel. Deacons assist the bishop and priest at Mass, in the distribution of Holy Communion, in assisting at and blessing marriages, in proclaiming and preaching the Gospel, in presiding over funerals, and in various works of charity.

The Importance of the Papacy

In Jesus' message to St. Peter—"I will give you the keys to the kingdom of heaven. Whatever you bind on earth shall be bound in heaven; and whatever you loose on earth shall be loosed in heaven" (Mt 16:19)—it seems certain that Jesus is granting Peter a unique authority over the Church.

OTHER NEW TESTAMENT PASSAGES SPEAK TO PETER'S IMPORTANCE:

In Luke's Last Supper account, Jesus confronts Peter and predicts that Peter will deny him, but then reassures him: "I have prayed that your own faith may not fail; and once you have turned back, you must strengthen your brothers" (Lk 22:32).

St. Paul acknowledges that Peter is the first to have received an appearance from the Risen Lord: "he appeared to Cephas (Peter), then to the Twelve" (1 Cor 15:5).

Paul also mentions an early trip to Jerusalem to "confer with Cephas" (Gal 1:18). He remained with Peter for fifteen days, suggesting that he respected Peter's authority as first among the Apostles.

In the final chapter of John's Gospel, full attention is given to Peter as Jesus asks a threefold question: "Simon, son of John, do you love me?" (see Jn 21:20–23). After each instance, with Peter's affirmative response, Jesus commands Peter to feed and tend Jesus' sheep. The passage is constructed to parallel Peter's three denials of Jesus prior to the Passion. In the Old Testament, kings were known to shepherd their people. The passage suggests the same type of authority is given to Peter, though it is a unique authority that is based in Peter's love for the Lord. These and other texts amply demonstrate the special role of leadership and authority of Peter in the early Church. From Peter's time on, the pope as been the "perpetual and visible source and foundation of the unity of bishops and the multitude of the faithful" (*Lumen Gentium*, 23).

Defending the Primacy of the Pope

There have always been opponents to the pope's authority and universal jurisdiction over the Church, also called papal primacy. This teaching has origins directly from Christ's commissioning of Peter to be the visible head of the Church. The teaching was reaffirmed several times. Pope Leo the Great (440–461) used biblical, historical, and legal arguments to assert the primacy of the pope among all bishops, taking the title *Pontifex Maximus* ("Highest Bridge Builder"), a title formerly used by the emperor to describe his role as high priest in the Roman religion. The Council of Florence (1439), the Fifth Lateran Council (1512–1517), and the First Vatican Council (1869–1870) also reaffirmed papal primacy. The First Vatican Council further defined papal infallibility, which holds that the pope is preserved from error when teaching dogmatically on matters of faith and morals. More information on this teaching will be presented in Chapter 5.

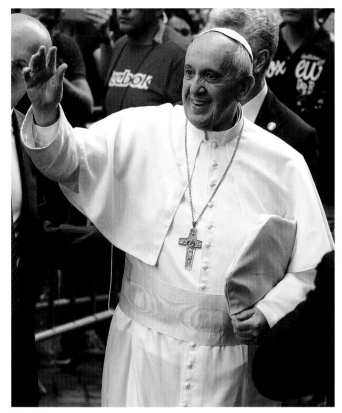

Pope Francis

The Second Vatican Council (1962–1965) likewise taught on the primacy of the pope. A difference was that the Second Vatican Council began its teaching first on the ministry of the bishops and then addressed the pope in relationship to the bishops. Two Council documents—the *Christus Dominus* ("Decree on the Pastoral Office of Bishops in the Church") and *Lumen Gentium* ("Dogmatic Constitution on the Church")—addressed how the bishops rule and bring unity to the Church only in their connection with the pope. The *Catechism* sums this up as follows: "The college or body of bishops has no authority unless united with the Roman **Pontiff**, Peter's successor as its head" (883). A bishop exercises pastoral care in his diocese, but in all cases his authority depends on his union with the pope.

The papacy in recent years has gone further to bridge unity both among Catholics and with the entire world. In his encyclical on ecumenism, St. John Paul II emphasized again the papal title taken by St. Gregory the Great's title: "Servant of the Servants of God." St. John Paul II wrote:

> This designation is the best possible safeguard against the risk of separating power (and in particular primacy) from ministry. Such a separation would contradict the very meaning of power according to the Gospel. (*Ut Unum Sint*, 88)

This title invokes the humble service of Christ himself:

> You know that the rulers of the Gentiles lord it over them, and the great ones make their authority over them felt. But it shall not be so among you. Rather, whoever wishes to be great among you shall be your servant; whoever wishes to be first among you shall be your slave. (Mt 20:25–27)

St. John Paul II invoked in his *Decree on Ecumenism* the image of the shepherd, pasturing his flock out of love for his sheep. He also described the pope as the "first servant of unity" who acts not in competition with, but in a spirit of communion with his fellow bishops. And, he wrote of the willingness of the papacy to reach out to other Christians and to use the office as a bridge of unity:

> The mission of the Bishop of Rome within the College of all the Pastors consists precisely in "keeping watch" (*episkopein*), like a sentinel, so that, through the efforts of the Pastors, the true voice of Christ the Shepherd may be heard in all the particular churches. . . . With the power and authority without which such an office would be illusory, the Bishop of Rome must ensure the communion of all the churches. For this reason, he is the first servant of unity. (*Ut Unum Sint*, 94–95)

pontiff A term that literally means "bridge-builder." It refers to the Bishop of Rome, or pope.

EXPLAINING
APOSTOLIC
SUCCESSION

Read both the *Catechism of the Catholic Church*, 857, and the following quotations on how the Church's authentic teaching and authority comes through apostolic succession:

Our Apostles knew through our Lord Jesus Christ that there would be strife for the office of bishop. For this reason, therefore, having received perfect foreknowledge, they appointed those who have already been mentioned, and afterwards added further provision that, if they should die, other approved men should succeed to their ministry.

—St. Clement of Rome

It is necessary to obey those who are presbyters in the Church, those who, as we have shown, have succession from the Apostles; those who have received, with succession of the episcopate, the church charism of truth according to the good pleasure of the Father. But the rest, who have no part in the primitive succession and assemble wherever they will, must be held in suspicion.

—St. Irenaeus

For this is the way the apostolic Churches transmit their lists: like the Church of the Smyrnaeans, which records that Polycarp was placed there by John; like the Church of the Romans, where Clement was ordained by Peter. In just this same way the other Churches display those whom they have as sprouts from the apostolic seed, having been established by the episcopate of the Apostles.

—Tertullian

Suppose that one of your peers has disputed the role of the pope and bishops as authentic leaders in the Church. *Write a letter* to the person explaining how the Church is founded on the Apostles and how the pope and bishops are their successors. *Cite* the material you have read above in your letter.

The ministry of the bishop of Rome, the pope, is essential to the life of the Church. The pope is both a symbol of the Church's unity and her principal guarantor. In a world that is often overwhelmed by conflicting voices, the pope speaks to Catholics and non-Catholics alike with an unparalleled spiritual and moral authority.

Although the College of Cardinals elects the pope, he is no mere elected official in the secular sense. The pope is the spiritual leader of the Catholic Church who acts with the authority of Christ. He is the shepherd of the whole Church who leads his flock to her final home with God.

The unity of the Church, expressed in this first mark of the Church, has different dimensions, beginning with her source in the unity of the Triune God.

The doctrine of the **Blessed Trinity** models the Church's unity and teaches three important truths:

 1 The Trinity is one. The Divine Persons are each God, whole and entire.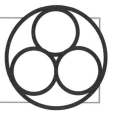

2 The Divine Persons are really distinct from one another. The Father is not the Son, nor is the Holy Spirit the Father or the Son.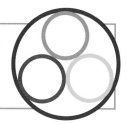

3 The Divine Persons are relative to one another. They share the same nature or divine substance.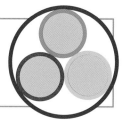

The doctrine of the Holy Trinity reminds us that unity is not the same as uniformity; God's oneness is not opposed to difference but expresses itself in difference. When you think of this unity-in-difference in the life of the Church, you are naturally led to another of the Church's traditional marks, her catholicity. (This mark of the Church is the subject of Chapter 4.)

SECTION ASSESSMENT

NOTE TAKING

Use your completed organizer to help you to answer the following questions.

1. How do the roles of the pope, bishops, priests, and deacons differ from the laity in defending the faith?

2. How do priests and deacons forge unity with the bishop?

COMPREHENSION

3. What are the three degrees of the Sacrament of Holy Orders?

4. Why was it incorrect in the early Church to view a local church as an independent congregation?

5. What were ways the bishop in the early Church preserved the unity of the local churches?

6. How did the Second Vatican Council reemphasize the role and authority of the bishop in the Sacrament of Holy Orders?

7. Cite a New Testament passage that speaks to the primacy of Peter.

8. How did the teachings of the Second Vatican Council about the primacy of the pope differ from those of the First Vatican Concil?

CRITICAL THINKING

9. How can having the skills of an *apologist* help you to *evangelize*?

10. What do you think St. John Paul II's use of the title "Servant of the Servants of God" signifies?

Section Summaries

Focus Question

With more than one billion members, how can the Church be unified?

Complete one of the following:

 Create a collage of many different types of people that represent Our Lady, Queen of Peace parish and the Catholic Church at large.

 Browse a liturgical hymnal. Cite two Communion songs with lyrics that represent the Church's unity. Use some of the lyrics in your answer to the Chapter Focus Question.

 Interview a member of a parish hospitality committee. Ask the person to describe the committee's mission and three ways the mission is put into practice.

INTRODUCTION (PAGES 47–49)
Solidarity

Unity, one of the four marks of the Church, involves interconnectivity with one another and with God. A term used by St. John Paul II to describe this relationship is *solidarity*. The Church's unity is primarily guaranteed by her love, expressed most perfectly in the love among the Persons of the Holy Trinity.

 What does it mean to say that the "Church is one because of her source"? (See also *CCC*, 813.)

SECTION 1 (PAGES 50–53)
Unity in God

The Church's unity begins and is best understood from her origins in the unity of the Blessed Trinity. A practical way for you to participate in the love of the Three Persons of the Trinity is to love God with your whole heart and your neighbor as yourself.

 Describe the depth and breadth of the love that God has for humans and how you model this love.

SECTION 2 (PAGES 54–66)
Unity of Belief

The Nicene Creed and the Apostles' Creed are a source of Church unity. False teachings regarding some creedal statements have led to apostasy, heresy, and schism. The Church has responded, primarily through the teachings of ecumenical councils. A renewed sense of ecumenism is at work to repair the divisions and bring new unity.

 Tell which image used by St. Ambrose to describe the Apostles' Creed is most meaningful to you: "spiritual seal," "our heart's meditation," or "an ever present guardian."

SECTION 3 (PAGES 67–73)
Unity in Common Worship

Participation in the Sacraments, especially the Eucharist, has been a source of unity for those who worship and pray together. Participation in the Sacraments strengthens both the Church's unity with the Blessed Trinity and her communion with fellow Catholics, those on earth, in Purgatory, and in Heaven.

 Review the story of the Notre Dame football team's pre-game Mass. Explain ways the story alludes to Catholics united with one another, Catholics united with non-Catholics, participants at Mass united with the Communion of Saints, and participants at Mass united with God.

SECTION 4 (PAGES 74–83)
Unity with Apostolic Succession

Jesus Christ commissioned Apostles to lead the Church. Through the Sacrament of Holy Orders, their ministry is extended to bishops, priests, and deacons. A bishop receives the fullness of the Sacrament and works in a college of bishops along with the pope to lead the Church.

 Imagine that a non-Catholic peer questions you about why Catholics respect the supreme authority of the pope. What would you say to explain Catholic belief in the primacy of the pope?

Chapter Assignments

Choose and complete at least one of the three assignments assessing your understanding of the material in this chapter.

1. Conflicts That Disrupted Church Unity

How much do Catholics know about conflicts that led to the Eastern Schism in 1054? Prepare a series of questions having to do with the four issues that led to the schism (see pages 56–57) and then videotape a series of "man/woman in the street" interviews with teachers, staff, and students at your school. For extra credit, expand your scope of interviewees to include others. The more unique and relevant your subjects, the more credit you merit. For example, consider also interviewing: parish staff members, parish priests, diocesan leaders, Orthodox Christians, Orthodox priests, local Catholic politicians, other well-known Catholics, Catholic school children, grandparents, random people on the street.

Sample Questions

1. What city was the seat of the Orthodox Church? of the Western Church?

2. Who were the principle parties in the Eastern Schism of 1054?

3. What do apostasy and heresy have to do with the Eastern Schism?

4. What is the meaning of the term *iconoclasm*?

5. The Orthodox creed stated that the Son "proceeds from the Father." What addition does the Roman Catholic creed make?

Edit your video in a fast-paced format, with a maximum length of seven minutes. Follow up with the interviewees to correct erroneous answers and to provide information that supports your knowledge of the material. Plan to play your video for your classmates.

2. Correcting Heresies

The chart below lists many of the heresies the Church faced from the third to the ninth centuries. Recreate this chart on paper, then use this chapter and other sources to complete the elements of the chart. In the second column, summarize the heretical teaching. In the third column, summarize the approved teaching of the Church and quote one or more of the sources listed. Then name at least three realities in today's world that threaten Catholicism. Tell how the Church can combat these realities.

HERESY	HERETICAL TEACHING	CHURCH TEACHING
Gnosticism		Quote: St. Irenaeus from *Against Heresies*

HERESY	HERETICAL TEACHING	CHURCH TEACHING
Arianism		Quote: St. Athanasius, Council of Nicaea
Apollinarism		Quote: Quote First Council of Constantinople
Nestorianism		Quote: Council of Ephesus, St. Cyril
Monophysitism		Quote: Council of Chalcedon, Pope Leo I in *Tome of Leo*

3. Understanding the Holy Trinity

One of the most famous Russian icons of all time is Andrei Rublev's *Trinity*, painted in the thirteenth century. Then, as now, understanding the Holy Trinity was difficult, especially for those with little education. Faced with the Orthodox prohibition of depicting images of God, Rublev turned to the story of the hospitality of Abraham in Genesis 18:1–15 to help with the understanding of the Trinity. The three visitors to Abraham and Sarah are believed to foreshadow contemplation of the mystery of the Holy Trinity. The visitor in the center is associated with Christ, the visitor on the left with God the Father, and the visitor on the right with the Holy Spirit. Note how Rublev's placement of the three visitors in a circle depicts the eternal unity of the Persons of the Trinity.

Create your own image of the Holy Trinity. Choose one of the ideas below or develop your own idea.

- A painting or mural

- A poem, rap, or song

- A photo essay

- A short story

- A prayer

Faithful Disciple

St. Gregory the Great

Those gathered in St. Peter's Square at the 2005 funeral of Pope John Paul II began to chant in unison: "Magnus, Magnus, Magnus" which is translated from Latin as "Great, Great, Great." Such a chant is an unofficial acclamation of a title that is testimony to the work of a pope. Only three popes of the first millennium carry that title. One of these is St. Gregory the Great (540–604), an influential leader who brought unity to the Church when interior and exterior factors were of great threat.

St. Gregory was born in Rome. His father was an elected official and his mother, Sylvia, is honored as a saint. Both of his parents gave up a vast amount of wealth to serve the Church in religious life in their later years. Rome in the sixth century was still reeling from the collapse of the Empire in 476. Rampaging Germanic tribes raided and pillaged many parts of the Empire, and brought with them customs that often conflicted with Christian beliefs and practices. Some of these groups had been Christian, many were pagan, and still others practiced a heretical Christianity. Arian cults were present in Italy, Spain, North Africa, and Eastern France. St. Gregory would eventually to bring order to this world.

Like his father, Gregory entered public service as an adult. After completing law studies, he accepted the position of Prefecture of Rome, the highest civil office. But soon after he abandoned this life and entered the nearby Monastery of St. Andrew to become a Benedictine monk. He called the three years he spent there the "happiest portion of my life."

Gregory's life in quiet contemplation in the monastery ended when Pope Pelagius II sent him to Constantinople as the papal representative to ask the emperor for military aid to help Rome defend itself against the Lombards. The lavish lifestyle of the bishops and their patronization of the Patriarch of Constantinople discouraged Gregory. He also became acutely aware and alarmed at the need of each patriarch to further separate himself from the bishop of Rome. The experience would be beneficial to him as pope. After seven years, Gregory was called back to Rome. When the pope died, Gregory was chosen to succeed him. Gregory at first refused, hiding for three days, before accepting. He was fifty years old when he became pope.

St. Gregory continued to have to deal with many severe problems in Rome. The Lombards were threatening to attack. Gregory took over many civil roles, thereby increasing the temporal power of the papacy, and negotiated a peace treaty with the Lombards. He also refused to recognize the representative from Constantinople in Rome, who was there promoting the Patriarch of Constantinople as the prime see of the Church, a right reserved to Rome.

Perhaps St. Gregory's greatest legacy was the reemphasis of Rome's primacy that he brought to the papacy. He wrote to the Emperor Maurice to combat the Patriarch of Constantinople's claim to be the bishop of the "New Rome":

> It is common knowledge that the charge of the whole church was entrusted by the voice of the Lord to the holy Apostle Peter, chief of all the Apostles. . . . Peter received the keys of the kingdom of Heaven; and yet [the bishop of Constantinople] endeavors to be called the universal bishop!
>
> We know indeed that many bishops of Constantinople have fallen into the gulf of heresy; have become not only heretics but also heresiarchs. Thence came Nestorius, who, deeming Jesus Christ, the Mediator of God and man, to be two persons, because he did not believe that God could become man, went even to the extent of Jewish unbelief. Thence came Macedonius, who denied the Godhead of the Holy Spirit, consubstantial with the Father and the Son. . . .
>
> For I am the servant of all bishops so long as they live like bishops. But whoever, through vainglory and contrary to the statues of the Fathers, lifts his neck against Almighty God, I trust in Almighty God that he will not bend me even with the sword.

St. Gregory is credited with many accomplishments that strengthened the Church. He sent missionaries to Great Britain to evangelize the Anglos and the Saxons, Germanic tribes that had settled there. Through the missions he sponsored, Christianity was brought to those lands. He is also remembered for establishing a system for providing care for the poor in the Empire, and for introducing liturgical reforms that still influence the Church today. He also reformed the seminaries and encouraged the newly ordained to open schools of their own at their parishes. Gregory also organized a written record of the Church's liturgy and music and is credited with creating a form of music called the Gregorian chant.

St. Gregory's choice of the title "Servant of the Servants of God" to describe his papacy was apt. Reflective of his background as a monk, a spirit of prayer and contemplation marked St. Gregory's reign. He truly lived and supported his progression in a line directly from St. Peter as bishop of Rome, Vicar of Jesus Christ, Successor of the Prince of the Apostles, Supreme Pontiff of the Universal Church, an Archbishop and Metropolitan of the Roman Province and (since 1929) Sovereign of the State of the City of the Vatican.

Gregory was canonized by popular acclaim after his death in 604 and was later named a Doctor of the Church. His feast day is September 3.

Reading Comprehension

1. Was St. Gregory born in the (a) fifth century, (b) sixth century, or (c) tenth century?

2. Gregory called the years he spent at _____ the "happiest portion of my life."

3. What lesson did Gregory learn as papal representative in Constantinople that helped forge his greatest legacy as pope?

Writing Task

- Write a poem or prayer that uses Pope St. Gregory's title "Servant of the Servants of God" as part of the text.

Explaining the Faith

How can the mystery of God being one yet three at the same time be understood?

The mystery of the Holy Trinity can be explained using analogies but in fact it is a mystery beyond human comprehension.

St. Patrick used one famous analogy. He would hold up a shamrock to potential converts and ask them: "Is it one leaf or three"? "It is both one leaf and three," they would reply. "And so it is with God," Patrick concluded. Similarly, the three Divine Persons have the same essence, that is, the same divine nature.

Another way to understand the mystery is to explore how all Three Persons share in the common work of Salvation. Each Divine Person performs this common work according to his unique mission. Therefore, creation and its continual existence are attributed to God the Father. Salvation is attributed to the Son, who became human to reveal the Father's merciful love. And to the Holy Spirit is attributed the work of making you and all other people holy and Godlike.

Although creation is attributed to the Father, Salvation (Redemption) to the Son, and sanctification to the Holy Spirit, it is important to remember that all Three Persons of the Trinity act as one and are fully present in each of these works. God is a unity-in-community. St. Augustine suggested thinking about the Holy Trinity as the Lover (Father), the Beloved (Son), and the bond of Love between them (Holy Spirit). In short, God is love.

 ## Further Research

- Why is the Most Holy Trinity the central mystery of Christian faith and life? Read *Catechism of the Catholic Church*, 232–260.

Prayer

Prayer of the Council Fathers

We are here before you, O Holy Spirit, conscious of our innumerable sins, but united in a special way to your holy name. Come and abide in us. Deign to penetrate our hearts.

Be the guide of our actions, indicate the path we should take, and show us what we must do so that, with your help, our work may be in all things pleasing to you.

May you, who are infinite justice, never permit that we be disturbers of justice. Let not our ignorance induce us to evil, nor flattery sway us, nor moral and material interest corrupt us. But unite our hearts to you alone, and do it strongly, so that, with the gift of your grace, we may be one in you and may in nothing depart from the truth.

—Attributed to St. Isidore of Seville
(prayed before several Church councils, including the Second Vatican Council)

THE
CHURCH
IS
HOLY

OUT OF THE DEPTHS

The rescue of thirty-three miners—trapped for nearly seventy days in a Chilean gold and copper mine—on October 13, 2010, was a result of the calculated, precise, and coordinated efforts of many. Credited for much of the positive outcome was an American company, Drillers Supply International, that brought all of its equipment to assist the rigs in going down 2,000 feet to the place where the miners were thought to be.

The job was risky and, at first, thought to have little chance of success. Then, after seventeen days of drilling, Greg Hall, co-owner of the company and a Catholic who was in the final months of preparation for his February 2011 ordination as a deacon, received some news. "I was getting ready to go to Mass at 7 a.m. when one of my guys called me and said, 'Greg, we think we hit a void, and we think we hear some banging on the drill pipe.' We pulled the pipe up and in between the hammer and drill pipe was a note saying 'All thirty-three of us are alive.'"

There were other connections to faith with this remarkable story. Pope Benedict XVI sent each of the trapped miners a rosary that he had blessed himself. They were delivered to the miners personally by the cardinal of Santiago. The miners later told how they prayed the Rosary daily, even creating a little chapel in the corner of their cave. The families of the miners also prayed the Rosary while waiting for the miners to be rescued. Family members wore crosses and had religious altars dedicated to their loved ones. They also celebrated Mass together at the mine on Sundays.

On the day of the rescue (interestingly, the Feast of Our Lady of Fatima), Santiago Bishop Cristián Contreras Villarroel preached that the lives of the miners should be a sign that all people need Redemption. "There is no saint without a past, nor sinner without a future," the bishop said. Certainly, he added, the miners buried beneath the ground were a product, like all people, of both sinfulness and holiness. Their rescue was remindful of Jonah's expulsion from the belly of the large fish, King David's rescue from the enemies who surrounded him, and Jesus' rising from the dead out of a sealed cave.

When Esteban Rojas reached the earth's surface, he didn't immediately run to the dignitaries present or even to his family. Instead, he knelt in prayer, this time in thankfulness, after days of petition. In both the immediate minutes after the rescue and in the days that followed, the words of Psalm 130 rang clear:

Out of the depths I call to you, Lord;
Lord, hear my cry!
May your ears be attentive
to my cry for mercy.
If you, Lord, mark our sins,
Lord, who can stand?
But with you is forgiveness
and so you are revered (Ps 130:1–4).

FOCUS QUESTION

How can a Church made up of sinners REMAIN HOLY?

INTRODUCTION
Holiness Is from God

MAIN IDEA
Holiness is a gift from God, not something that can be earned.

Thomas Merton (1915–1968), whose image is shown above, became a Cistercian monk after years on a unique spiritual journey. Merton's family was not religious. Merton was raised in both the United States and Europe and studied at Columbia University in New York and Cambridge in England. At school he had a reputation for partying and womanizing.

After reading a book by a Catholic philosopher, Etienne Gilson, Merton grew more interested in Catholicism. His life decisions moved at a rapid pace from that time on. In 1938 he was baptized a Catholic at Corpus Christi Church in New York City. Feeling called to the priesthood, Merton faced rejection from the Franciscan religious order, primarily for the questionable choices of his earlier life. In 1941 he went on a retreat to the Abbey of Gethsemani, a Trappist monastery near Bardstown, Kentucky. He immediately felt drawn to monastic life. The Trappists maintained strict silence, communicating with one another only through sign language. They gathered multiple times during the day to pray the **Liturgy of the Hours**. The rest of the day was spent in common labor or study.

Merton joined the Trappists in December 1941. He began to keep journals of prayer and reflection. The abbot recognized his literary gifts and encouraged him

> **Liturgy of the Hours** The prayer of the Church; it is also known as the Divine Office. The Liturgy of the Hours utilizes the Scriptures, particularly the Psalms, for praying at specific times of the day from early morning to late evening.

NOTE TAKING

Analyze Information. Three ways to live a life of holiness are listed in this chart. Recreate it for yourself, then write an example of how Thomas Merton lived each one of these ways. Also list examples of how you are or will live out each way of holiness in your own life.

Ways to Be Holy	Thomas Merton	You
Prayer		
Good works		
Living a Christian vocation		

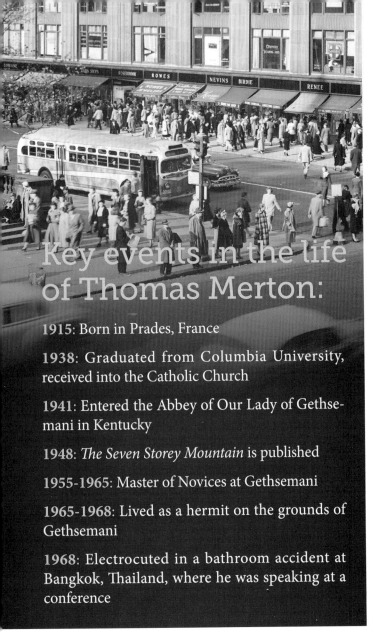

Key events in the life of Thomas Merton:

1915: Born in Prades, France

1938: Graduated from Columbia University, received into the Catholic Church

1941: Entered the Abbey of Our Lady of Gethsemani in Kentucky

1948: *The Seven Storey Mountain* is published

1955-1965: Master of Novices at Gethsemani

1965-1968: Lived as a hermit on the grounds of Gethsemani

1968: Electrocuted in a bathroom accident at Bangkok, Thailand, where he was speaking at a conference

to pursue his writing further. In 1948 his spiritual autobiography, *The Seven Storey Mountain*, was published. To the surprise of many, it became a bestseller. In the book, Merton explained that his life apart from others was the opportunity to reach greater holiness than could be achieved by those who "lived in the world."

But years later Merton came to question his understanding of monasticism and its relationship to holiness. Did a person really have to be a monk to be holy? During one of his trips to the doctor in Louisville, he had a dramatic change of heart. Gazing at all of the strangers walking on the city streets, Merton instantly felt a mystical union with them. He realized that his view of the monk as a separate, spiritual person was

not only an illusion but a dangerous illusion as well. While he recognized that certainly there was something distinctive about being a monk ("for we all belong to God. Yet so does everybody else belong to God. We just happen to be conscious of it, and try to make a profession out of this consciousness"), he began to reflect more on his Louisville experience and the miraculous dignity of every human being. "If only everybody could realize this!" he wrote. "But it cannot be explained. There is no way of telling people that they are all walking around shining like the sun."

Holiness is a second mark of the Church. This chapter traces the roots of holiness to God himself and the ways the Church, like God, is holy because of her intimate connection with him. Merton's insight captured an important aspect of holiness—namely, that it is not something that can be earned; rather, holiness is a gift of God.

The gift of holiness translates to the opportunity to be holy in your own particular way. Being holy primarily means living in loving communion with God and one another. As you know, those tasks are not always so easy. Undermining your relationships with God and others is ever-present sinfulness that affects each person in the Church. Through prayer, good works, living a Christian vocation, and God's gift of Redemption, you are still able to live a holy life. Think of the Chilean miner story as a parable for what you have to do to be holy. You can rise from sin to a life of holiness. This chapter reminds us that Christ himself called sinners and the Church continues to invite and welcome sinners to membership.

It is important for you to know that holiness is not about becoming *super*human. Holiness is about becoming *fully* human. Holiness flows from the Christian understanding of the Incarnation. Jesus was fully human and fully divine. He did not come to reject humanity, but rather to live his human life in the fullest and most authentic way: "I came so that they might have life and have it more abundantly" (Jn 10:10). To live authentically human lives means to remain in a life-giving relationship with God. Thomas Merton adds this further insight:

> A tree gives glory to God by being a tree. For in being what God means it to be it is obeying him. . . . But what about you? What about me? Unlike the animals and the trees, it is not enough for us to be what our nature intends. . . . Therefore the problem of sanctity and salvation is in fact the problem of finding out who I am and of discovering my true self. Trees and animals have no problem. God makes them what they are without consulting them, and they are

perfectly satisfied. With us it is different. God leaves us free to be whatever we like. We can be ourselves or not, as we please. . . . Our vocation is not simply to *be*, but to work together with God in the creation of our own life, our own identity, our own destiny.

The mark of holiness calls you to saintliness. Don't let this word scare you. This goal of being a saint is really your destiny. It is achievable not only by turning to an austere life of prayer, as in a monastery, but in whatever your Christian vocation. To be a saint, to achieve holiness, is to live your ordinary life such that your relationship with God shines through.

Times of Prayer

The Church's prayer is centered in Jesus Christ. It is the Lord who teaches, guides, consoles, and blesses the Church through prayer. The Church's prayer life is organized around a liturgical calendar that takes in the entire year. In the Church Year or Liturgical Year, the entire mystery of Christ from the Incarnation and Nativity and through the events of the Paschal Mystery unfolds around six main parts or seasons: Advent, Christmas, Lent, Triduum, Easter, and Ordinary Time.

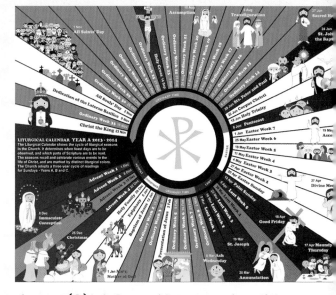

The liturgical calendar also is arranged for daily prayer. Like Thomas Merton, the monks of the Abbey of Gethsemani today (and many other priests, religious and laypeople worldwide) pray throughout on a schedule based on the Church's Liturgy of the Hours. Examine the names of the hours of prayer italicized in the weekday schedule below. Do the following: (1) write a definition for each name (2) explain the significance of that hour of prayer (3) briefly provide an overview of the background and organization of the entire Liturgy of the Hours.

Weekday Schedule

- 3:15 a.m. Vigils
- 5:45 a.m. Lauds
- 6:15 a.m. Eucharist

- 7:30 a.m. Terce
- 12:15 p.m. Sext
- 2:15 p.m. None

- 5:30 p.m. Vespers
- 7:00 p.m. Rosary
- 7:30 p.m. Compline

SECTION ASSESSMENT

NOTE TAKING

Review your responses from your completed chart. Then answer the following question:

1. Besides the ways for holiness listed on the chart, what gift does God provide to help you to live a holy life?

VOCABULARY

2. In the Liturgy of the Hours, what is the name for evening prayer?

COMPREHENSION

3. What was the realization Thomas Merton had about holiness as he gazed at strangers on the streets of Louisville?

4. What are the roots of holiness?

5. What is the primary meaning of holiness?

APPLICATION

6. What do you find appealing about a life of solitude, as Merton lived at the monastery?

7. If you could, how would you communicate to people that "they are all walking around shining like the sun"?

8. In your opinion, what is the difference between being *super*human and being *fully* human?

SECTION 1
Tracing the Church's Holiness

MAIN IDEA
Holiness is a gift of the Father, Son, and Holy Spirit that the Church offers to both saints and sinners.

The Church has been called holy from the earliest centuries of her existence. Some of the primary creeds refer to the *sancta ecclesia*, the "holy Church." It was only natural to refer to the Church as holy because "Christ, the Son of God, who with the Father and the Spirit is hailed as 'alone holy,' loved the Church as his Bride" (*Lumen Gentium*, 39).

The definition of God—Three Divine Persons in One—as holy is important to understand and trace in order to know why the Church can also be called holy. In his **transcendence** and rule over the world, God is not dependent on the world. Though all beauty, goodness, and love itself have their origins in God, his holiness lies in the fact that he did not in any way depend on the world to create these things, but rather brought them into existence by his own power out of nothing.

God's holiness is part of his very identity. He has revealed to the world that he is holy. In fact, only God is all-holy. This is supported in the Old Testament in several places:

- Since I, the LORD, brought you up from the land of Egypt that I might be your God, you shall be holy, because I am holy. (Lev 11:45)
- There is no Holy One like the LORD, there is no Rock like our God. (1 Sm 2:2)
- "Holy, holy, holy is the LORD of hosts!" they cried to one to the other. "All the earth is filled with his glory!" (Is 6:3)
- I am the LORD, your Holy One, the creator of Israel, your King. (Is 43:15)
- For I am God and not man, the Holy One present among you. (Hos 11:9)

> **transcendence** A trait of God that refers to his total otherness and being infinitely beyond and independent of creation. While God is immanent to humanity with a deep and loving relationship with man and woman that resembles that of a parent to a child, God is neither male nor female. He is pure spirit. He is God.

NOTE TAKING

Summarize Information. As you read the section, write one-sentence summaries that trace the Church's understanding of holiness and answer the following questions.

How is God holy?
How was holiness understood in the Old Testament?
What does the Son of God incarnate teach about holiness?

We can speak of people and the Church herself as holy, but only insofar as they are related to God. In the Old Testament, places like the Temple and things like the altar for sacrifice were holy only because they were set apart and consecrated for God and dedicated as places where people could encounter God. Likewise, people were holy only as they were related to God:

 A priest was holy because of the sacrifices he offered to God.

 A prophet was holy because he spoke God's Word.

 A king was only holy when he obeyed the Lord's commands.

The Chosen People themselves were only holy when in relationship with God.

God's relationship with the Chosen People was defined as a covenant. The covenant God established was an irrevocable bond. God promised his love and care and in return expected lives of gratitude in which the people would live out the truth of the covenant by way of ethical living, epitomized by the Great Commandment of loving God and neighbor.

The New Testament largely embraces the same understanding that holiness comes from God alone. Yet the very fact that God became incarnate in Jesus Christ makes it clear that humans are also called to holiness. How so? Jesus is the "Holy One of God" (Mk 1:24), but also fully human besides divine, a man "who has similarly been tested in every way, yet without sin" (Heb 4:15). Moreover, he was not the incarnate Son of God as royalty, but as a poor Galilean Jew who lived most of his life as a humble craftsman (see image on page 101). Jesus' holiness was certainly evident in his ministry; he blessed children, welcomed sinners, and healed the sick. But his holiness must also be recognized in his hidden years at home where he lived with his family, respected his parents, and practiced a trade. If you want to know what it takes to be holy, just look at his example and consider how it applies to your own current life.

A final lesson of Jesus' incarnate holiness takes place at the time of this Death. Recall that in the ancient Jewish Temple, the most sacred area was the Holy of Holies, reserved originally for the Ark of the Covenant. It was an inner place that only the high priest could enter, and then only on the **Day of Atonement**. When Jesus "gave up his spirit" at the moment of his Death, "behold, the veil of the sanctuary was torn in two from top to bottom." (Mt 27:51). The tearing of the veil of the Holy of Holies suggests that from that time on, it would not be only a select person, the high priest, or even a few who could encounter the Holy One. Now, through Christ the Redeemer, all people can come near to God's presence. All people are called to holiness.

As Thomas Merton discovered in his own experience on the streets of Louisville, there is deep value in humanity and the lives of individual people. God's holiness truly shines through all of his creation: "Thus it is evident to everyone, that all the faithful of Christ,

> **Day of Atonement** Known as Yom Kippur, this is the holiest day of the year for the Jewish people. It is a day when Jews ask forgiveness for both communal and personal sins.

In 2002, a severe crisis in the Church came to light with the discovery of a sexual scandal involving a small fraction of the clergy worldwide.

CORPUS PERMIXTUM

In July 2014, Pope Francis held the first of several private meetings with victims of clergy sexual abuse. Each meeting lasted about thirty minutes. During the same year, Pope Francis directed bishops around the world to reach out in compassion to sexual abuse victims and to report any future crimes of sexual abuse to civil authorities.

whatever rank or status, are called to the fullness of Christian life and to the perfection of charity" (*Lumen Gentium*, 40).

Saints and Sinners Intertwined

Danielle, a tenth-grader preparing for the Sacrament of Confirmation at her parent's request, had some serious doubts about whether or not she would receive the Sacrament. She questioned the parish catechist, Mrs. Anne Tapia: "How can anybody who knows anything about the history of the Catholic Church possibly call it holy? There have been **Crusades** championed by popes who gave indulgences to soldiers for killing so-called infidels. There was the **Inquisition** that led to heretics being tortured. I could go on and on, and I don't have to remind you of the sexual abuse scandal that has been a plague in the Church in these recent decades."

Just as Danielle had researched her question well, Mrs. Tapia was able to respond in a thoughtful way. Here is what she said:

Danielle, you raise an important question, one that *does* have an answer. It is true that over the course of nearly two thousand years, people in the Church, including leaders, have not always lived up to the Gospel. The reality is that all of us are sinners, including popes and bishops. With sinners, comes sin. Some of the examples

Crusades The nine armed expeditions by Christians beginning in 1095 and ending in 1291 that were intended to drive the Muslims out of the Holy Land and in the process reunite Christians of the East and West.

Inquisition A Church tribunal established in the thirteenth century that was designed to curb heretical teachings and beliefs. In collaboration with secular authorities, papal representatives employed the Inquisition to judge the guilt of suspected heretics with the aim of getting them to repent. Unfortunately, before long, many abuses crept into the process.

that you brought up were very important to St. John Paul II as well. Did you know that over his long reign as pope he gave public speeches asking for forgiveness for sins committed by Catholics, past and present, over ninety times? St. John Paul II apologized for the sin of anti-Semitism, for not acknowledging the dignity of women, and for crimes committed by Christians against non-Christians.

In some ways, the Church's history and relationship with God is like that of ancient Israel in the Old Testament. The Israelites sometimes let God down too, whether it was worshipping the fatted calf, grumbling to Moses in the desert, or abusing the poor as the prophet Amos pointed out. Yet each time they departed from God's way, God would draw them back to him.

Remember, too, that Jesus was often disappointed by his chosen disciples, including the Apostles. Think back to the Last Supper. There is Jesus sharing his final meal before he is to undergo his terrible ordeal. What does he see around the table but one Apostle who will betray him and another who will deny him. And, if that wasn't enough, Luke's Gospel reports that right after that an argument broke out among the disciples about which of them was the "greatest." Can you imagine how Jesus must have felt at that moment?

Actually, Jesus must have been tempted to give up on them right then and there. But he didn't. He stayed at the table, not because of who they were, but because of who, by God's grace, they might be someday.

This is who we are as a Church, Danielle. We are a broken and sinful people. The Church *is* holy, but not because of our individual merits, but because of the forgiveness of Christ.

In March 2000, St. John Paul II visited the Western (Wailing) Wall in Jerusalem. He left a letter of apology in one of the cracks of the Wall that asked the Jewish people to forgive Christians for behaviors that caused them hurt over the centuries.

It is the Holy Spirit who makes us the Body of Christ. It is the Holy Spirit that makes us a holy Church, not our own efforts. It is the Holy Spirit that allows the Church to remain sinless even if her members sin.

Mrs. Tapia made an important point: it is incorrect to think that the holiness of the Church depends on the holiness of her members. Throughout the history of the Church there have been several times when that school of thought has been held; that is, that only "holy" people are worthy of Church membership. If that approach were implemented there would be a Church without any people in it! The Church is not like the United States Marine Corps ("the few, the proud, the Marines"). The Church is not an elite and select organization. What Mrs. Tapia rightly expressed is that the Church is a Church of sinners, from the pope in Rome to the baby baptized last Sunday at your parish.

In fact, Catholics have always held the Church to be, as St. Augustine put it, a *corpus permixtum*—a "mixed body" of saints and sinners. This understanding comes from the teachings of Jesus, who told a parable about the Kingdom of Heaven where sinners (weeds) intermingled among the righteous (wheat). One of the slaves of the household addressed the master in the story, wondering if the weeds should be pulled up before the harvest. The master's answer was no. He explained:

> [if] you pull up the weeds you might uproot the wheat along with them. Let them grow together until harvest; then at harvest time I will say to the harvesters, "First collect the weeds and tie them in bundles for burning; but gather the wheat into my bar." (Mt 13:29–30)

MISGUIDED VIEWS ON HOLINESS

Throughout the Church's history, Catholic men and women have lived lives that exemplify the true vocation of holiness. Unfortunately, some attempts to call the Church back to true holiness were in error.

For example, in the seventeenth century, *Jansenism*, inspired by Cornelius Jansen, a bishop of Yrpes, France, taught that human nature was utterly depraved and that God's grace extends to only a few. Jansenists held that God predetermined some people to Heaven and most others to Hell. They believed that most Catholics were not worthy to receive Holy Communion. They held a negative view of the human body and sexuality.

Quietism, inspired by a Spanish priest, Michael Molinos (1628–1696), held that human nature was so powerless a person could do nothing to grow in holiness. Under this view, you should not try to resist temptations since they are God's will. You should not try to live virtues or concern yourself with Heaven and Hell. You should actually do nothing except remain quiet in abandonment.

The Church condemned both of these heretical views. Holiness is not just for a few chosen ones. Spiritual effort is worthwhile. God gives grace to every Catholic. Prayer, frequent reception of the Sacraments of Penance and Holy Eucharist, and works of self-denial and charity toward others are ways in which all Catholics can grow close to God. Your growth in holiness takes effort, but God helps you through his grace.

One of the most distinctive characteristics of the Church is that she doesn't just tolerate the presence of sinners in her midst, she eagerly reaches out to welcome sinners into the field of God's Salvation. This does not mean that the Church celebrates sin. Catholics are called to respond to God's grace and his invitation to live holy lives. But it does mean that the Church continues to recognize the words of Jesus, preached from the very beginning of his public ministry: "Those who are well do not need a physician, but the sick do. I did not come to call the righteous but sinners" (Mk 2:17).

The Church's holiness is more than just the sum—adding up the plusses and minuses—of her individual members. This is important to remember because the Church will always have sinful members who will act in ways that are contrary to the Gospel. What is more crucial in understanding the mark of holiness for the Church is to understand how the Church can remain holy even with sinners in her midst.

SECTION ASSESSMENT

NOTE TAKING

Use the chart and summary statements you created to help you write the following definition.

1. Write a one-sentence definition of holiness that combines the understandings of the term from both the Old Testament and New Testament.

VOCABULARY

2. Write the phonetic spelling of the two Latin terms: *sancta ecclesia* and *corpus permixtum*. Practice their pronunciation with a partner. Also, write a meaning of the terms in your own words.

COMPREHENSION

3. What is the lesson of holiness that takes place at the time of Jesus' Death?

4. What is the meaning of St. Augustine's description of the Church as *corpus permixtum*, a "mixed body"?

ANALYSIS

5. Differentiate between Jansenism and Quietism.

CRITICAL THINKING

6. How does your understanding of the Church's holiness differ from Danielle's? In your opinion, how effective was Mrs. Tapia's response to Danielle?

Ways the Church Is Holy

MAIN IDEA
Sacramental graces, the practice of a Christian vocation, and moral behavior based on the Ten Commandments and Beatitudes are ways the Church reaches for holiness.

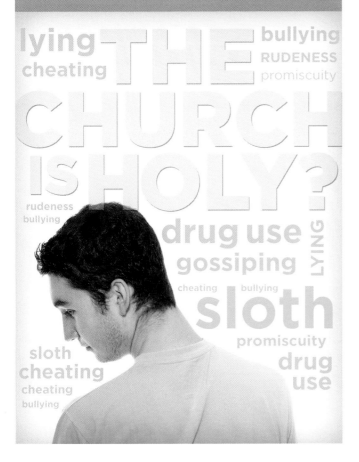

The image above is not accurate. The sinfulness of some Catholics *never* reduces the Church's holiness. The Church will always be complete and filled with holiness. The Church is always holy because of Christ's presence. It is the very essence of the Church to be holy, to be set apart as a community united with him. Because Catholics are united with Christ and made holy by him, they strive to avoid tapping into sin.

Instead, Catholics travel on the road to perfection and reach for holiness with the help of the many graces present in the Church.

There are many lifestyle choices that can help you to be holy. Remember to throw away the thoughts of Jansenism (page 105) that falsely taught that holiness is reserved for only a few. You are not only called to holiness, but you are called to perfection, too. Later in this section some specific vocation choices to live a holy life will be discussed. But for now consider some **sacramental graces** God offers you right now to be holy.

NOTE TAKING

Recognize Connections. As you read through the section, match the term in the right column with the vocation *most* associated with it from the left column. In your notebook, write one sentence for each vocation that includes the name of the vocation and the corresponding term.

Bishop	evangelical counsels
Priest	dedicated career focus
Deacon	governance
Sister or Brother	service
Husband or Wife	preaching
Single Person	domestic church

sacramental graces The grace of the Holy Spirit, given by Christ, that is proper to each sacrament.

The sacraments all point to a life of holiness. Sacramental graces are foremost among the graces. Here are some associated with each sacrament.

BAPTISM

- Forgives sins (both Original Sin and personal sins)
- Makes you a "new creature" who can share in the divine life
- Makes you a member of the Church, the Body of Christ
- Strengthens the opportunity for unity among all Christians
- Seals you with a spiritual mark that can never be repealed

CONFIRMATION

- Roots you more deeply as a child of God
- Unites you more firmly to Christ
- Increases the Gifts of the Holy Spirit in you
- Renders your bond with the Church more perfect
- Gives you a special strength of the Holy Spirit to defend and spread the Faith by word and action

EUCHARIST

- Brings you to greater, more intimate union with Christ
- Separates you from sin (forgives venial sins)
- Builds the Church through your relationships with others

PENANCE

- Reconciles you with God through the forgiveness of your sins
- Reconciles you with the Church
- Brings about peace and serenity of conscience

ANOINTING OF THE SICK

- Offers a particular gift of the Holy Spirit to assist those who are sick in accepting the trials they face
- Provides a grace to unite the suffering of those who receive it with the Passion of Christ
- Delivers to you and the Church a grace to be able to serve the sick
- Helps you accept and conform to your impending death (when it is time) as a preparation for the final journey

HOLY ORDERS

- Configures the man to Christ as priest, teacher, and pastor dependent on the three degrees of the sacrament so that he can serve as Christ's instrument for the Church
- Confers an indelible spiritual character, and therefore cannot be repeated
- Gives the bishop the power to govern
- Empowers the priest to offer the Sacrifice of the Eucharist
- Gives the deacon the grace to serve the people

MARRIAGE

- Shares a bond established by God himself and indissoluble by human authority
- Assures the couple of a lifetime of God's grace by which their love is perfected and their unity strengthened
- Consecrates concrete, real ways to live lives of love

Surrounded by the sacramental graces and many other graces of the Holy Spirit shared through the Church, Catholics set out along a road to perfection, which is the result of holiness. In today's world, it seems that reaching for perfection is discouraged. You might imagine parents of a young student not wishing to put too much pressure on their child to achieve all A's in school or to practice a piano piece until it can be played with absolutely no flaws. Reaching for perfection in living a life of holiness, however, is not discouraged; it is *required*. Jesus said: "So be perfect, just as your heavenly Father is perfect" (Mt 5:48).

In your quest to live a good and holy life, Catholic moral teaching—including the Ten Commandments and the Beatitudes—are your essential guide. They challenge you to do what is right and help you to avoid sin. Jesus asks you to do even more. Jesus expanded on the Great Commandment by redefining the requirement of love to include love for your enemies and those who persecute you. This is difficult to do. Christ's willingness to suffer and die for friends and enemies alike is the greatest example and inspiration for you to strive for perfection.

Remember, seeking this form of perfection is different than the allure of working out to achieve a flat stomach and toned abs. This type of perfection involves uniting yourself to the Cross of Christ by suffering some yourself. It involves praying for others and reaching out in love to all people, both friend and enemy. Thomas Merton chose the austere life of the monastery as a way to seek his own perfection. He realized later that the life of a monk was not the only way to do this.

All people, you included, are called to both the challenges of striving for perfection of holiness and the rewards. This is a **vocation** given to Catholics in Baptism as part of the **common priesthood of the faithful**. Living this gift is "exercised by the unfolding of baptismal grace—a life of faith, hope, and charity, a life according to the Spirit" (*CCC*, 1547). This is the way to holiness. The next sections explore how

> **vocation** The calling or destiny we have in this life and in the hereafter.
>
> **common priesthood of the faithful** The priesthood of all the baptized in which we share in Christ's work of Salvation.

the Sacrament of Baptism calls all Catholics to lead holy lives and, further, how the vocations of ordained ministry, consecrated life, marriage, or a single life dedicated to a life of chastity and service to others are connected with holiness.

Living the Graces of Baptism

Identifying with and sharing in the Cross of Christ and the entirety of the Paschal Mystery is not like going to a concert and then living vicariously through the musician on stage. In Baptism, you take on an actual share in the Paschal Mystery and membership in the common priesthood of the faithful. In Baptism, you receive God's grace. The priestly work left for you to do is to live in Christ. The New Testament Letter to the Hebrews describes Jesus as a "high priest forever according to the order of Melchizedek" (Heb 6:20). By his sacrifice on a Cross, a single offering, Jesus merited all the grace for the Salvation of humankind. He established a new understanding for priestly living.

In the Old Testament, priestly living had different connotations than it does for Catholics today. Jewish priests performed a number of roles but over time their primary ministry was restricted to service in the Temple. They offered animal sacrifices on behalf of all of God's People. They were considered holy because of this special role. In other words, they were holy because they were *consecrated* or set apart for the sake of serving God and the community. Their holiness was not related to their moral lives.

The practice of sacrifice also affected how the rest of the Jewish community understood holiness. Many Jews came to accept a belief that the sacrifices were in themselves almost magical ways of gaining God's favor and, hence, their own holiness. They forgot that beyond worship, another aspect of the covenant

One type of Hebrew sacrifice was a whole offering. An entire animal except its hide was consumed in fire on the altar.

relationship was to live as God would have them live—as good, moral, and holy people.

Some of the Old Testament prophets voiced this concern. They worried that Israel had put so much emphasis on sacrifices through the priest that they had neglected their own personal obligations to live lives of holiness. The prophet Hosea spoke for the Lord: "For it is love that I desire, not sacrifice, and knowledge of God rather than holocausts" (Hos 6:6).

When Christ took on the role of the High Priest who offers not another victim but himself as the one sacrifice, he ended the need for humans to ever have to offer sacrifices to God again (see Heb 9:11–14). Christ was not offered as a *victim* by another person in order to appease God; Jesus freely offered *himself* as both priest and victim. His offering, punctuated by his Resurrection, demonstrated that his self-giving love triumphs over sin and death.

You can draw on the life of Christ so that you, too, can live his self-giving love. The First Letter of Peter names your title and your task:

> But you are a "chosen race, a royal priesthood, a holy nation, a people of his own, so that you may announce the praises" of him who called you out of darkness into his wonderful light. (1 Pet 2:9)

So how are you to live out the common priesthood of the faithful? Put simply, you are to participate in the one sacrifice of Christ. Living the graces of the Paschal Mystery is the true path to holiness. Catholics have specific vocations or God-given callings to live the Paschal Mystery in a way unique to their lives. These vocations for living out holiness are most clearly defined around the ordained priesthood, consecrated or religious life, marriage, and the dedicated single life.

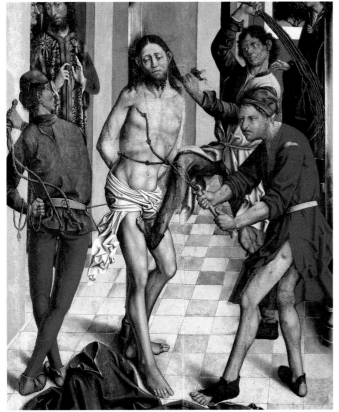

Jesus Christ "entered once and for all into the sanctuary, not with the blood of goats and calves but with his own blood, thus obtaining eternal redemption" (Heb 9:12).

Sacrificing and Celebrating for God's Kingdom

Through Jesus' Death and Resurrection, our life on earth is permanently linked to the Kingdom of God, though no one on earth will experience the fullness of the Kingdom until Jesus' Second Coming. In the meantime, the Church foreshadows the Kingdom's presence on earth. The Church is the place where we are called to live a life of holiness. What does that entail? It means both living out the sacrifice of Christ and beginning our celebration of the Kingdom. Compare a story told by twentieth-century author James Alison that tells about what it is like to both sacrifice and celebrate in connection with the fall of the Soviet Union with Christians living as a priestly people.

To understand Alison's image, you first have to recall that for much of the twentieth century, the world was haunted by the oppressive reign of the Soviet Union that was held together by military might and fear of repression from a brutal communist government. Within the same sphere were puppet communist governments in countries like Poland, Hungary, Yugoslavia, and Albania that were dependent on the Soviet Union and followed its lead in all matters.

From 1989 to 1990, there was a dramatic shake-up of this world as the communist empires of the Soviet empire began to crumble. This era was symbolized by the tearing down of the Berlin Wall that had separated the communist and democratic sides of the German city of Berlin. The fall of the Berlin Wall became a powerful symbol of the liberation of whole nations from the terror of communism. In spite of this great liberating event, some countries remained under communist rule even as the central Soviet regime collapsed. One of these countries was Albania.

With that background, imagine along with Alison that you are living in Albania in 1989 and have just heard over the airwaves that the Berlin Wall has fallen. The evil communist regime has been defeated. The Albanian communist government may still technically be in power in your country, but it doesn't matter because you know, and they know you know, that it is all over. You, your family, your neighbors, and your friends begin to celebrate because you all know that the days of oppression are numbered. For now, the government may still be acting in the same brutal ways as before, but everyone knows that it is only a matter of time before the effects of the torn-down Berlin Wall reach the streets of Albania. And so you begin to celebrate now because maybe by your celebration you will even hasten the spread of this decisive victory to your own land.

This is something of what it is like for Catholics to live as a priestly people. A very big event has happened in Jesus that has changed the course of all human history, even if there are people who are not yet aware of it. God sent his only Son, the Second Person of the Blessed Trinity, to live in the world. As true God and true man, Jesus had both a divine and human nature that made him uniquely chosen to share the Good News of God's Kingdom with all. To live the common priesthood of Baptism is to participate "in the beginning of the celebration of a new regime even while the old regime hasn't yet grasped the news of its own fall."

Holiness of the Ordained Ministry

For men called to the ministerial priesthood, the vocation offers several graces both for personally living a holy life and for helping others to a life of holiness as well. Realize that the ministerial priesthood is different from the common priesthood. The ministerial priesthood is directed at serving the common priesthood by "unfolding the baptismal grace of all Christians" (*CCC*, 1547). In the life of the Catholic priest, Christ builds up and leads the Church. For that reason, the ministerial priesthood has its own sacrament, the Sacrament of Holy Orders.

Men who are ordained to the priesthood in the Sacrament of Holy Orders are consecrated to serve the Church in three basic ways:

- preaching the Gospel;
- celebrating divine worship; and
- providing pastoral governance, typically as the pastor of a parish.

In fulfilling these roles in the Spirit of Christ, priests grow in their own holiness and build up the laity so they can live lives of faith, hope, and love, and reach for perfection.

In receiving the fullness of the Sacrament of Holy Orders, bishops share in a similar role of consecrated service to the Church. Priests function in their ministry only because of their relationship to their local bishop. Each may administer the sacraments, though only a bishop can administer the Sacrament of Holy Orders, and he is also the ordinary minister of the Sacrament of Confirmation. Whereas the priest is responsible for sharing in the governance of a parish, the bishop is the ordinary pastor of the dioceses and therefore he has responsibility for all of the ministries in the dioceses that are oriented toward building up the Church in holiness.

Deacons, too, receive the Sacrament of Holy Orders, but unlike the bishop and priest, deacons are not ordained for priesthood but for service. In the Rite of Ordination, the deacon promises obedience to the bishop. He serves at liturgy and is also in service to the needs of the entire Church and world. While until recently the diaconate was almost exclusively a transition to priestly ordination, many deacons today remain permanently in the diaconate. They may be mature single or married men. A single man ordained in the permanent diaconate may not marry. A married man ordained to the permanent diaconate may not remarry if he should become a widower. St. John Paul II praised the ministry of the deacon, saying that "such a ministry, whether in the form of the simplest acts of charity or the most heroic witness to the radical demands of the Gospel" is much needed in today's world.

Living the **evangelical counsels** applies to all Catholics. For consecrated religious, this takes the form of a vow. Bishops, priests, and deacons may take one or more of these vows. Each of the counsels stands in opposition to something that can draw a person away from God. A commitment to *poverty* frees a person from the temptation to sin for the sake of material wealth. A commitment to *chastity* frees one from the temptation to sin for the sake of physical pleasure. In the Latin Church, celibacy—the state of being unmarried for the sake of the Kingdom of God—is required for bishops and priests. A commitment to *obedience* frees one from the temptation to sin for the sake of power. These evangelical counsels also make up the heart of consecrated or religious life, described below.

> **evangelical counsels** Vows of personal poverty, chastity understood as lifelong celibacy, and obedience to a bishop or to the superior of a religious community.

St. Jerome (342–420) was commissioned by Pope Damasus to translate the Bible from Greek to Latin. He did most of this tedious work living as a hermit in a cave near Bethlehem. The task took twenty-three years.

Holiness of Consecrated Life

There have always been Christians who have renounced worldly goals and pleasures for the sake of God's Kingdom. Some of them have made vows or promises committing themselves to the evangelical counsels. Today, there are still both men and women who live a consecrated life to God, typically in religious communities. You may react to this as an extreme way to live a life of holiness. In many ways it truly is. This radical form of discipleship has roots in the words of Jesus who, in explaining the lifetime commitment of marriage, said

Some are incapable of marriage because they were born so; some, because they were made so by others; some, because they renounced marriage for the sake of the kingdom of heaven. Who can accept this ought to accept it. (Mt 19:12)

Around the third century, there were already a few Christians who were renouncing marriage, personal property, and even most social interactions in the name of discipleship. Some went off to the desert to live alone as hermits. Eventually, others formed small communities whose members took vows of poverty, chastity, and obedience. Living these vows was meant not only to further their own holiness, but also to give dramatic witness to all Christians to pursue lives of holiness. Their intention was to also offer prayer for the Church and the world.

Over time consecrated religious life blossomed into many different forms. Monastic communities such as the Benedictines, Trappists, and Carmelites continue to be present for both men and women. In the Middle Ages, St. Francis of Assisi and St. Dominic founded two religious communities that combined prayer and solitude with active ministry in the world. Other communities later emerged that were founded based on a charism or commitment to a particular ministry or apostolate in the world. Two visible results today of these apostolates are Catholic schools and Catholic hospitals that were originally totally staffed by women and men from various religious communities. In male communities, some men are also ordained to the priesthood. Those who are not are called "brothers." Among the "sisters" who are professed religious, the term "nun" technically refers to women who live a monastic or cloistered life dedicated to prayer and contemplation.

There are other forms of consecrated life that continue as a part of Church life and are ways to holiness. Members of *secular institutes* are men or women who consecrate themselves to God through the profession of vows, particularly to celibacy, but generally do not live in community. Rather, they dedicate themselves to evangelization and promoting the Gospel through secular careers. Members of *apostolic societies* are faithful Catholics who pledge to live the evangelical counsels, but who do not take formal vows. *Consecrated virgins* are women who dedicate themselves to virginity or perpetual chastity. Members of *third orders* are laypeople who live according to the rules of a religious order, but don't necessarily live in community. Living lives of prayer, penance, and apostolic service, they are consecrated by the bishop as an image of the heavenly bride and of the Kingdom of God that is to come.

Holiness of Married Life

Like Holy Orders, Matrimony is one of the sacraments at the Service of Communion. In marriage the husband and wife focus on one another. It is this self-giving love that brings them their holiness and salvation. Through their service to each other and their intimate union, a husband and wife "experience the meaning of their oneness and attain to it with growing perfection day by day" (*Gaudium et Spes*, 48).

The effects of the Sacrament of Matrimony are an encounter with God's grace. This isn't something that happens only on the wedding day. In fact, it is the very ordinariness of married life that witnesses to the graced character of a sacramental marriage. Daily

"With parents leading the way by example and family prayer, children and indeed everyone gathered around the family hearth will find a readier path to human maturity, salvation, and holiness" (Gaudium et Spes, 48).

activities like preparing dinner, shopping for groceries, folding laundry, picking up the children at school, and listening to a spouse share the events of his or her day can be moments of grace that lead to the perfection of holiness. These activities can also be done by single people, but take on a different meaning when engaged in by a married couple. These simple actions become the sacramental expressions with meaning because they are lifelong and unconditional. They become symbolic actions that say in effect, "In this simple act of care, I want you to know that I am now and will always be concerned about your needs."

The sexual relationship of a husband and wife is the more profound example of the sacramental reality of marriage. When a husband and wife make love, they consummate or seal their sacramental commitment. The love and union between the two of them, expressed in their sexual sharing, is also intended to be fruitful, that is open to children.

A married couple's sacramental union constitutes the beginning of what the Second Vatican Council called "an intimate partnership of married life and love" (*Gaudium et Spes*, 48). Marriage is also the root of the **domestic church**, a "church of the home" that ordinarily bears fruitfulness of the couple's love in the children they will welcome and raise. But even couples that are unable to have children must see that their love can be put to the service of others.

Catholic married couples are called not only to ensure the happiness of one another, but also to ensure one another's *holiness* as well. This takes place through the sharing of the kind of love that is concerned with the care and well-being of another. Recall that the

Greek word used in the New Testament for this kind of love is *agape*. This kind of love goes beyond romantic desires and fantasies. It offers ways to celebrate an ever-deepening intimacy. It leads the spouses to grow in holiness and work toward salvation in partnership with one another. Thus in marriage the husband and wife are truly holy companions.

Holiness of Single Life

As the average age for marriage continues to rise for both males and females, the number of single Catholics also increases. Eventually, most Catholics, as with other young adults, do marry. But, being single, even for a lifetime, does not prohibit a person from living a life of holiness that, like those who take public vows in the consecrated life, is rooted in a commitment to chastity.

For example, Catholic singles are often involved in a number of parish-sponsored programs that are typically educational, service-oriented, or social in nature. This type of Church participation promotes holiness among single Catholics.

Consider the experience of Michael Quinn, a young lawyer who attended a parish series on Catholic social teaching. The series inspired him to look into ways he could personally help the poor. He began to

Committed Catholic singles are often involved in various forms of service.

> **domestic church** A name for the Christian family. In the family, parents and children exercise their priesthood of the baptized by worshiping God, receiving the sacraments, and witnessing to Christ and the Church by living as faithful disciples.

Single life is an authentic and valuable vocation that more and more Catholics are freely choosing.

volunteer regularly to prepare meals at the local homeless shelter. Later he developed a presentation for the senior partners in his law firm to increase the amount of *pro bono* work they would do on behalf of the poor.

Michael also wound up meeting Maureen, the woman he would eventually marry, at one of the diocesan "Theology on Tap" events—gatherings usually held in a social setting, such as a bar or restaurant, during which a priest or another speaker leads conversation about faith. Michael and Maureen considered the information they heard at one of these sessions promoting Church teaching on chastity as impetus for them *not* living together and for abstaining from sex until they got married.

Michael and Maureen might be called "transitional singles" because they eventually did marry. Other Catholics make the commitment to remain single for a lifetime. Both groups of singles must practice chastity that is witnessed in celibacy. Transitional singles keep the promise of celibacy until they are married. Lifetime singles make a personal consecration or commitment to celibacy.

The *Catechism of the Catholic Church* explains some of the reasons a person might choose to remain single:

> Some forgo marriage in order to care for their parents or brothers and sisters, to give themselves more completely to a profession, or to serve other honorable ends. They can contribute greatly to the good of the human family. (*CCC*, 2231)

Single persons have a greater opportunity for silence and solitude that may translate to a deeper prayer life. Because they are not committed to one relationship, single persons are free to love all and develop friendships with men and women of a variety of ages. People committed to remaining single are often people with a dedicated focus on a career or interest that may have great benefits to humanity; for example, as a medical researcher or as a missionary to a foreign country. All of these elements of the committed single life lead to growth in holiness for both the single person and for all those he or she knows, loves, and serves.

SECTION ASSESSMENT

NOTE TAKING

Use the matching activity you completed with this section to help you complete the following assignment.

1. Of the six distinctions of vocations in your notes, name those that are part of the ministerial priesthood.

VOCABULARY

Rewrite each sentence to make it true.

2. **Sacramental graces** are the grace of the Holy Spirit, given by Christ, given only to men at their ordination.

3. A **vocation** is the calling to an individual career that is intended to build up a Christian's life while on earth.

4. The **common priesthood of the faithful** is exercised when a Catholic commits himself or herself to one of the Church's vocations: ordination, consecrated life, marriage, or single life.

5. The **evangelical counsels** are faith, hope, and love.

6. The **domestic church** is another name for the local parish.

COMPREHENSION

7. Why were the Old Testament prophets concerned that Israel had put too much emphasis on the sacrifice of the priest?

8. How is Jesus' sacrifice different from those offered in the Old Testament?

9. Name three acts of service that help a priest grow in holiness.

APPLICATION

10. Give an example of an ordinary event of married life that might be an opportunity for married couples to grow in holiness.

11. Share a situation whereby a person might choose to commit to the single life for good reason.

SECTION 3
Canonized Saints: Models of Holiness

MAIN IDEA
In every age the Church venerates men and women who are called saints and asks for their intercession.

Every era in the Church's history has produced saints, holy persons who live by the grace of the Holy Spirit and who offer inspiration for others to live good and holy lives. The practice of honoring saints and recognizing them for their holy lives goes back to the early Church. In the years when Christianity was illegal, many Christians dedicated their lives to the Gospel and were arrested, persecuted, and even killed for their Faith by the Roman government. Those who died this way were martyrs, and their names and brief stories of their lives were recorded in local martyrologies.

As martyrdom diminished when Christianity became legal, Christians began to define holiness in other ways. For example, a person's holiness was typically marked by

- a life of prayer,
- self-denial in giving witness to Christ, and
- publicly living the virtues.

Also, miracles associated with a Christian began to be regarded as the proof of a person's worthiness for sainthood. One of the miracles commonly associated with a saint was the incorruption of the body; that is, the body did not decay after death. The relics of the saint then became regarded as objects that not only connected a person to the saint, but as sacred items of healing power themselves. During the Middle Ages, relics were collected and shared with many local churches. Because of this, the *veneration* or honoring of saints began to spread beyond their own regions and nations.

NOTE TAKING

Draw Conclusions. As you read the stories of the three models of holiness profiled in this section (pages 121–124) create a table like the one below to help you list examples of how they exemplify the following characteristics of holiness.

	Prayer	Self-Denial	Living the Virtues
St. Francis de Sales			
St. Thérèse of Lisieux			
Bl. Pier Giorgio Frassati			

As more and more saints were venerated, the Church recognized a need to regulate who could be called a saint. Christians needed to be assured they were not honoring or asking for intercession of fictional characters or of people who did not truly live holy lives. It was left to the bishop of a particular region to determine whether or not a person can be named a saint. Bishops received and studied the biographies of those considered for sainthood and heard testimony about miracles associated with them. If the bishop approved the person for sainthood, the body of the person would be exhumed and moved to an altar and a feast day for the saint would be assigned on the Church calendar within that diocese or province.

Eventually the pope became more involved in approving a person for sainthood. At first he became responsible for allowing the transfer of a person's relics and the introduction of the saint to a particular area. Later he took on the right to formally declare that a person is in Heaven and worthy of veneration as a saint. This declaration is known as *canonization*. The first saint to be officially canonized was St. Ulrich of Augsburg by Pope John XV in 933.

Today, the canonization process includes a detailed examination of a person's life, teachings, and works. The Church also investigates whether miracles took place through this person's intercession. After successful scrutiny, the process proceeds to *beatification*, which allows the faithful to call the person "Blessed." Finally, after the validation of further miracles, the cause of the holy person proceeds to canonization and the new saint is officially enrolled in the canon or list of saints. The pope continues to oversee the process of canonization.

Praying to the Saints

The fact that some followers of Christ have been canonized to sainthood does not mean that they were perfect people. Twentieth-century Church historian Perry

Pilgrims sleep outside the Our Lady of Guadalupe Basilica in Mexico City in preparation for the feast day, December 12.

Miller once observed that "a saint is a sinner, writ large, someone who struggles exceptionally hard to turn a bad thing into a good one." St. Augustine, who lived a publicly scandalous life before conversion, comes to mind (see page 257). Theologian Lawrence Cunningham defined saints in this way: "A saint is a person so grasped by a religious vision that it becomes central to his or her life in a way that radically changes the person and leads others to glimpse the value of that vision." Put another way, saints are members of our Catholic family who inspire and lead us to holiness.

Sometimes Catholics are criticized for holding saints in honor. You may have heard a question like, "Why do Catholics worship saints?" or "Why do Catholic pray to saints?" The first question is inaccurate;

Catholics do not worship saints. Only God merits worship as accorded in the First Commandment. The second question usually refers to the veneration or honor Catholics offer saints and the **intercession** asked of saints. In these cases, Catholics do pray to saints.

But, remember, the word "pray" means something very different from worship. To seek the intercession of the saints should come naturally to any Christian since we all have the obligation to pray for one another. Is there any more basic expression of our Christian solidarity than to pray for the needs of another and to ask others to do the same for us? This commitment rises from our unity in the Body of Christ, a grace given to us at Baptism. And neither this unity nor commitment to pray for one another ends at death. We do not cease to be members of the Body of Christ when we enter the divine presence of Heaven. Those who are in Heaven do not stop caring for their family who remain on earth. It is only natural to pray to saints we know to be in Heaven to ask for their intercession. Belief in the communion of saints is a belief that those who have died and come into the **beatific vision** in Heaven, by virtue of their remarkable intimacy with God, are uniquely equipped to pray for people on earth on our behalf to the Heavenly Father. All the saints model Christian living and are examples of holiness, worthy of emulation.

Models of Holiness

You can probably name several people of all ages whom you can describe as holy. You might think of a neighbor who always is available when someone is in need. Perhaps she prepares full meals for a family when the mother has just given birth to a child, or for another family who has experienced an unexpected death. You likely also can name several of your peers who emit holiness by their words and actions; perhaps a friend who walks away whenever someone begins to gossip or another who avoids sinful pressures of drugs and sex before marriage. Of the many holy people in the Church's history, three described here not only lived holy lives, they also consciously encouraged others to do so as well.

St. Francis de Sales

St. Francis de Sales (1567–1622), a bishop of Geneva, made ecumenical work a focus of his ministry. He worked to restore peace to the Church after the Council of Trent through preaching and writing. One of his special concerns was to reconvert the Calvinists, a splinter church established by John Calvin in Switzerland during the time of the Protestant Reformation.

St. Francis de Sales

intercession A prayer of petition for the sake of others.

beatific vision Seeing God "face-to-face" in Heaven, the source of our eternal happiness; the final union with the Triune God for all eternity.

Calvin denied the sacraments and condemned the papacy, monasticism, and clerical celibacy. Calvin's best-known doctrine is *predestination*, which falsely taught that God determines people for Salvation or damnation before they are born. Francis de Sales countered Calvinism with conciliatory words and was not harsh or condemning. He never preached with a desire to "win" as if in battle with the Calvinists. He said: "Whoever wants to preach effectively must preach with love." A Calvinist minister in Geneva said of St. Francis: "If we honored anyone as a saint, I know of no one since the days of the Apostles more worthy of it than this man."

Francis believed that every Christian had a vocation to holiness. He counseled many laypeople and wrote the *Introduction to the Devout Life* and the treatise *On the Love of God*. Both are still popular today. In each of these he taught that holiness is not reserved for monks or hermits, but is for every person no matter his or her state in life. A famous quotation of Francis that describes the universal call to holiness that he preached to all people is "bloom where you are planted."

St. Thérèse of Lisieux

The *Catechism of the Catholic Church* calls love "the soul of holiness to which all are called" (*CCC*, 826). Love "governs, shapes, and perfects all the means of sanctification" (*Lumen Gentium*, 42). Love as the path to holiness is something understood by St. Thérèse of Lisieux (1873–1897). She called love "the vocation which includes all others; it's a universe of its own, comprising all time and space—it's eternal."

A young Carmelite nun who died at an early age, Thérèse and her words would have never been known if not for the publication of her autobiography, taken from journal entries she composed. It was published as *The Story of a Soul* just one year after her death. The autobiography reveals that from her earliest days she was fascinated by love and determined to plumb its

St. Thérèse of Lisieux

depths, regardless of personal cost. "How can a soul as imperfect as mine aspire to the possession of love?" she wondered.

Thérèse adopted a symbol for her life, the "little flower." She said she was like the little flower that survives the harshest conditions of winter only to appear again in the spring. Her goal in life was to go to Heaven and her plan to achieve this was, in her words, "the little way." Thérèse's little way translated to accepting some of the bothersome events of her life in Jesus' name. For example, one time Thérèse leaned over a wash pool with a group of sisters washing some clothing. One of the sisters splashed the hot, dirty water on Thérèse not one time, but multiple times. Thérèse was near to exploding, but she said nothing, offering up the sister's lack of consideration to Christ. Doing so brought her peace.

The "little way" is a road to holiness attainable for anyone in any state of life. Keeping love of Christ as the motivation for all thoughts and actions is the force that St. Thérèse encouraged all Catholics to act upon.

The Church recognized her holiness in a surprisingly quick manner. Just twenty-six years after her death from tuberculosis, Pope Pius XI beatified Thérèse. On May 17, 1925, he canonized her in Rome. In 1997, St. John Paul II named St. Thérèse of Lisieux a **Doctor of the Church**. *The Story of a Soul* remains a best-seller.

Bl. Pier Giorgio Frassati

As an Italian teenager, Bl. Pier Giorgio Frassati (1901–1925) loved the outdoors. He was adept at both hiking and skiing. He once wrote to a friend: "I left my heart on the mountain peaks and I hope to retrieve it this summer when I climb Mount Blanc. If my studies permitted, I would spend whole days on the mountain admiring in that pure atmosphere the magnificence of God."

In addition to a passion for the outdoors, Bl. Pier was also passionate about social causes and went to great lengths to support justice. Though he came from a rich family, Pier felt kinship with the poor. He was known for giving away his train fare to strangers in

St. John Paul II called Pier Giorgio Frassati the "Man of Eight Beatitudes."

need, then hopping off the train and running all the way home.

Pier Giorgio also participated in many different kinds of protests against Italy's Fascist regime. When the government police knocked down the banner of a fellow protestor at an outdoor rally, Pier retrieved it and held it higher, even as he was warding off the police with a pole he wielded in his other hand. At another time, a group of Fascists broke into his home intending to kill or injure Pier and his father. Instead, Pier turned the tables on them and defended himself and his father. Then he chased them away.

Pier Giorgio had a great love for the Eucharist and deep devotion to the Blessed Sacrament. He attended Mass frequently and would spend hours in prayer before the Blessed Sacrament. St. John Paul II recognized the inspiration Pier has for teens today at his beatification in 1990, calling him the "Man of Eight Beatitudes." St. John Paul II said:

> By his example he proclaims that a life lived in Christ's Spirit, the Spirit of the Beatitudes, is "blessed," and that only the person who becomes a "man or woman of the Beatitudes" can succeed in communicating love and peace to others. He repeats that it is really worth giving up everything to serve the Lord. He testifies that holiness is possible for everyone, and that only the revolution of charity can enkindle the hope of a better future in the hearts of people.

In his own words, Bl. Pier had more advice for reaching for holiness:

> With all the strength of my soul I urge you young people to approach the Communion table as often as you can. Feed on this bread

> **Doctor of the Church** A Church writer of great learning and holiness whose works the Church has highly recommended for studying and living the Faith.

of angels whence you will draw all the energy you need to fight inner battles. Because true happiness, dear friends, does not consist in the pleasures of the world or in earthly things, but in peace of conscience, which we have only if we are pure in heart and mind.

Bl. Pier Giorgio Frassati died of polio in 1925. He was only twenty-four years old. His funeral attracted thousands of mourners. Many of the poor people of Turin immediately petitioned the archbishop to begin the cause for Pier's canonization.

Holiness Demands Constant Renewal

It's important to remember that the canonized saints were ordinary people, like you, who used the means of grace found in the Church to be holy and Christ-like. It's also important to keep in mind that the Church is, in the words of St. Augustine, *corpus permixtum*, a "mixed body" of saints and sinners.

This means that while Christ is "holy, innocent, undefiled, separated from sinners" (Heb 7:26), all others, including the saints, are not. The Church that gathers weeds along with wheat is in constant need of purification and conversion. In order for this to occur in your own life, you must acknowledge your sinfulness and accept the call of Christ to continue your movement to God with a contrite heart.

Though a Catholic's sins are forgiven in the Sacrament of Baptism, they remain tangled in the world of sin, and in need of a "second conversion." Catholics are able to return to the Father in Christ through a sacrament of conversion, the Sacrament of Penance. This

> **mortal sin** A serious violation of God's law of love that results in the loss of sanctifying grace (God's life) in the soul of the sinner. To commit a mortal sin, there must be grave matter, full knowledge of the evil done, and full consent of the will.

Holy Confession during World Youth Day at Rio de Janeiro, Brazil, 2013.

sacrament has three actions of the penitent—repentance, confession, and penance—and one action of the priest who is the minister of the sacrament, the absolution of the sins in God's name.

The Sacrament of Penance assures that Catholics will be properly prepared to receive the Eucharist. Catholics must confess their sins any time they have committed a **mortal sin**. The sacrament can also be used to confess venial sins. Additionally, the sacrament is an opportunity to receive the graces of renewal, especially during the seasons of Advent, Christmas, Lent, and Easter.

Like the Sacrament of Penance, the holiness of the Church is a gift from God. Because of the presence of sin, this gift can sometimes be obscured, for although the Church is always holy, she remains also a pilgrim Church of sinners. Unlike other earthly pilgrims who may be unsure of their final destiny, the Church is

CATHOLICS WEAR
♥RELIGIOUS MEDALS

Have you ever been given a religious medal, perhaps a medal of Mary or one of the saints, to wear on a chain around your neck? Did you in fact wear your medal? If so, this is one way to remind yourself of your Catholic faith and of the Lord's desire that you keep him close to your heart. The practice of wearing devotional medals dates back to very early in Church history. Archeologists discovered medals with the likeness of Sts. Peter and Paul dating back to the second century.

Wearing a religious medal is an example of a **sacramental**, a sacred sign that signifies the spiritual effects we receive through the sacraments. Sacramentals help Catholics remember their Faith and religious duties. Religious medals remind Catholics to pray and do works of charity. If the medal is of a saint, it is a reminder for the person to ask the saint to intercede for him or her.

Probably the most popular religious medal worn by Catholics is the Miraculous Medal. In 1840 the Blessed Mother appeared to a young nun, St. Catherine Labouré, and told her to have a medal struck honoring the Immaculate Conception. In one of a series of visions, Mary said to St. Catherine, "Have a medal struck after this model. All who wear it will receive great graces; they should wear it around their neck." In the vision, Catherine saw Mary as the Immaculate Conception with letters of gold written around her saying: "O Mary, conceived without sin, pray for us who recourse to thee." She also saw the tableau turn and on the reverse of the medal a large "M" on a bar and a cross; below the "M" were the hearts of Jesus and Mary, one crowned with thorns, the other pierced with a sword.

After Catherine's story was verified by the archbishop, the medal was produced. It has been worn by millions of people ever since and is now referred to as the Miraculous Medal. One of the most famous stories of grace surrounding the wearing of the medal is the conversion of a Jewish man, Marie-Alphonse Ratisbonne of Strasburg. After he consented to wear the medal he had a vision of Mary in church in the same posture as on the medal.

Do one or more of the following:

- Wear a religious medal, either one depicting a favorite saint or the Miraculous Medal.

- Pray for a special grace in your life using the simple prayer on the Miraculous Medal: "O Mary, conceived without sin, pray for us who recourse to thee."

- Offer a **novena** of the Miraculous Medal.

- Pray the Miraculous Medal Prayer:

    O Mary, conceived without sin, pray for us who have recourse to thee, and for those who do not have recourse to thee, especially the enemies of the Church and those recommended to thee.
    Amen.

> **sacramental** A sacred sign (e.g., an object, a place, or an action) that resembles the sacraments. Through the prayers of the Church, spiritual effects are signified and obtained.
>
> **novena** A nine-day prayer for a certain intention.

assured of her final home in the Kingdom of God while foreshadowing this final destination along the way.

And don't forget that the saints can help you in this constant renewal. The saints can help you as both intercessors and inspirations to live holy lives. St. Gregory the Great (540–604) wrote:

"In the Holy Church, we are all nourished by each one, and each one is nourished by all."

SECTION ASSESSMENT

NOTE TAKING

Use the information from the chart you completed with this section to help you answer the following questions.

1. How do you interpret St. Francis de Sales' call to holiness: "bloom where you are planted"?

2. How could you apply St. Thérèse of Lisieux's "little way" as a model for your own life of holiness?

3. What was Bl. Pier Giorgio Frassati's advice for reaching holiness?

SUMMARIZE

4. Briefly describe the process of canonization today.

5. What are the three actions of the penitent and the one action of the priest in the Sacrament of Penance?

VOCABULARY

6. What is a sacramental? Give two examples of sacramentals.

COMPREHENSION

7. How did saints come to be recognized after martyrdom diminished in the Church?

8. Why is it natural for Catholics to pray to saints known to be in Heaven to ask for their intercession?

APPLICATION

9. How have you or how would you respond to someone who said to you: "Why do you pray to saints"?

Mary, the Mother of God: Queen of All Saints

MAIN IDEA
Mary's life of holiness is rewarded in this world and beyond. She is the Mother of God, the Queen of All Saints, and the Mother of the Church.

The Blessed Virgin Mary, the Mother of God, is all the Church strives to be. She is a sign that the Church is "without spot or wrinkle or any such thing" (Eph 5:27). Mary shines out to the entire Church as a model of virtues. St. Ambrose, a fourth-century bishop and a **Church Father**, called Mary a figure of the Church because she announces Christ's presence with her faith, charity, and perfect union with Christ. She is the first disciple of her Son, Jesus, and the one whom we need to intercede for us and bring us closer to him. She is the Queen of the Saints.

Mary's absolute openness to God's plan was present at the crucial moment of her life. She heard a message from an angel asking her to be the Mother of the Savior. Her Son, Jesus Christ, would be divine, but he also was to be human. He needed a human Mother for this to take place. Mary was predestined from the beginning of creation to be this one-of-a-kind woman from whom the Savior could be born. Yet in the God-given freedom of her own life she had the power to cower in fear, to close down, and to say "no" to this mission.

Mary's response to the angel was "Yes." Her faithfulness allowed Jesus to be conceived, first in the willingness of her spirit, and then in her flesh. This

Church Fathers A traditional designation given to theologians of the first eight centuries whose teachings made a lasting mark on the Church. Also called Fathers of the Church.

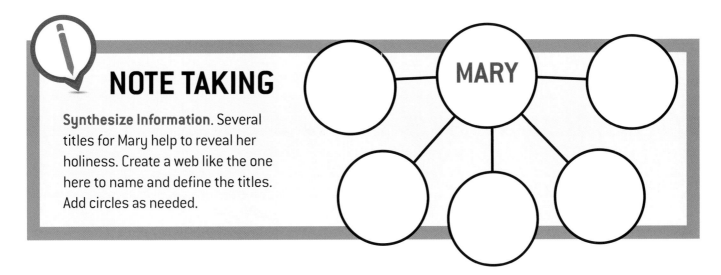

NOTE TAKING

Synthesize Information. Several titles for Mary help to reveal her holiness. Create a web like the one here to name and define the titles. Add circles as needed.

MARY

The Annunciation *(1438–1445) by Fra Angelico.*

climactic moment of the **Annunciation** is something all people are called to imitate: to be open to God's call, to not be afraid, and to be welcoming of Jesus into our lives. The poor, humble girl from Nazareth was the first of many like her who would accept her Son into their lives: shepherds, Simeon and Anna in the Temple, the bride and groom at Cana, little children, the fishermen, the sick, prostitutes who would all be attracted to Jesus and become his disciples. All of them followed the example of Mary.

Mary Is Preserved in All Time for Holiness

By choosing Mary to be the Mother of God, God the Father made the unbreakable commitment to involve human beings in the plan of Salvation, that is, in all that he does. St. John Paul II wrote that Mary's election "is more powerful than any experience of evil and sin" (*Redemptoris Mater*, 5). It is no wonder that Mary was preserved from the stain of Original Sin from

the moment of her conception. This doctrine of the Church is called the **Immaculate Conception**.

Related to the Immaculate Conception is the Annunciation, or announcement that Mary would give birth to the Savior. Just as death entered the world when the first woman, Eve, sinned, so renewed life came through Mary's response to the angel's request: "May it be done to me according to your word" (Lk 1:38). Mary's freedom from sin is the sign and the promise that everything that could separate humanity from God has become powerless. Mary's "Yes" allows

Annunciation The visit by the angel Gabriel to the Virgin Mary to announce that she would be the Mother of the Savior. After giving her consent, Mary became Mother of Jesus by the power of the Holy Spirit. The Feast of the Annunciation is on March 25.

Immaculate Conception The belief that Mary was conceived without Original Sin. The Feast of the Immaculate Conception is on December 8 and is a Holy Day of Obligation.

the Incarnation, the birth of the Savior. It is through her Son, Jesus, that the world is offered Salvation.

Mary's holiness was preserved on earth in her perpetual virginity. Mary was "ever-virgin" meaning that she was a virgin before, during, and after the birth of Jesus. This has always been the belief of the Church from the time of the Apostles. The Gospels share that the virginal conception of Jesus was the work of the Holy Spirit and a fulfillment of the Old Testament prophets: "Therefore the Lord himself will give you this sign: the virgin shall be with child, and bear a son, and shall name him Immanuel" (Is 7:14).

What does Mary's perpetual virginity teach us about holiness in God's plan? Here are five teachings:

1 Jesus has only one Father, who is in Heaven.
Jesus was never separated from his Father even in his humanity.

2 From the virginal conception, Jesus is filled with the Holy Spirit.
The Holy Spirit caused Mary to conceive the Second Person of the Blessed Trinity, who himself was anointed with the Holy Spirit from the beginning of his human existence. "From his fullness, we have all received grace in place of grace" (Jn 1:16) that communicate to us what we need to reach Heaven.

3 The virginal birth of Jesus signifies a new birth for humanity, an offer of Salvation.
This new birth takes place in the Holy Spirit through Faith. In fact, the virginal conception is only accessible to those with Faith who understand how all of the mysteries associated with the Life, Death, and Resurrection of Christ are connected.

4 Mary's virginity is a sign of her Faith.
Mary's virginity allows the world to witness her blessedness.

5 Mary's perpetual virginity is symbolic of the Church.
The Church who "by receiving the word of God in faith becomes herself a mother" (*Lumen Gentium*, 64).

In summary, Mary's life of holiness—begun at the time of her Immaculate Conception and lived through her perpetual virginity—is rewarded and continues after her time on earth. Mary is the first to share in the rewards of her Son's Resurrection. In 1950 Pope Pius XII officially proclaimed this belief: "The Immaculate Mother of God, the ever Virgin Mary, having completed the course of her earthly life was assumed body and soul into heavenly glory." This is the doctrine of the **Assumption**. Mary embodies the hope of all Catholics who one day hope to experience the resurrection of the body.

Mother of the Church

The Scriptures reveal Mary's special place in the Church. The Gospel of John tells that it was Mary who first persuaded Jesus to begin his public ministry at the wedding feast in Cana (Jn 2:1–11). Jesus' concern for his Mother's wishes at Cana remained with him to his final moments on the Cross:

> When Jesus saw his mother and the disciple there whom he loved, he said to his mother, "Woman, behold, your son." Then he said to the disciple, "Behold, your mother." And from that hour the disciple took her into his home. (Jn 19:2–27)

This incident indicates Mary's special place in the communion of saints as the Mother of the Church. It is because of her role as Mother of the Church that Catholics seek her intercession above all the saints in Heaven.

Catholic devotion to Mary is motivated first and foremost by her place as the Mother of God. Authentic devotion to Mary never distracts Christians from the saving work of Jesus. Mary is nothing without Jesus and is able to be the Mother of the Church only because she is filled with God's grace. At the same time, Jesus' humanity would not be the same without Mary. God the Father prepared this unique Mother for the Second Divine Person of the Blessed Trinity. In the Incarnation, Christ and Mary are indissolubly linked. They are united by blood; nothing can ever undo the essential nature of their relationship. In this way, Mary prefigures the Church, which is indissolubly linked to Christ through the blood of the Cross from which the

Mary remained with Jesus until he took his final breath.

Church was born. Like Mary, the Church can never be separated from Christ.

Mary is the Mother of the Church, but her role in the Church is in no way equal to the role of Christ. Yet her life provides a model of faith Catholics and all people can strive to imitate.

Assumption The Church dogma that teaches that the Blessed Mother, because of her unique role as the Mother of God, was taken directly to Heaven when her earthly life was over. The Feast of the Assumption is on August 15 and is a Holy Day of Obligation.

MOTHER OF THE POOR

Pope Paul VI described Mary as a contemporary model of Christian discipleship, as a Mother who has special care for the poor:

> [S]he was a woman who did not hesitate to proclaim that God vindicates the humble and the oppressed, and removes the powerful people of this world from their privileged positions (cf. Lk 1:51–53). The modern woman will recognize in Mary, who "stands out among the poor and humble of the Lord," a woman of strength, who experienced poverty and suffering, flight and exile. (cf. Mt 2:21–23; *Marialis cultus*, 37)

REFLECTION

Read the Magnificat in Luke 1:46–55. List at least three verses that give hope to the poor. Explain why you chose the verses that you did.

PROJECT

Do one of the following service projects in support of children or teenagers in need:

- Contact an organization that fights against a childhood disease (for example, juvenile diabetes). Ask how you can aid its efforts on either a group or individual basis. For example, you might be able to coordinate a fund-raising walk or 10K race to raise funds for the organization or support an ongoing fund-raising effort.

- Arrange with a teacher or parish youth minister ways to provide care packages to juveniles in a local detention facility. Sample items usually of need include: toothbrushes, deodorant, combs, and shampoo. Sponsor a collection day at school and/or your parish. Package the items and work with your teacher or youth minister to arrange delivery.

- Tutor younger children on their schoolwork. Contact the local school district or parks and recreation department and find out opportunities to work one-to-one with students in need at the end of the school day.

You can also choose a service project on your own that shows care and concern for children or teenagers in your area. Share your ideas with your teacher prior to beginning any project.

SECTION ASSESSMENT

NOTE TAKING

Use your flow chart to help you to complete the following assignment.

1. Define the following terms related to Catholic beliefs about Mary: Annunciation, Immaculate Conception, and Assumption.

COMPREHENSION

2. What are the Gospel origins of Mary's place as Mother of the Church?

CRITICAL THINKING

3. How does Mary's "Yes" counteract the decision of Eve?

4. What does Mary's perpetual virginity teach about holiness?

REFLECTION

5. Describe your admiration of Mary as a role model for your life.

Section Summaries

Focus Question

How can a Church made up of sinners remain holy?

Complete one of the following:

 Research the life of one of the miners or of Greg Hall, the American who helped to facilitate the rescue, since the event. Write a two- to three-paragraph report on any spiritual or religious changes that have occurred in the person's life based on the experience.

 Choose any art medium and create a presentation illustrating Jesus' parable of the weeds among the wheat (Mt 13:24–30, 36–43) and how it applies to the world's need for Redemption today.

 Create a penitential plan to express your desire for conversion around these three areas: fasting (e.g., sacrificing something the body desires for the sake of a spiritual good), prayer (e.g., devoting time to adoration of the Blessed Sacrament, reading the life of a saint), and almsgiving (e.g., volunteering to help the disadvantaged, visiting someone who is lonely). Write a description and schedule of your plan. Work to implement it.

INTRODUCTION (PAGES 97–100)
Holiness Is from God

Holiness is a second mark of the Church. Everyone is called to holiness, not only monks like Thomas Merton. Through prayer, good works, living a Christian vocation, and through the grace of God, we are capable of achieving holiness.

 Pope Paul VI wrote: "The Church is holy, though having sinners in her midst, because she herself has no other life but the life of grace" (*Credo of the People of God*, 19). Explain how this statement compares with Jesus' parable of the weeds among wheat (Mt 13:29–30).

SECTION 1 (PAGES 101–106)
Tracing the Church's Holiness

The Church's holiness has origins in God alone. The Old Testament described how God's holiness made him who he is. The Incarnation of Jesus and the entire scope of his life, from home to ministry to redeeming Death have lessons for achieving holiness. Jesus' role as the Great Physician reminds us that he ministers to a Church of sinners and saints, with the former called to give up their sin and work toward holiness.

 Why is it incorrect to think that the holiness of the Church depends on the holiness of her members?

SECTION 2 (PAGES 107–118)
Ways the Church Is Holy

The Church is holy because of the graces offered by God. Foremost among these graces are sacramental graces. The Church is also holy because of the holy lives lived by her members and witnessed most profoundly by the living of the Great Commandment. Particularly, the Church is holy in the ways Catholics live out their personal vocations that emanate from Baptism: ordained ministry, consecrated life, marriage, and committed single life.

 Compare your life story with James Alison's story of the people of Albania around the time of the end of communism. How does your quest for the perfection of God's Kingdom involve both sacrifice and celebration?

SECTION 3 (PAGES 119–126)
Canonized Saints: Models of Holiness

The practice of honoring saints and asking for their intercession dates back to the earliest centuries of the Church when Christians were martyred for their Faith. After martyrdom diminished, saints began to be recognized for the holiness of their lives and for miracles attributed to them. A process of formally recognizing saints called *canonization* emerged in the Church. It is always appropriate to pray for others; this is what saints do for us. For that reason Catholics pray to saints asking for their intercession on their behalf. The Sacrament of Penance is a way Catholics can seek conversion and purification for sins.

 Briefly share biographical information about three saints: (1) a saint honored on your birthday; (2) a saint for which you were named (or a close relative was named); and (3) a patron saint of an activity that you enjoy.

SECTION 4 (PAGES 127–132)

Mary, the Mother of God: Queen of All Saints

Mary, the Mother of God, is, in the words of St. Ambrose, a "type of Church" who models the Church of her Faith, charity, and perfect union with Christ, her Son. Her "Yes" to God's will is a model of holiness. Her holiness was in place from the moment of her conception, through the perpetual virginity of her life on earth, to her Assumption—body and soul—to Heaven at the end of her earthly life. As Mother of Church, Catholics seek her intercession above all the saints.

 Read the announcement of the birth of Jesus from Luke 1:26–38. Then listen to a recording of the Beatles "Let It Be." Write a short meditation on what it means for you to say "Yes" to God in your life.

Chapter Assignments

Choose and complete at least one of the three assignments assessing your understanding of the material in this chapter.

1. Universal Call to Holiness Collage

➜ If you visit the National Shrine of the Immaculate Conception in Washington, DC, you will have the opportunity to view the sculpted marble relief (above) from Maryland artist George Carr that ranks among the largest in the world, measuring seventeen feet from top to bottom and fifty-two feet across, and weighing more than thirty-seven tons. Its theme is taken from the Second Vatican Council's call to universal holiness: "All the faithful of Christ of whatever rank or status are called to the fullness of the Christian life and to the perfection of charity; by this holiness as such a more human manner of living is promoted in this earthly society" (*Lumen Gentium*, 40). Included among the nearly fifty figures portrayed in the relief are a young couple, an elderly woman, some children of different races and cultures, along with recognizable faces like St. John Paul II, Mother Teresa of Calcutta, and even James Cardinal Hickey, the archbishop of Washington, DC, at the time. All are gathered with the Blessed Mother receiving the grace of the Holy Spirit. The Universal Call to Holiness sculpture was dedicated on November 14, 1999, in celebration of the fortieth anniversary of the dedication of the National Shrine. After you have examined the collage at the National Shrine website (www.nationalshrine.com), create a similar collage representing some holy people in your life (friends, family members), favorite saints, and other people (the poor, ill, children) who represent holiness to you. Choose a medium that fits your style, such as:

1. photos

2. watercolor

3. pencil sketch

You may also wish to include other elements (e.g., words) and textures (e.g., cloth) to complete your collage.

2. Vocations of Holiness

Prepare a project to support the Catholic vocations described in this chapter (ordained ministry, consecrated life, marriage, or committed single life). There are several things you can do. For example, compile a resource notebook for with positive news articles about priests or religious that share the joy and scope of their vocation. The articles might refer to their ministry, hobbies, call, or even their obituary. Just make sure the articles provide an interesting and inspiring view of this vocation. Similarly, you could gather personal letter correspondences from priests, religious, married couples, and committed single people that speak of some aspect of their vocation. Begin by sending a handwritten letter of your own to people in these vocations that explains this assignment and asks them to share some aspects of their life, both the rewards and challenges. Alternatively, rather than write and collect letters, you may wish to interview these people and record the interviews on videotape. Edit and plan for a showing. Finally, one other possibility is to arrange for a "vocations panel" and invite people representing each vocation to address your classmates at school or parish around the topics already mentioned.

3. Investigating the Process of Canonization

The procedure for beatification and canonization was revised by St. John Paul II in 1983. Typically an investigation for sainthood begins five or more years after the person has died. A simple summary of the steps along the way follows:

1. A local bishop conducts an investigation of the heroic virtues of the person, including research from the person's writings. A summary of the findings are sent to the Vatican. The person may be given the title "Servant of God" to indicate his or her life is being considered for sainthood.

2. A panel of theologians and cardinals of the Congregation for the Causes of Saints evaluates the findings. If the panel finds the person is a role model of Christian virtues, he or she is given the title "venerable."

3. The cause moves on to beatification. In order to beatified, the person must be credited with a posthumous miracle. Martyrs can be beatified without evidence of a miracle. A person who is beatified is called "blessed" and may be honored in a particular region or by a particular group—for example, by the religious community of which the person was a member.

4. To be considered for sainthood, there must be proof of a second posthumous miracle. If this is found, the pope himself can choose to canonize the person to sainthood.

Examine the names that follow of people who have been canonized or have cases open for canonization and who have also ministered in America. Choose one person from each part of the process and write two paragraphs for each one. Paragraph one should summarize the person's life story. Paragraph two should summarize status of the canonization process. For extra credit, research and write about Americans who have been given the title "Servant of God."

American Saints

North American Jesuit Martyrs. Sts. Isaac Jogues, René Goupil, and Jean de Lalande were killed near Auriesville, New York. Canonized in 1930.

St. Frances Cabrini (1850–1917). Italian immigrant who founded the Missionary Sisters of the Sacred Heart. Canonized in 1946.

St. Elizabeth Ann Bayley Seton (1774–1821). First native-born American to be canonized. Established many Catholic schools, which came to serve as the prototype of the American Catholic school system. Canonized in 1975.

St. John Nepomucene Neumann (1811–1860). Native of Bohemia who served as a pioneer diocesan priest in Rochester and Buffalo, New York. Named the fourth bishop of Philadelphia in 1852. Canonized in 1977.

St. Rose Philippine Duchesne (1769–1852). French-born foundress of the Religious of the Sacred Heart. Devoted her years of service to educate Native Americans. Canonized in 1988.

St. Katharine Drexel (1858–1955). Inherited a fortune that she eventually used for missionary endeavors through the community of Sisters of the Blessed Sacrament. Dedicated to the education of Native Americans and African Americans. Canonized in 2000.

St. Anne-Thérèse Guérin (1798–1856). French nun who helped establish the Academy of St. Mary-of-the-Woods (1841) at Terre Haute, Indiana, the first Catholic women's liberal-arts college in the United States. Canonized in 2006.

St. Damien De Veuster (1840–1889). "The Leper Priest" who heroically served outcast lepers on the colony at Molokai in Hawaii. Canonized in 2009.

St. André Bessette (1845–1947). Holy Cross brother who lived a humble life of service dedicated to honoring St. Joseph, the foster father of Jesus. Canonized in 2010.

St. Kateri Tekakwitha (1656–1680). Iroquois Indian born in New York who was converted by the early Jesuit missionaries. Canonized in 2012.

St. Mother Marianne Cope (1838–1918). Worked nonstop for thirty years serving the lepers in Hawaii helping St. Damien. Canonized in 2012.

American Blesseds

Bl. Junípero Serra (1713–1784). Spanish-born Franciscan who established nine missions in California while showing great love for Native Americans. Beatified in 1988.

Bl. Francis Xavier Seelos (1819–1867). Born in Bavaria and ordained a Redemptorist priest in Baltimore. Died of Yellow Fever after caring for its victims in New Orleans. Beatified in 2000.

Bl. Carlos Manuel Rodriguez (1918–1963). First Puerto Rican to be beatified. Known as the "lay Apostle of the liturgical movement." Beatified in 2001.

American Venerables

Venerable Solanus Casey (1870–1957). Capuchin priest from Detroit.

Venerable Cornelia Connelly (1809–1879). Founder of the Society of the Holy Child Jesus.

Venerable Samuel Charles Mazzuchelli (1806–1864). Missionary and church architect in Iowa, Wisconsin, and Illinois.

Venerable Michael McGivney (1852–1890). Founder of the Knights of Columbus, the largest Catholic fraternal organization in the world.

Venerable Pierre Toussaint (1766–1853). Haitian born abolitionist and Catholic convert.

Venerable Félix Varela (1788–1853). Human rights activist in Cuba.

American Servants of God

Servant of God Vincent McCauley (1906–1982). Holy Cross missionary priest who was also the first bishop of Fort Portal, Uganda.

Servant of God Patrick Peyton (1909–1992). The well-known "Rosary Priest" who promoted the Family Rosary campaign.

Faithful Disciple

Adele Brise

December 8, 2010, the Feast of the Immaculate Conception, was a momentous day for the Church and for the United States of America. It was on that day that Bishop David Ricken of Green Bay issued a decree that authenticated the nineteenth-century apparitions of the Blessed Virgin Mary to a young woman, Adele Brise, in the farmlands near Champion, Wisconsin. A shrine built there, the Shrine of Our Lady of Good Help, reminds the Church that the apparitions of Mary to Adele Brise are now worthy of belief, in the same way that Guadalupe in Mexico, Lourdes in France, and Fatima in Portugal are because of their approval by a local bishop. Mary's appearances to Adele Brise are the first Marian apparitions approved by the Church for the United States.

Adele Brise's story is a remarkable one. The oldest of four children of Belgian immigrants, at age twenty-four she came with her family to the Green Bay peninsula in 1855. Her father purchased 240 acres of land in the town of Red River for 120 dollars. Adele had intended to join a religious community when she came to America, but her first days in Wisconsin were taken up with the hard work of farming and pioneer life.

Adele's life changed in early October 1859. While carrying grain to a mill about four miles from her home, Mary appeared to her. A few days later, on October 9, while walking to Sunday Mass in Bay Settlement, about eleven miles from home, Mary appeared to her again. After Mass, Adele told the pastor

Bishop David Ricken of the Diocese of Green Bay reads the official pronouncement on December 8, 2010, to approve the Marian apparitions of 1859 to Adele Brise.

about what she had seen. He said to her, "Ask in God's name who it was and what it desired of you." On the way, home, Mary appeared a third time and Adele asked the question as the pastor had suggested. Mary responded:

> I am the Queen of Heaven who prays for the conversion of sinners and I wish you to do the same. Gather the children in this wild country and teach them what they should know for salvation. Teach them their catechism, how to sign themselves with the Sign of the Cross, and how to approach the sacraments.

Adele Brise dedicated the rest of her life to doing what Mary instructed. She gathered the children near her home and taught them the Faith. She also traveled to other farms, sometimes as far as fifty miles away, to do the same. She faced the challenges of the forest and weather that were often easier to handle than ridicule that came from those who didn't believe that Mary had really appeared to her.

Eventually, a school and chapel were built at the site of the appearances. Most of the students were orphans. Adele, who gathered a lay community known as the Sisters of Good Help around her, often went begging for what she and the school needed. When food was scarce, Adele would pray to Mary for help. Inevitably someone would drop by a sack of flour or some meat to get them through the next days.

A huge forest fire known as the Peshtigo Fire threatened the area on October 8, 1871 (the same day as the Chicago Fire). People brought animals and their families to the grounds of the chapel. Adele carried a statue of Mary around the perimeter of the grounds. On the outer portion of the perimeter everything burned. The fire did not advance inside the five-acre section near the school and chapel. Many considered this a miracle. Every year since, on October 8 pilgrims gather to re-enact the original procession.

Bishop Ricken began looking into Mary's appearances to Adele in 2009, and much of his investigation involved the life of Adele Brise. The bishop said this about her:

> What has struck me about the story of the life of Adel Brise is her lifelong fidelity to what the Blessed Mother asked her to do with her life. She dedicated her life to prayer, especially for the conversion of sinners, and to the catechesis of children. She made great sacrifices and attracted other young women to follow her in fidelity to the Blessed Mother's call.

Reading Comprehension

1. What is unique about the location of Mary's appearance to Adele Brise?
2. What did Mary ask of Adele?
3. Describe the miraculous event that convinced others to believe that Mary had truly appeared to Adele.

Writing Task

- Imagine you are teaching younger children about what they should know for their Salvation. What would you tell them?

Explaining the Faith

The Church teaches that Mary was "ever-virgin" but the Bible says that Jesus had "brothers and sisters." How can both be true?

Mary remained at the foot of the Cross with St. John the Apostle and other women companions of her Son.

There *are* Gospel passages that mention the "brothers and sisters" of Jesus (e.g., Mt 13:55–56, Mk 3:31–35, 6:1–6). The Church has always believed that these so-called brothers and sisters of Jesus were actually his cousins or other relatives or the children of another Mary. There is evidence to support both statements.

First, Jesus spoke Aramaic. In this ancient language there was no special word meaning "cousin." The word available, *ah*, was used for various types of relations. The patriarchal family dominated Jesus' world. His society considered the oldest living male the patriarch. The patriarch may or may not have been a person's own father. He could have been a grandfather or an uncle. In this type of family structure, relatives like cousins referred to themselves as brothers and sisters.

Also, two of the men in Matthew's Gospel mentioned as brothers of Jesus—James and Joseph—could not be sons of Mary, Jesus' Mother, because other places in the Gospels (Mt 27:56 and Mk 15:40) clearly reference them as sons of another Mary.

Mary is "ever-virgin" and Jesus is her only Son, "but her spiritual motherhood extends to all men whom indeed he came to save" (*CCC*, 501).

 ## Further Research

- Why in the plan of God the Father did he want his Son to be born of a virgin? Read *Catechism of the Catholic Church*, 502–507.

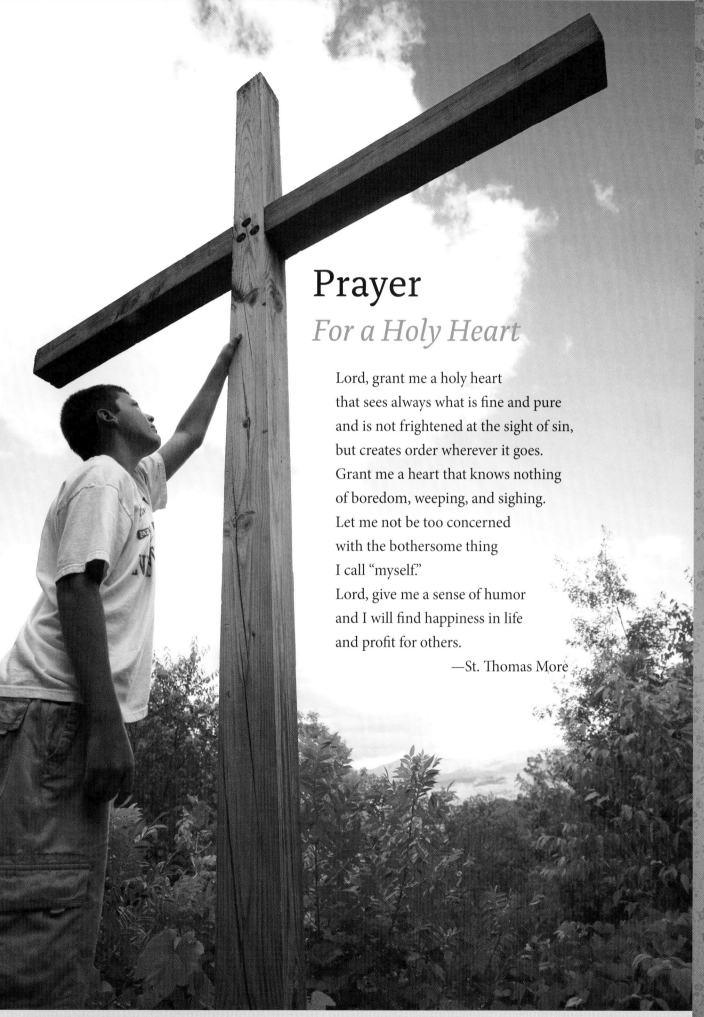

Prayer

For a Holy Heart

Lord, grant me a holy heart
that sees always what is fine and pure
and is not frightened at the sight of sin,
but creates order wherever it goes.
Grant me a heart that knows nothing
of boredom, weeping, and sighing.
Let me not be too concerned
with the bothersome thing
I call "myself."
Lord, give me a sense of humor
and I will find happiness in life
and profit for others.

—St. Thomas More

THE
CHURCH
IS CATHOLIC

4

Mission and Challenges in Catholic SCHOOLS

Is a Catholic school system still needed in America? To combat discrimination against Catholics in the public school system, in 1884, the Third Plenary Council of Baltimore mandated that every parish construct a Catholic school and that Catholic parents send their children to these parochial schools. Catholic secondary schools were also built, with parish grade school students being sent on a "feeder system" to local Catholic high schools. With priests and religious as teachers, the school system flourished. The peak of the Catholic primary and secondary school system was in 1965 when nearly 5.5 million students attended about 13,000 Catholic schools in the United States. Those numbers began to decline dramatically, beginning in the 1970s, as the number of priests and religious also dropped. By the 2009–2010 school year, there were about 2.1 million students enrolled in 7,094 Catholic schools, of which 1,205 were Catholic high schools.

Certainly the Catholic school system has been a great success. Leaders in every business field, politics, and entertainment are among the products of Catholic education. But Catholics no longer face the discrimination that marked the earlier time. In fact, both primary and secondary Catholic schools have greater non-Catholic student bodies than ever before.

Many non-Catholics—especially those from urban areas—choose a Catholic education for its superior academics, safety, and spiritual formation. The evangelization outreach of Catholic schools has also always been one of its benefits. Cardinal Timothy Dolan of New York cited another reason Catholic schools should remain in operation: helping Catholics to combat widespread **secularization**:

Cardinal Timothy Dolan

The Catholic Church is now confronted by a new secularization asserting that a person of faith can hardly be expected to be a tolerant and enlightened American. Religion, in this view, is only a personal hobby, with no implications for public life. Under this new scheme, to take one's faith seriously and bring it to the public square somehow implies being un-American. To combat this notion, an equally energetic evangelization—with Catholic schools at its center—is all the more necessary.

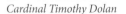

secularization A process of drawing society away from religious orientation in order to make it more worldly and less influenced by religion.

FOCUS QUESTION

How does the
Catholic Church invite
ALL PEOPLE TO BELONG?

INTRODUCTION

What It Means to Be Catholic with a Small "c"

MAIN IDEA
The Church is catholic because Christ is present in the Church and because her mission extends to all people.

Catholic schools have always done a good job of promoting the "Catholic identity" of their students. This identity is forged within the school communities in theology courses, through regular prayer, and in student participation in liturgy and retreats. Catholic identity is also witnessed in outward signs for the larger community, such as athletic teams that pray publicly before a game or even Catholic school students wearing distinctive uniforms to school.

Catholicity is one of the four marks of the Church. Its meaning is much more expansive than the identifying features of the Church mentioned above, though identity as a Catholic on both a local and worldwide basis is an element of catholicity. To begin to understand the meaning of the designation, consider two different usages. The first way designates Catholic with a capital "C" and refers to the Catholic Church, which simply defined comprises those Christians who accept the entire visible and institutional apostolic structure of the Church, headed by the pope and bishops, as well as the Church's sacraments and doctrinal teachings.

To say that the Church is "catholic" with a lower case "c" is to say that what the Church teaches is based on the whole of Revelation: all of Scripture, the teachings of the Apostles, and the understanding and witness of Christians from all times and places. This second meaning, not unrelated to the first, refers to the mark of the church that means "universal." The Church is universal in two distinct ways: She is universal because Christ is present in the Church. Second, the Church is universal because of her mission to the entire human race.

The word "catholic" does not appear in the Bible.* The early Church first started describing herself as "catholic" to highlight the differences between the

---

* Much of the material in the succeeding sections draws from Cardinal Avery Dulles, S.J., *The Catholicity of the Church* (Oxford: Chaldeon Press, 1985).

NOTE TAKING   **Apply Information.** While reading this section, define *Catholic* with a capital "C" and *catholic* with a lowercase "c."

Catholic:

catholic:

Church and many of the heretical sects that were springing up, particularly those involving Gnosticism. A recorded use of the term appears in the second-century writings of St. Ignatius of Antioch who explained that the fullness of Christ's Body is present in the Church: "Where there is Christ Jesus, there is the Catholic Church."

What can an understanding of the mark "catholic" help you to understand about the Church herself? Three main considerations will be addressed in the context of the chapter sections that follow:

1. How Christ's presence in the Church is a way to understand her catholicity.

2. How the relation and participation of baptized Catholics and all people in the Church is a way to understand her universal nature.

3. How the Church's missionary mandate to "make disciples of all nations" is a concrete way she lives the mark of catholicity.

As you study these ways that the Church is catholic, take time to think about how all people—from the past to the present—are able to find a home in the Church through a relationship with Jesus Christ.

SECTION ASSESSMENT

NOTE TAKING

Use the two definitions you wrote to help you answer the following question.

1. How are the two usages of *catholic* (uppercase and lowercase) related?

COMPREHENSION

2. Why did the early Church start to describe herself as "catholic"?

APPLICATION

3. What are two ways your school promotes Catholic identity?

4. How can family, schools, and the Church promote pride in being Catholic?

SECTION 1
Catholicity in Creation, Christ, and the Church

MAIN IDEA
The mark of catholicity is expressed in the fullness of creation, in the divinity of Christ, and in the "unity with diversity" of the Church.

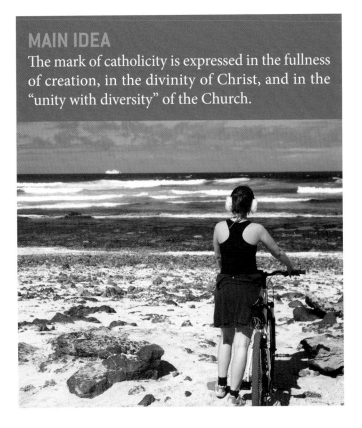

Think of the Church's catholicity or universal nature as grand, and without bounds. This mark of the Church begins with God's very act of creation, which is itself all-encompassing. Also, the catholicity of the Church is also present in the fullness in the divinity of Jesus Christ. As a member of Christ's Body, the Church, you are able to participate in the largeness of the mark of catholicity.

How so? Everywhere you turn you encounter the multilayers and rich diversity of God's creation, from the millions of galaxies of the universe to the millions of species of living organisms that populate the earth. Humans are surrounded by a diversity of creation and survive and thrive together with these many elements of life.

The diversity of creation is so interwoven into the fabric of daily life that it is easy to take it for granted. Think of the different experiences of nature you might have when you go to the lakeshore, hike in the Canadian Rockies, scuba dive on the Great Barrier Reef, or gaze at the vastness of the universe through a powerful telescope. What holds these different experiences of creation together is the sense of beauty, wonder, and goodness that they evoke as they connect you

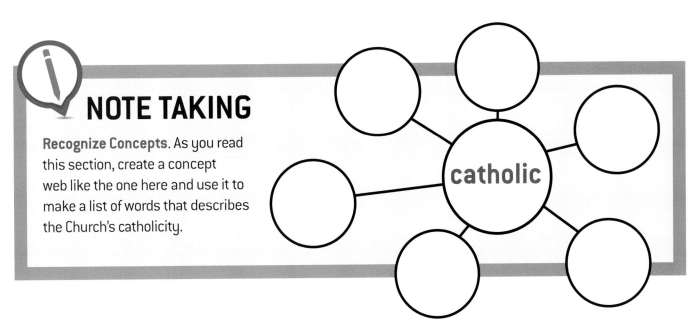

NOTE TAKING

Recognize Concepts. As you read this section, create a concept web like the one here and use it to make a list of words that describes the Church's catholicity.

catholic

with God. In this majestic diversity of creation you truly experience an understanding of catholicity that expresses how all of life is drawn together in a mystical unity by God its Creator.

Now think about the universal all-encompassing Divine Person of Jesus Christ, the Second Person of the Blessed Trinity. Jesus is one Divine Person with a divine nature and a human nature. He is "consubstantial with the Father." He is **begotten** not made. *All* of life was created through him and *all* creation reaches its pinnacle in him. In the Letter to the Colossians, St. Paul expressed the preeminence of Christ with a poetic hymn that was probably used by the early Church in liturgy:

> He is the image of the invisible God,
>   the firstborn of all creation.
> For in him were created all
> things in heaven and on earth,
>   the visible and the invisible,
>   whether thrones or dominions
>   or principalities or powers;
>   all things were created through
>   him and for him.
> He is before all things,
>   and in him all things hold together.
>   He is the head of the body, the church.
>   He is the beginning, the firstborn
>   from the dead,
>   that in all things he himself might be
>   preeminent. (Col 1:15–18)

This moving hymn points to Christ as the Redeemer of all creation, both humans and the very cosmos itself. All things in Heaven and on Earth are summed up in Christ (see Eph 1:10). To celebrate the sacredness of creation is to celebrate Christ in whom "were created all things in heaven and on earth" (Col 1:16). This celebration takes place in the Church where Christ is present. Terry, the teen from Chapter 1 who described the outdoors as his "church" did have some insight in this observation. However, his approach bordered on **pantheism**, which not only sees God *in* the world of nature, but actually identifies God *as* nature. This can end up as a form of idolatry. Rather, an accurate sense of wonder at the beauty, expansiveness, and completeness of creation is to direct one's gaze at Christ.

Fullness in Christ

Expanding on the understanding of catholicity further, there is nothing in creation that is good—no virtue, no spiritual gift, no wisdom, no cure for sin—that exists outside of Christ. In Jesus, God the Father has spoken his definitive Word; there is nothing more to say. Because this is true, there is nothing lacking in Christ's Body, the Church. The poetic hymn from Colossians concludes:

> For in him all the fullness was pleased to dwell,
> And through him to reconcile all things for him,
> making peace by the blood of his cross
> [through him], whether those on earth or those in heaven. (Col 1:19–20)

> **begotten** A term that means "to bring about"; Jesus is begotten because he was not generated by God the Father as human fathers generate their children. He has always existed.
>
> **pantheism** The belief, in opposition to Christian doctrine, that God and nature are one and the same.

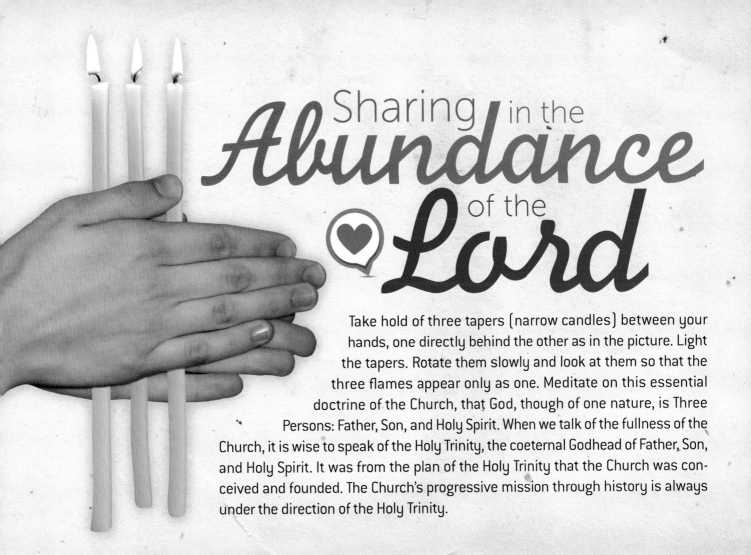

Sharing in the Abundance of the Lord

Take hold of three tapers (narrow candles) between your hands, one directly behind the other as in the picture. Light the tapers. Rotate them slowly and look at them so that the three flames appear only as one. Meditate on this essential doctrine of the Church, that God, though of one nature, is Three Persons: Father, Son, and Holy Spirit. When we talk of the fullness of the Church, it is wise to speak of the Holy Trinity, the coeternal Godhead of Father, Son, and Holy Spirit. It was from the plan of the Holy Trinity that the Church was conceived and founded. The Church's progressive mission through history is always under the direction of the Holy Trinity.

This fullness that the hymn describes is connected to a fullness of the Son of God who assumed human nature in order to become present to the world at the Incarnation. You can share in the fullness of Christ through your participation in the life of Christ through the Church. Anyone who enters into Faith through Baptism experiences the fullness of Christ and communion with him. St. Paul explained this in the Letter to the Colossians:

> For in him dwells the whole fullness of the deity bodily, and you share in this fullness in him.... You were buried with him in baptism, in which you were also raised with him through faith in the power of God, who raised him from the dead. (Col 2:9–10, 12)

This fullness cannot be measured in spiritual "units" as if you have an opening at the top of your head and God pours in his grace in that fashion. For example, you are not 50 percent filled with God's grace, or 70 percent, or even 90 percent. Rather, with the grace of Faith present at Baptism, you are *fully* incorporated into Christ himself through your participation in the Body of Christ, the Church. Your participation in the fullness of Jesus Christ through belonging to the Church is a living example of the mark of catholicity. As Cardinal Avery Dulles put it in *The Catholicity of the Church*: "Even if there were only one true Christian in the world, that individual would be Catholic in the qualitative sense."

Fullness in the Church

When you are connecting the mark of catholicity with the Church, think big! This mark of universality is meant to be expansive, welcoming, and inclusive. In *Finnegan's Wake*, Irish novelist and poet James Joyce described the Church as "here comes everybody"—a beautiful way to express the Church as having plenty of room for all. From the catholic mark of the Church comes her description as a Church of "unity with diversity."

One way to imagine the Church's unity within her diversity is to compare it with a free-flow jazz band composed of several musicians all playing different instruments. In such a performance the drummer, bass player, lead guitarist, saxophonist and others improvise what they are playing, often describing their individual contributions as "losing themselves in the music" or "not being conscious" of how their own sound fits in with the music being made by the rest of the band. This improvised interplay creates a unique and wonderful sound. Compare the workings of the free-flow jazz band with how Catholics each use their very unique gifts in a personal way that enhances their individuality while interacting beautifully with the gifts of others in the Church.

St. Paul expressed this understanding of "unity with diversity" in several places, including his description of how the diversity of gifts in the Body of Christ builds up the Church:

> For as in one body we have many parts, and all the parts do not have the same function, so we, though many, are one body in Christ and individually parts of one another. Since we have the gifts that differ according to the grace given to us, let us exercise them: if prophecy, in proportion to the faith; if ministry, in ministering; if one is a teacher, in teaching; if one exhorts, in exhortation; if one contributes, in generosity; if one is over others with diligence; if one does acts of mercy; with cheerfulness. (Rom 12:4–8)

Also in the Letter to the Galatians, Paul taught that things like ethnicity and gender can no longer be a source of division because these differences are being drawn into a more profound reality, an expanding Church that finds her unity in Christ:

> For all of you who were baptized into Christ have clothed yourselves in Christ. There is neither Jew nor Greek, there is neither slave nor free person, there is not male and female; for you are all one in Christ Jesus. (Gal 3:27–28)

It is important to remember your personal responsibility for enhancing the mark of catholicity. You can do this by using your personal gifts to the best of your ability. This was Jesus' message in the Parable of the Talents (Mt 25:14–30): "For everyone who has, more will be given and he will grow rich."

SECTION ASSESSMENT

NOTE TAKING

Use at least one of the terms you listed in your concept web for the following assignment.

1. In the spirit of James Joyce, write a sentence describing the Church's catholicity.

SUMMARIZE

2. How does the totality of creation help to explain catholicity?

3. How is the Church's catholicity expressed in Jesus Christ?

4. What is the guarantee to those who enter the Church through Baptism?

REFLECTION

5. How do you understand Cardinal Dulles's statement: "Even if there were only one true Christian in the world, that individual would be catholic in the qualitative sense"?

APPLICATION

6. Present another image (like the free-flow jazz band) of how the "unity with diversity" of the Church is expressed.

7. How can you personally enhance the mark of catholicity?

The Local Church: A Firsthand View of Unity in Diversity

MAIN IDEA

In union with the pope, bishops help to bring about unity in the local Church amidst a great amount of diversity of language, culture, and custom.

In just about any diocese in the United States there is remarkable diversity. For example, in the Archdiocese of Los Angeles (the Cathedral of Our Lady of the Angels is above), Mass is celebrated in more than sixty languages. The diversity is a great gift to the Church, but it also means that the "unity with diversity" feature of the Church's catholicity operates on a fine line that must be protected by the local bishop in union with the college of bishops and the pope.

It is the task of the bishop to draw these diverse groups of beliefs, practices, and people together into an enduring communion without depriving his local Church of the richness the diversity brings. Both alternative extremes would damage the mark of catholicity. If the bishop mandated uniformity in all parishes, the Church could be reduced to sterile and lifeless uniformity. If he allowed the diversity to stray away from the Church's magisterial teachings and belief, the danger of splintered or independent local churches arises. Priests (especially pastors of parishes), deacons, and many others in the Church share responsibility with the bishop. All Catholics have a special obligation to challenge subtle forms of bigotry, racism, sexism, and any attitude that is motivated by fear of differences in people or cultures.

The bishop's role in preserving the Church's catholicity is not limited to his own diocese. Recall that every diocesan bishop is both pastor of the local Church and a member of the college of bishops. When the bishop meets with his brother bishops in an episcopal synod or, more rarely, an ecumenical council called by the pope, he always brings with him the Faith of the people

NOTE TAKING

Applying Information. As you read the section, name two parishes in your diocese that contrast for each difference. Fill out a chart like this one.

Differences	Parish 1	Parish 2
Language/Ethnicity		
Socioeconomic		
Education levels		
Theological perspectives		
Other		

The Bishop and BEING Catholic

In his "Letter to the Smyrnaeans" St. Ignatius of Antioch was the first to refer to a *Catholic* Church. His letter also expresses how the office of the bishop is essential in promoting the Church's unity:

> You must all follow the lead of the bishop, as Jesus Christ followed that of the Father; follow the presbytery as you would the Apostles; reverence the deacons as you would God's Commandment. Let no one do anything touching the Church, apart from the bishop. Let that celebration of the Eucharist be considered valid which is held under the bishop or anyone to whom he has committed it. Where the bishop appears, there let the people be, just as where Jesus Christ is, there is the Catholic Church.

Check the website for your diocese and record the events on your bishops' episcopal calendar for the next month. Categorize the events using a table or flow chart by the type (e.g., sacramental, pastoral visit, social). Interview two people who have been at recent events with the bishop. Ask: "How was the bishop's visit an occasion of unity for the Church?" Record the responses. Turn them in with the table or flow chart.

in his own diocese. In any meeting of bishops there is a kind of "gift exchange." Each bishop then returns to his own particular church carrying with him the richness of the other local churches. When that happens the life of the whole Church is enriched immeasurably.

Certainly a responsibility of the pope and the college of bishops is to teach and make judgments about matters of Faith that enhance the Church's catholicity. However, more often than not the pope and bishops support catholicity by keeping the universal and local churches in dialogue with one another. The fruits of their efforts are witnessed among Catholics where they practice their Faith, in their own parishes and dioceses.

In recent history, popes beginning with Pope Paul VI also have supported the Church's catholicity by personally visiting local churches throughout the world. St. John Paul II made 104 pastoral visits to 129 countries from 1978 to 2005. In 2008, Pope Benedict XVI visited the United States. He addressed several pertinent issues to Americans, including the separation of church and state that allows all religions to practice their mission freely in the United States. Not long after his election to the papacy, Pope Francis made his first pastoral visit to Brazil, to celebrate World Youth Day.

Local Catholicity

Old St. Patrick's Catholic Church in downtown Chicago (see photo and feature on page 157) is also one of approximately eighteen thousand Catholic parishes in the United States in 195 archdioceses and dioceses. The latter are the designations for the local "particular Church," which are modeled on the larger universal Church and which are "fully catholic through their communion" with the Church of Rome (*CCC*, 834). It is in a diocese and more to an extent, a parish, that Catholics typically experience the Church. As a member of a parish, it is important for you to know that the universal Church is not simply an alliance of different particular churches, even though on appearance, it may sometime seems so.

For example, in the nineteenth century in Chicago, Old St. Pat's was made up of Irish immigrants who spoke English. (Old St. Pat's was the first English-speaking parish in Chicago.) There were many other Chicago parishes with different ethnic roots. St. Jerome Croatian Catholic Church was founded in 1903 after thousands of Croats came to Chicago to work in the steel factories or slaughterhouses. German immigrants to Chicago built St. Joseph's Church on Orleans Street in 1872. The first Polish Catholic Church was St. Stanislaus Kostka on Noble Street, founded in 1877. Each of these particular churches had their own customs, spoke their own language, celebrated their own festivals, and honored their own saints. But they were still Roman Catholic churches united under the local bishop of Chicago, who, because of his ordination, was a successor of the Apostles, and representative of the Church in the diocese. The bishop represents a diocese just as the pope represents the universal Church.

OLD ST. PAT'S:
(English)
Peace be with you

ST. JEROME:
(Croatian)
Mir s vama

ST. JOSEPH'S:
(German)
Friede sei mit euch

ST. STANISLAUS KOSTKA:
(Polish)
Pokój niech będzie z tobą

Today, there are not as many ethnic parishes in the United States. But that doesn't mean there isn't diversity of language, liturgical rites, and other cultural traditions among neighboring parishes or even within one parish. Your firsthand experience of the diversity of the universal Church in your local diocesan and parish Church "shows all the more resplendently the catholicity of the undivided Church" (*Lumen Gentium*, 62).

THE REMARKABLE STORY OF Old St. Pat's

That the church and supporting buildings of Old St. Patrick's Catholic Church in downtown Chicago are still standing is remarkable. Located along a busy corridor of the Dan Ryan Expressway, the parish escaped demolition as construction of the expressway edged ever closer in the early 1950s. Of course, that was nothing in comparison to what happened on October 10, 1871: Old St. Pat's was one of the few structures standing in the four-square-mile area destroyed in the Great Chicago Fire, making the church the oldest public building in Chicago.

Old St. Patrick's Catholic Church, Chicago, Illinois

That Old St. Pat's remains alive as one of the most vibrant parishes in the United States may be even more remarkable. The parish was founded for Irish immigrants in 1846, but the changing neighborhood eventually saw parishioners moving out as warehouses and other businesses took their place. By 1983 when Fr. John Wall became pastor, the parish had only four registered members.

Fr. Wall unveiled a plan of rebirth called the "church for the marketplace." He began a strong outreach to young adults working in the city, launching a program called Center for Work and Faith. In 1985 the parish began to sponsor the World's Largest Block Party. More than 5,000 people came to the first event, most of them young adults. By 1989 the parish had rebounded with 1,000 registered families, nearly 2,000 attending Sunday Mass, and more than 10,000 on the parish mailing list. In 1989 the parish reopened its long-closed school. It was the first new Catholic grammar school in Chicago in over twenty-five years.

The parish, many times in danger of closure, remains one of Chicago's most vibrant Catholic parishes today. People come into the city from miles around to participate in Sunday Mass. The future of Old St. Pat's is bright!

SECTION ASSESSMENT

NOTE TAKING

Apply the comparison of parishes in your local area to help you to answer the following question.

1. Despite the differences, why are Catholic parishes not simply part of an alliance of particular churches?

COMPREHENSION

2. Explain why a bishop must balance diversity in his diocese with supporting the Church's magisterial teachings.

3. How is the sharing of gifts between one diocese and another made possible?

4. In what ways does the pope support the Church's catholicity?

REFLECTION

5. What does it mean to you that the Church is both united and diverse?

APPLICATION

6. Using Fr. John Wall as an example, how would you "market" the Church to people your own age?

SECTION 3
Who Belongs to the Catholic Church?

MAIN IDEA
All people are called to know Jesus Christ in the Catholic Church and all people belong to the Church in different ways.

As the previous section revealed, the Catholic Church is not an exclusive club or limited to certain races, genders, national, or ethnic groups. The Church is open to everything that Jesus taught, and she contains the fullness of a faith relationship to him. The Church sees a relation to all people with the Body of Christ, even with those who have not yet received the Gospel. All people are called to know Christ in the Church and all people belong or are connected to the Church:

- first, the Catholic faithful,
- then others who believe in Christ, and finally,
- all people who are "called by God's grace to salvation" (CCC, 836).

Those who are fully incorporated in the Church are baptized Catholics who accept the whole structure of the Church and all her means of Salvation and are united by Faith, sacraments, and obedience to the bishops under the pope. Being fully incorporated in the Catholic Church is a great gift attributed to a special grace given by Christ that should not be taken for granted. "If they fail to respond in thought, word, and deed to that grace, not only will they not be saved, they will be more severely judged" (*Lumen Gentium*, 14).

The Church's Relationship with Other Christians

Other Christians who do not believe in the Catholic Faith in its entirety or have broken ties of unity with the pope remain in communion with the Catholic Church, though the communion is imperfect. Baptism is the foundation of the unity among all Christians.

NOTE TAKING

Compare and Contrast. Create a Venn diagram like the one here to show how other Christians and non-Christians share some things in common with the Catholic Church. Some things in common are: belief in one God, the Bible, Baptism, family of Abraham, moral judgment. Also include other commonalities not mentioned in the section.

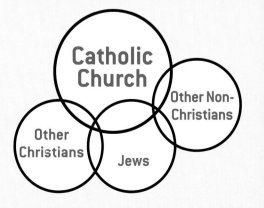

A recent ecumenical prayer service in France included leaders from several Christian traditions.

For this reason, the Church believes in *one Baptism for the forgiveness of sins* and generally accepts as valid most Christian baptisms for anyone who later enters the Catholic Church. Besides Baptism, there are many other key elements of Salvation found in these ecclesial communities, including honoring Sacred Scripture as a rule of Faith, and acts of charity inspired by the Holy Spirit. Recall also that the bond between the Catholic Church and Orthodox Churches is very close to full communion.

The Church's Relationship with Non-Christians

Those who have not accepted the Gospel are nevertheless connected to the Catholic Church in various ways.

First of all, Catholics have a deep bond with Jewish people. Judaism has special honor because it was to Jews that God first revealed the Old Covenant. The intercessions of the Good Friday liturgy remind us that the Jews were "the first to hear the Word of God." Jews and Catholics have similar goals of faith: awaiting the Messiah. However, while Catholics await the Second Coming of the Messiah, Jesus Christ who rose from the dead, Jews await a coming of a Messiah whose features are hidden.

Islam also has a connection with the Church because Muslims believe in one God as Catholics do. Muslims acknowledge God as Creator, the right of God to judge mankind, and their ancestry in Abraham.

Other non-Christian religions are recognized by the Church for their own goodness and truth that prepares them "for the Gospel and given by him who enlightens all men that they may have life" (*Lumen Gentium*, 16).

The Catholic Church invites all people, including non-Christians, to reach out to her like a bark in the sea. The Church continues to affirm that outside her there is no Salvation, meaning that everyone who is to be saved is to be saved through Christ the Head of the Catholic Church, the universal sacrament of Salvation.

The Church Is Necessary for Salvation

Traditionally, the Church has stated that the Catholic Church is necessary for Salvation and that "outside of the Church there is no Salvation." This is so because

Jesus is necessary for Salvation. Without Jesus, who has made the Church his Body, there is no Salvation.

All who recognize that the Church is the Body of Christ are called to be part of that Church. If they reject the Church, knowing that it is the Body of Christ, they are rejecting Salvation. This does not mean that those who, through no fault of their own, do not know Christ or his Church have rejected Salvation. Jesus and the Church are necessary for God's plan for Salvation; however, through ways known only to God, the Holy Spirit can lead those who know neither Jesus nor the Church to unity with the Father.

In order to be faithful to Christ and to truly be his Body on earth, the Church must reach out with compassion to everyone; the Church must also challenge Catholics to live as Christ lived. The Church must be willing to teach against certain things that are not compatible with the truth of Christ. The Church, in Christ, is like a sacrament—a sign and instrument of God's love for humanity. As the sign, the Church must strive for perfection; as the instrument, the Church must offer God's all-encompassing love to all.

A Catholic priest in the Akata Djokepe leper's village, Togo, West Africa, greets a resident.

SECTION ASSESSMENT

NOTE TAKING

Use your completed Venn diagram to help you answer the following questions:

1. If you were speaking at a gathering of the major world religions about what they have in common, name a title or theme for your presentation.
2. What are ways the Church is in communion with other Christians? With Jews? With Muslims?

COMPREHENSION

3. Who are full members in the Catholic Church?
4. Why is it accurate to say that "outside the Church there is no Salvation"?

APPLICATION

5. What greater responsibility do you have because you are Catholic?

The Catholicity of the Church's Mission

culture, race, and nationality. Instead, her catholicity also involves sharing the Good News of Christ with the entire world. After Jesus called together a group of disciples, he sent them out to continue his own work. They were sent on a mission:

> He summoned the Twelve and gave them power and authority over all demons and to cure diseases, and he sent them to proclaim the kingdom of God and to heal [the sick]. . . . Then they set out and went from village to village proclaiming the good news and curing diseases everywhere. (Lk 9:1–2, 6)

Jesus did not intend for the Church to be a kind of support group in which the disciples would focus only on their own lives. Rather, Jesus endowed the Church with his own authority, power, and responsibility. The Church was born by the power of the Holy Spirit on Jesus' twin actions of *calling* and *sending*. The ultimate purpose of the mission of Christ and the Holy Spirit is for all people to share the love between the Father and the Son through the Holy Spirit.

MAIN IDEA

The catholicity of the Church is intertwined with Jesus' sending out his disciples to preach the Good News to all people in all cultures.

The Church does not exist for her own sake. What this means is that the catholicity of the Church does not only involve having a diverse membership based on

NOTE TAKING

Identifying Main Ideas. As you read, create an outline like the one started for you below to record the main sub-points for how chapters 1 to 15 of the Acts of the Apostles recorded the Church's missionary mandate.

I. How did the Church expand in her first century?

  A. Pentecost

    1.

    2.

  B. Preaching to the Samaritans

    1.

    2.

Acts of the Apostles: The Church's First Missionary Manual

The Church's mission began at the feast of Pentecost, detailed in Acts 2:1–41. The Holy Spirit came upon the Apostles and anointed them, and filled them with the gifts of the Spirit. Pentecost began a series of events in Acts that tell how the Holy Spirit is able to go beyond human, religious, and cultural differences to expand the boundaries of the Church's communion, much like the ripples of a pebble dropped in a pond extend outward. Four examples from Acts 1–15 of how the Church fulfilled in sharing the Gospel to all people are described in the sections that follow.

1. Preaching to the Samaritans

After "about three thousand" new members were added to the Church at Pentecost (Acts 2:41), the Spirit was at work again in Acts 8 with the Apostles preaching successfully in several Samaritan villages. Samaritans were a mixed population of Israelites and Assyrians who accepted the Law of Moses and belief in one God, but rejected the writings of the prophets and the wisdom writings. They also rejected the Temple in Jerusalem and constructed their own shrine on Mount Gerizim.

There was a mutual distrust and dislike between Jews and Samaritans. But when the Apostle Philip came to the region of Samaria and proclaimed the Messiah to them, the Samaritans paid attention. They accepted the Gospel and were baptized. When the Apostles in Jerusalem heard what was going on, Peter and John went to Samaria "and prayed for them, that they might receive the holy Spirit" (Acts 8:15). The Apostles laid hands on them and they received the Holy Spirit, the early roots of the Sacrament of Confirmation.

2. Philip and the Ethiopian

Also in Acts 8, Philip encountered an Ethiopian eunuch who was likely a "God-fearer," that is a person who followed some elements of Judaism but was not circumcised and who usually did not obey Jewish dietary laws. The man was reading from the text of Isaiah 53:7–8 and Philip ran up and instructed him on how those words applied to Jesus. As they traveled on, they came upon some water and the Ethiopian said to Philip: "What is to prevent my being baptized?" (Acts 8:36). They stopped and Philip baptized the man. Clearly, the boundaries of the Church were expanding well beyond Judaism.

3. The "Conversion" of St. Peter

Another widening ripple is reflected in Acts 10–11. Following the conversion of St. Paul, previously an observant Pharisee, St. Peter had his own personal conversion of sorts that had great implications for the Church's mission. After receiving a disturbing vision in which he was told by God to eat unclean food not approved by Jewish law, upon waking, Peter was invited to the house of a Gentile centurion, Cornelius. Only then did Peter begin to understand his dream. Applying the image in the dream of unclean food to Gentiles, Peter realized he was to give up his old assumptions about what was clean and unclean. In the Church, all such distinctions had been swept away: "In truth, I see that God shows no partiality. Rather, in every nation whoever fears him and acts uprightly is acceptable to him" (Acts 10:34–35). This insight was confirmed as Peter saw the Holy Spirit descend on all who heard him preach, an echo of Pentecost.

4. The Council of Jerusalem

A final ripple in the missionary narrative of Acts 1–15 was the official recognition that Gentiles could indeed find a place in the Church. This was stated at the Council of Jerusalem (Acts 15:1–29) where Paul and Barnabas argued that Gentiles should be able to be baptized without also having to become circumcised Jews. Peter reiterated that to the Gentiles, "God, who knows the heart, bore witness by granting them the holy Spirit just as he did us. He made no distinction between us and them, for by faith he purified their hearts" (Acts 15:8–9).

Chapters 1 to 15 of Acts are an inspirational chronicle of the Holy Spirit's action in teaching the Apostles to draw all people into communion with God: Father, Son, and Holy Spirit. As the universal sacrament of Salvation, the Church, "in her whole being and in all her members . . . is sent to announce, bear witness, make present and spread the mystery of the Holy Trinity" (*CCC*, 738). The principal agent directing the message is the Holy Spirit.

What Is NET?

National Evangelization Teams (NET) is a ministry of young people that originated in the Archdiocese of St. Paul and Minneapolis in 1981. Basically, NET operates like this: youth—at minimum graduates from high school—dedicate nine months from September to May to work in teams of eight to fourteen volunteers traveling the country in vans to give retreats six days in every week. In the nine months, each team logs more than twenty thousand miles on the road. Each year the NET teams conduct approximately a thousand retreats!

The mission of NET is to "proclaim the Gospel of Christ through a personal witness of faith" and to "challenge young Catholics to love Christ and embrace the life of the Church."

You may have an interest in serving on a NET team. Take some time to research the NET ministry. Imagine yourself as a NET team member. Who knows? You may end up traversing the country for the Lord like many NET ministers before you!

Catholicity and Culture

As part of her ongoing missionary efforts, the Church embraces a variety of cultures. Distinct features like the spoken language, ethnic foods, and styles of music help to define a particular culture. Certain practices—such as the way weddings are celebrated and the way death is marked by a ceremony or funeral—can also be described as being culturally driven. Being fully human means being part of a culture.

Jesus himself belonged to a particular culture. He studied the Hebrew Scriptures in the synagogue like other Jewish boys; he spoke Aramaic, the language typical for Galilee; and he ate food prepared according to Jewish dietetic laws. It is worth taking a pause to think about what it meant for Jesus to belong to this culture. Consider the particular century, place, ethnicity, and socioeconomic level that God Incarnate chose to become a part of. The fact is that the Incarnate God,

the fullness of Divine Revelation, came to Earth as a first-century Middle Eastern Jew.

Because Jesus was raised and participated in a particular culture, the culture itself is good. Indeed, the Church can only complete her mission to share the Good News with the world by sharing it through culture. St. John Paul II said: "A faith which does not become culture is a faith which has not been fully received, not thoroughly thought through, not faithfully lived out." On the other hand, no human culture is above criticism and every culture must submit itself to the challenging Gospel of Jesus Christ. The missionary work of sharing the Good News will always involve a tension with culture; that is, both fitting in with the culture while not compromising the Gospel message.

In a recent census, 4.2 million residents of England and Wales identified themselves as Roman Catholic, about eight percent of the total population. This Church of St. Thomas of Canterbury and English Martyrs in St. Leanoards-on-Sea, England, has been a Roman Catholic parish since 1848.

Balancing the Gospel with Culture

How does the Church work to balance the sharing of the Good News with the contemporary issues associated with culture? Consider the following example: In the late sixth century, St. Gregory the Great sent St. Augustine of Canterbury on a missionary excursion to England. On the way to England, Augustine was able to visit numerous local churches in different places. He noted for Pope Gregory that there was a great diversity in the local churches. Many did not celebrate the liturgy in the exact way that it was celebrated in Rome, for example. According to *Ecclesiastical History of the English People*, Pope Gregory responded to Augustine's concern:

You know, my brother, the custom of the Roman church in which you remember you were trained. But if you have found anything in either the Roman or the Gallican or any other church which may be more acceptable to Almighty God, I am willing that you carefully make choice of the same and diligently teach the English church, which is as yet new in the faith, whatever you can gather from several churches. For things are not to be loved for the sake of places but places for the sake of good things. Select, therefore, from every church the things that are devout religious and upright, and when you have, as it were, combined them

Living the
CATHOLIC FAITH

Cardinal Joseph Bernardin (1928–1996)

Another aspect of catholicity relates to both the Church's social teaching and her moral teaching. To truly live the Church's moral and social teaching demands a "both/and" rather than an "either/or" approach. It means both having faith and putting that faith into action, through good works. Pope Francis tweeted a reminder to us of the importance of charity in a life of holiness: "Prayer, humility, and charity toward all are essential in the Christian life: they are the way to holiness."

The catholicity of faith requires that Catholics keep together both a vertical faith that attends to our relationship with God and with a horizontal faith that attends to love of neighbor.

In the United States, the late Cardinal Joseph Bernardin of Chicago embodied a "both/and" catholicity in speaking of Catholic social and moral teaching. He promoted a consistent ethic of life that described by using the image of a "seamless garment," referring to the tunic that Jesus wore at his crucifixion (cf. Jn 19:23). This means that society must not only guarantee an unborn child the right to life, but it must support the life of the weak and powerless in our midst: old and young, homeless and hungry, undocumented immigrants and those unemployed. The Church prods government to guarantee the right to life (and Cardinal Bernardin reminded all of this necessity in a Respect Life statement that stated that "no earthly value is more fundamental than human life itself"). And the Church also teaches that governments must create the economic, social, and political conditions that enable those born to have a decent life of dignity.

Nigerian Catholics celebrate Mass at St. Theresa's Catholic Church in Jos. St. Theresa's was the city's first Catholic church, built in 1923.

into one body, let the minds of the English be trained therein.

Recall that one of the responses of the Council of Trent to the Protestant Reformation was uniformity of language in the Tridentine Mass. But this example of St. Gregory shows that in her history the Church has also been sensitive to diversity of customs and practices, including in the liturgy. Church history also includes examples of missionaries, often filled with zeal, who failed to appreciate the goodness of local customs and cultures. Instead, these missionaries worked to either stamp them out completely or impose European cultural attitudes on those people they were supposed to be serving. (See Faithful Disciples: Sts. Cyril and Methodius, pages 176–177.) When abuses would occur the pope and the Church's Magisterium would respond in correction. For example, according to *The Christian Faith in the Doctrinal Documents of the Catholic Church*, in 1659, the Vatican's Congregation for the Propagation of Faith offered instructions on dealing with indigenous customs to two bishops from Europe who had been appointed to dioceses in Vietnam:

Do not attempt in any way, and do not on any pretext persuade these people to change their rites, habits, and customs, unless they are openly opposed to religion and good morals. For what could be more absurd than to bring France, Spain, Italy, or any other European country to China? It is not your country but the faith you must bring, the faith which does not belittle the rites or customs of any nation as long as these rites are not evil, but rather desires that they be preserved in their integrity and fostered.

The Second Vatican Council also addressed furthering the catholicity of the Church while also embracing many new cultures. Indeed the Council taught that various customs could be introduced into Catholic worship as long as they were not "indissolubly bound up with superstition and error" (*Sacrosantum Concilium*, 37). For example, Mass celebrated in Nigeria sometimes includes in the offertory procession the fruits of harvest. Traditional music is part of the liturgies of different African nations and several other specific cultures.

The mark of catholicity demands that the Church see any and all cultures as potential mediums of the Gospel of Jesus Christ and as signs of grace. The beauty of the mark of catholicity in the Church is the conviction that the Gospel can be at home in any land, in any culture, and among any people.

SECTION ASSESSMENT

NOTE TAKING

Use the section outline to help you to answer the following question.

1. Summarize two examples from Acts 1–15 of how the Church's mission expanded.

COMPREHENSION

2. What was St. Augustine of Canterbury concerned about on his trip to England?

3. How did Pope St. Gregory respond to the concern?

4. What rule did the Second Vatican Council provide for incorporating new customs into worship?

REFLECTION

5. What meaning do you find in the fact that the Incarnate God came to Earth as a first-century Jew?

Section Summaries

Focus Question

How does the Catholic Church invite all people to belong?

Complete one of the following:

 View a recent study (see, for example, a sampling of studies on the topic by the Center for the Applied Research in the Apostolate [CARA]) of Catholic school enrollment in the United States. Create a chart or graph that illustrates current trends. Project outward to develop a hypothesis of future enrollment numbers in Catholic elementary and high schools over the next ten years. Write a one-page report that details your findings.

 Read about the Nativity Miguel and Cristo Rey Network of Schools. Both organizations, one for Catholic elementary schools and the other for Catholic high schools, provide opportunities to young people, mostly from urban areas, with limited educational opportunities. Write a letter (not an e-mail) to the principal of three of the schools in one or both of the networks. Ask them to tell you how the school welcomes all people of many backgrounds and religions while also furthering its Catholic mission and identity.

 Develop a media presentation with images and quotations of actors, politicians, business leaders, and other well-known people who are products of Catholic schools. Search for quotations where the persons credit Catholic education for some later success they have had in forging a career and developing their values and character. Add your own personal statement about what you believe to be the value of a Catholic education.

INTRODUCTION (PAGES 147–148)

What It Means to Be Catholic with a Small "c"

The mark of catholicity refers to two definitions: that the Church's teachings are based on the whole of Revelation and the universal nature of the Church. The term "Catholic" typically refers to the Roman Catholic Church.

 Name one example of how the Roman Catholic Church has a universal mission.

SECTION 1 (PAGES 149–153)

Catholicity in Creation, Christ, and the Church

The universal nature of the Church begins with the fullness of all creation and in the fullness of the divinity of Jesus Christ. Baptized Catholics are able to share in this fullness through their unique participation in Christ' Body, the Church.

 Read the Parable of the Talents (Mt 25:14–30). What does it have to say about how you are to express the fullness of the mark of catholicity?

SECTION 2 (PAGES 154–158)

The Local Church: A Firsthand View of Unity in Diversity

Bishops have an important role in preserving the Church's catholicity by encouraging diversity within their dioceses while also shepherding communion with the universal Church through meetings with other bishops. The pope encourages the dialogue between the universal and local churches. It is in the local church—diocese and parish—that Catholics experience firsthand the Church's mark of catholicity.

 Name at least two specific issues in the Church (besides those listed in Section 2) that show off the Church's diversity. In regard to these issues, how does your local bishop protect the Church's unity?

SECTION 3 (PAGES 159–161)

Who Belongs to the Catholic Church?

All people are welcome in the Church and all people are members in different ways. Full membership involves Baptism and commitment to the sacraments and Church teaching. Salvation is only offered through the Church because Salvation is only in Christ. A mission of the Church is to make Christ's love available to everyone.

 How would you explain the necessity of the Catholic Church for Salvation to a non-Catholic friend?

SECTION 4 (PAGES 162–169)

The Catholicity of the Church's Mission

The Church's catholicity means more than the diversity of her current members. In addition, catholicity involves all Catholics accepting the call to go and proclaim the Gospel to all people and cultures and to invite them into relationship with Christ through the Church.

 How have you witnessed the diversity of culture and custom in the Church today?

Chapter Assignments

Choose and complete at least one of the three assignments assessing your understanding of the material in this chapter.

1. Noting Trends in the Church in America

Research and summarize trends in the Catholic Church in the United States. The Center for Research in the Apostolate (CARA), founded in 1964, is a national non-profit research center affiliated with Georgetown University that conducts social scientific studies about the Catholic Church. One of its goals is to increase the Church's self-understanding. Focus your investigation on statistics provided by CARA under the category of "Frequently Requested Church Statistics." Then do one of the following:

1. Organize what you consider to be five important categories into a graph, chart, or table. Write one sentence for each category summarizing the data.

2. Provide several different ratios that compare information in two columns. For example: priests/parish; high school students/school; Sunday Mass goers/Catholics; Catholic population/total US population. Compare the ratios over different years.

3. Make two columns: Negative Trends/Positive Trends. Include at least three summary points in each column supported by current statistics.

2. Helping the Holy Childhood Association

A motto of the Holy Childhood Association is "children helping children." One of the Pontifical Mission Societies in the United States, the Holy Childhood Association began in 1843 on the inspiration of French Bishop Charles Forbin-Janson who founded the HCA in order to help the missionary needs he had witnessed firsthand while in the United States. He had observed on a visit to New York that "there is not yet a minor or major seminary, and this diocese is larger than all of England." A common way children of the United States support the HCA is that, after learning about the needs of the poor children of the world, they offer prayers and financial help. You may have once contributed your gift of coins and dollars to one of the HCA boxes during Lent. Besides this help, there are other things you can do support Mission Awareness and the HCA. Choose and complete one of the following ideas:

1. Sponsor a living Rosary at your school where students wear shirts, hats, or bandanas representing various colors of the mysteries of the Rosary. Pray for the poor children of the world. Arrange a financial donation that can be collected and given to the HCA.

2. Sponsor an "international hat parade" in which students wear hats that represent a country in the world. Parade together to other classrooms during the school day. Have each person in your group prepare a brief report on the poor in the country he or she represents. Collect donations from the students intended for the HCA.

3. Sponsor a lunchtime or after-school walk-a-thon in support of the missions. Arrange for businesses and individuals to support the participants with donations for laps or yards walked. Share a short presentation at the beginning of the walk-a-thon about a famous missionary. Point out that the participants will be "walking in step with the missionaries" who have always shared the Gospel with others.

Write a three-page report that summarizes your role in the event you chose in support of the Holy Childhood Association.

3. Missionaries in the United States

 Introduce some famous Catholic missionaries in the United States by doing one of the following assignments.

1. Write a three-page report detailing the life of one of the missionaries. Include information about the missionary's early life, how the person came to America, the goal and results of the mission, how the person's life ended, and his or her legacy.

2. Prepare a flash slide-show or PowerPoint presentation displaying each of the missionaries in chronological or geographical sequence. Include two slides for each person. On one of the slides, include biographical information in the caption. On the other slide, include a quotation of the missionary.

Partial List of Catholic Missionaries in the United States

Juan Segura—One of eight Jesuit missionaries killed by natives near the future site of Jamestown, Virginia, in 1571.

Georgia Martyrs—Six Franciscans killed near their mission base of St. Augustine, Florida, in 1597.

St. Isaac Jogues—With the other North American Martyrs, he was put to death by the Iroquois in the seventeenth century.

Andrew White—English Jesuit who was known as the "Apostle of Maryland."

Sébastien Râle—Jesuit missionary who ministered to the native Abenak people around Maine at the beginning of the eighteenth century.

Eusebio Kino—Jesuit martyr who founded twenty-four missions in Mexico and the southwest United States.

Ferdinand Farmer—Eighteenth century priest who ministered to Catholics in eastern Pennsylvania, New Jersey, and New York.

Jacques Marquette—Jesuit priest who traveled with Louis Joliet on his exploration of the Mississippi River. He also founded the first European settlement in Michigan.

Gabriel Richard—French priest who became a delegate to the United States House of Representatives from the Michigan territory.

Frederic Baraga—First bishop of the Upper Peninsula in Michigan.

Stephen Badin—First priest ordained in the United States, he explored Kentucky and the Ohio Valley in the early 1800s.

Edward F. Sorin—French Holy Cross priest who founded the University of Notre Dame in northern Indiana.

St. Elizabeth Ann Bayley Seton—First American saint, instrumental in laying the groundwork for the Catholic school system in the United States.

Demetrius Gallitzin and Henry Lemke—Both helped Catholics to settle in western Pennsylvania.

Bl. Junípero Serra and Fermín Lasuén—Spanish Franciscans who founded twenty-one missions in California.

Pierre de Smet—Traveled nearly 180,000 miles in the Western United States to minister to Native Americans. Known as a friend of Sitting Bull.

St. Katharine Drexel and Samuel Mazzuchelli—Focused on missions to Native Americans and African Americans.

St. Damien De Veuster and Bl. Marianne Cope—First missionaries in Hawaii, focusing eventually on the leper colony there.

Fulton J. Sheen—Head of the Society for the Propagation of the Faith in the 1950s and 1960s, when he also had a nationally televised program of evangelization.

Faithful Disciples

Sts. Cyril and Methodius

In the ninth century, two brothers, Constantine (later known by his monastic name, Cyril) and Methodius, from the city of Thessaloniki in Asia Minor, both decided they wanted to be Christian missionaries. Methodius, the older of the two, had been a civil official, before entering a monastery. Cyril was a professor who taught and studied in Constantinople. In 860 they both left those lives behind and went as missionaries to Moravia, a region now part of the Czech Republic, at the invitation of Moravian Prince Rastislav.

Unfortunately Rastislav had other civil and political motivations for inviting the brothers to his country. He wanted to replace the German missionaries who were already there and who were teaching and preaching the Gospel in German. He felt that Slavic missionaries would encourage use of the Slavic language in the liturgy. Rastislav realized that a common language had a great deal to do with maintaining power and control of the people.

Cyril and Methodius intended to speak and use the Slavic language anyway. They recognized the importance of the native people learning the Christian faith in their own language. Cyril and Methodius even created an alphabet, now known as the Cyrillic alphabet, which they used to translate the Scriptures and certain liturgical texts into the Slavic language.

The German priests complained to Rome about their loss of influence in Moravia and expelled the two brothers from the region. However, Pope Nicholas I supported Cyril and Methodius's efforts to evangelize in the native Slavic language. The pope approved the use of Slavonic in the liturgy and in preaching and asked the brothers to return to Moravia.

The request was never fulfilled. Cyril became ill and died shortly after entering a monastery in Rome. Methodius did not return to Moravia either, due to political tensions. But he did minister in other Slavic lands, despite more harassment by German bishops. Before he died in 884, Methodius had translated most of the Bible and the writings of the Church Fathers into Slavonic.

Sts. Cyril and Methodius are known today as the Apostles to the Slavs. In 1980, St. John Paul II declared them co-patrons of Europe, along with St. Benedict of Nursia (480–543). St. John Paul II described their work in this way:

> Making use of their own Greek language and culture for this arduous and unusual enterprise, they set themselves to understanding and penetrating the language, customs, and traditions of the Slav people, faithfully interpreting the aspirations of human values which were present and expressed therein. . . . The effort to learn the language and to understand the mentality of the new peoples to whom they wished to bring the faith was truly worthy of the missionary spirit. Exemplary too was their determination to assimilate and identify themselves with all the needs and expectations of the Slav peoples. Their generous decision to identify themselves with those peoples' life and traditions, once having been purified and enlightened by Revelation, make Cyril and Methodius true models for all missionaries who in every period have accepted St. Paul's invitation to become all things to all people in order to redeem all.

The universal feast day of Sts. Cyril and Methodius is July 5.

Reading Comprehension

1. What ulterior motive did Prince Rastislav have for wanting Sts. Cyril and Methodius to come to Morovia?

2. The Cyrillic alphabet was the first alphabet used to translate the _____ and _____ into the Slavic language.

3. True or False: After Sts. Cyril and Methodius were expelled from Moravia they never returned there.

Writing Task

- Write a three-sentence statement that proclaims your faith in Jesus Christ. Translate your statement to a foreign language you study (or have studied) in school. Share your translation with classmates or friends. Ask them to state its meaning in English.

Explaining the Faith
Are Catholics Also Christians?

Believe it or not, this is a question that is often asked of Catholics. To determine the answer, ask yourself two questions: Do you believe in the divinity of Jesus Christ as the only Son of God? Have you been baptized in the name of the Father, and of the Son, and of the Holy Spirit? If you answer "yes" to both questions, then you are a Christian.

The related question is: "Are all Christians 'Catholic'?" The answer is no. A Catholic is a Christian who believes that Jesus himself established the Catholic Church and that this Church, as the one that Christ intended, possesses the fullness of truth and all the means necessary for Salvation. Practically, this means that Catholics:

- believe in the "one, holy, catholic, and apostolic Church" and all that she teaches through the pope and bishops who are successors to St. Peter and the Apostles;

- accept all Seven Sacraments of the Catholic Church; and

- submit to the teaching authority of the Magisterium in matters of Faith and morals.

 ## Further Research

- In addition to the requirements for being a Catholic listed above, what is one other prerequisite for being incorporated into the Church? Read *Catechism of the Catholic Church*, 837.

Prayer

Prayer for Christian Unity

Good and gracious God,

We pray for all our brothers and sisters,

who profess faith in Jesus Christ.

May our peace and unity increase

as we show the world our love for each other,

and that we are your faithful friends.

We ask this in the name of your Son, Jesus Christ, our Lord.

Amen.

—Adapted from the Good Friday Liturgy

5

THE
CHURCH
IS APOSTOLIC

The Church Passes on the Faith through Social Networking

Did you know that the Church celebrates World Communications Day? This is a worldwide celebration called for by the Second Vatican Council, in its "Decree on the Media of Social Communications" (*Inter Mirifica*). World Communications Day is celebrated in most countries on the Sunday before Pentecost.

By encouraging respectful dialogue among Catholics and with members of other faiths, the Church can bring the Gospel message of Jesus to those who may otherwise not have opportunity to hear it. In modern times, this dialogue has come to include a technological dimension, in the form of online social networks.

Pope Francis has embraced online social networks. Not long after his election, he re-established the Twitter account @Pontifex that Pope Benedict XVI began in 2012 and quickly began communicating with millions of followers. Through this social media, Pope Francis shares the Gospel message and teachings about the Catholic faith, and invites his followers to prayer. Through the website Pope2you.net, the Vatican links users to the pope's Twitter account and several social media sites it uses to reach the faithful.

But even while embracing the potential of technologically based social communications, Pope Francis also reminds Catholics and all others of the importance of personal contact as they share the journey of faith. In his 2013 address to participants at the Plenary Assembly of the Pontifical Council for Social Communications, he wrote: "We are called to rediscover, through the means of social communication as well as by personal contact, the beauty that is at the heart of our existence and journey, the beauty of faith and of the beauty of the encounter with Christ." He also encourages Catholics to use technology to build meaningful dialogue that enriches us and the world: "[We must] use modern technologies and social networks in such a way as to reveal a presence that listens, converses, and encourages."

FOCUS QUESTION

How does the Church PRESERVE AND PASS ON THE FAITH first shared by the Apostles?

INTRODUCTION
Preserving and Sharing

MAIN IDEA
With the help and guidance of the Holy Spirit, the Church preserves and passes on the Faith she heard from the Apostles.

Have you ever been back to a favorite restaurant that changed management but retained the name of the respected founder and previous owner? What if the new owners painted the trademarked sign out front

> **apostolic** One of the marks of the Church, this term comes from *apostle*, which means literally "having been sent."

a different color or tore out a classic columned entry-way? Or what if you found the food and service a poor imitation of how it had always had been before? Would you say that the restaurant had lost its way or was not being loyal to the tradition and quality established by its founder? The well-respected name and reputation of the restaurant could soon lose all of its connection with the past and either veer off in an entirely new direction or maybe even go out of business.

Think about how this example is related to the fourth mark of the Church: the Church is **apostolic**. The Church is apostolic because Christ sent her into the world. In fact, the Church has an identity and a reason to exist only because of this connection with Christ and his Apostles.

How so? Consider this: Jesus, God's only Son, was sent to live among us by his Father. He in turn sent the Apostles, giving them the mission to continue his work and preach the Gospel to the ends of the earth. If the Church were to forget the One who sends her or the reason for which she is sent, she would become nothing more than another organization among many in the world. Maybe she would persevere, maybe not.

It is the apostolic nature of the Church that helps her—through the intercession of the Holy Spirit—to remember and preserve all she has been taught all the way back to the Apostles and to Jesus himself.

NOTE TAKING

Key Words. Write three sentences describing how the Church is apostolic. Make sure that all of the following words are used at least once.

Foundation	Apostles
Capstone	Faithful
Holy Spirit	Successors

How the Church Is Apostolic

The *Catechism of the Catholic Church* stresses that the Church remains faithful to her apostolic nature in three ways:

- First, as the Letter to the Ephesians states: the Church is "built on the foundation of the apostles and prophets, with Christ Jesus himself as the capstone" (Eph 2:20). Jesus is both the source and focal point of all the Church does:

  > Through him the whole structure is held together and grows into a temple sacred in the Lord; in him you also are being built together into a dwelling place of God in the Spirit. (Eph 2:21–22)

- Second, guided by the Holy Spirit, the Church is apostolic because she remains faithful to the teachings of the Apostles. This was true from the time of Pentecost: "They devoted themselves to the teaching of the apostles and to the communal life, to the breaking of the bread and to prayers" (Acts 2:42). The Church keeps and hands on the teaching of the Apostles through her **Deposit of Faith**.

- Third, the Church remains apostolic by faithfully accepting the teaching, sanctification, and guidance of the Apostles through their successors, the bishops, and particularly the pope, the successor of St. Peter.

Every member of the Church has a responsibility to model the apostolic nature of the Church by sharing the Gospel and expressing the Church's teachings in the unique situations they find themselves in. But this isn't a solitary task where the individual Christian or even the individual pastor or bishop interprets and reinterprets what is to be shared. Rather, the apostolic nature of the Church allows the teachings of the pope and bishops to direct all Catholics despite the personal beliefs or preferences of individuals. This can be challenging and difficult for Catholics sometimes.

This chapter explains why it's important to appreciate the living nature of the Church's memory, preserved in the Deposit of Faith, the heritage of our Faith contained in both Sacred Scripture and Sacred Tradition.

> **Deposit of Faith** "The heritage of faith contained in Sacred Scripture and Sacred Tradition, handed down in the Church from the time of the Apostles, from which the Magisterium draws all that it proposes for belief as being divinely revealed" (*Catechism of the Catholic Church*, Glossary).

SECTION ASSESSMENT

NOTE TAKING

Use the notes you made to help you complete the following assignment.

1. Summarize the three ways that the Church remains faithful to her apostolic nature.

VOCABULARY

2. What is the meaning of the word *apostolic*?

PERSONAL RESPONSE

3. What do you find challenging about accepting the Church's apostolic nature?

SECTION 1
Remembering Who We Are

Therefore, O Lord, as we celebrate the memorial of the blessed Passion, the Resurrection from the dead, and the glorious Ascension into heaven of Christ, your Son, our Lord. . . .

Television and movies have long been fascinated by memory, and especially individuals' lack of it. If it weren't for movie plots you might have never heard of the term *amnesia* (from a Greek word meaning "not remembered"). A person who suffers from amnesia experiences a loss of memory of past events from his or her life. The experience can be devastating because our memory is so essential to our identity.

Memory is so important to knowing and understanding ourselves that people sometimes spend hundreds of hours (and thousands of dollars) in psychiatric therapy trying to uncover long-lost memories that might reveal to them the source of current difficulties in their lives. On the other hand, positive experiences from childhood and their memory help to form the foundation of a lifetime of personal success in career and vocation and in developing lasting and loving relationships.

Whether negative or positive, memory is essential to a person's identity. Similarly, the Church would also be incomplete with the lack of her memory. One of the terms used for memory in the Septuagint, the Greek translation of the Old Testament, is *anamnesis*. Opposite of amnesia, anamnesis is concerned with the recovery of memory. It can be translated as "remembrance" and it signals recovery of deep memory. Interestingly, every time a form of the word *anamnesis* is used in the Bible, it is connected to a sacrifice (see, for example Nm 10:10 or Lk 22:19. Likewise, all of the Eucharistic prayers of the liturgy contain an anamnesis, usually after the consecration in which the key events of the Paschal sacrifice are remembered.

NOTE TAKING

Recall and categorize. As you read the following section, make a list of four important stages of God's Revelation. On a second list, name four significant memories from your own life.

Four Stages of God's Revelation	Four Significant Personal Memories

Without some kind of personal memory, your own existence would be rootless; you would be forced to continually reinvent yourself. More importantly, without a community memory preserved in your family and in the Church, your own personal memory would more likely be mostly formed out of the stories and myths of the larger society. These memories of society too often don't reflect the love for God and for neighbor we are all called to live by. To be a member of the Catholic Church is to acknowledge the authority of a sacred communal memory that gives you a part in her identity. It helps you personally to discover who you are in the eyes of God. The apostolic nature of the Church is essential for preserving this sacred memory.

Revelation and the Sacred Memory of the Church

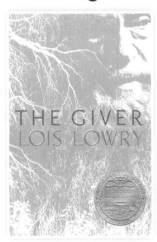

A popular science-fiction novel among middle-school students is *The Giver* by Lois Lowry. The novel is set sometime in a future society that first appears to be utopian. All people have food and shelter. Temperatures are controlled. There are no wars or even arguments. The central character of the novel, Jonas, a twelve-year-old boy, is chosen by the community to be the sole "Receiver of Memory." He will receive from his predecessor, "the Giver," knowledge of the memories from generations before that include tragedies and conflicts, but also true joy and love. The purpose of Jonas's position is for the community to be able to draw on the wisdom of ancient memories whenever it faces unique and difficult challenges. Central to the story's resolution is that Jonas and the Giver realize that the fullness of life demands that *everyone* have access to the memories and lessons of previous generations.

The pope and bishops, as the Church's Magisterium, are successors of the Apostles who were commissioned by Christ himself to keep alive the Church's sacred memories. The difference between the role of the pope and bishops and that of the "Receiver of Memory" in the science-fiction novel is that the Church's memories are to be revealed and shared with all. The sacred memory that is kept alive in the Church is the memory of God's Word and actions. It is the memory of God's Revelation.

The Church is grounded in a sacred memory of what God has revealed about himself through several stages of human history.

God revealed himself to Adam and Eve and did not withdraw his revelation even after they sinned.

God revealed himself to Noah and guaranteed that the unity of humankind would be reestablished bit by bit through time and place. He also promised that nature would never again destroy the world. The covenant with Noah prepared for the covenant with Abraham and remained in place until the coming of Christ.

God chose Abraham to be the father of all believers. From his descendants, God formed a chosen and holy People, Israel, in the hope of their Salvation. When Christ came, Gentiles were grafted onto the holy people through their belief in him.

What Are Private REVELATIONS?

God continues to reveal himself to all of humanity. *Private revelation* is the term used to describe supernatural communications that God gives to certain people. These revelations may take the form of *apparitions* (things that are seen) and *locutions* (things that are heard) that tell us more about God. The Magisterium of the Church at times recognizes such revelations as authentic; however, Catholics are not required to believe them nor are the revelations part of the Church's Deposit of Faith. Nevertheless, private revelations help people understand and live out the Church's public revelations.

Many saints have been blessed with private revelations. These saints are often called mystics because of their intense experience of intimate union with God. Often their revelations have come through **contemplation**. St. John of the Cross, a Doctor of the Church and a mystic, encouraged others to seek contemplation, though he disapproved of anyone seeking a private vision or revelation. He believed true growth in the Lord came through the practice of love, which is founded on the other theological virtues of faith and hope.

Assignment

Research a Catholic mystic. Write a brief report on one of the mystic's private revelations. Also answer: "What did this revelation reveal about God for me?" Some Catholic mystics include:

- **St. Bernard of Clairvaux**. He described the Church in spousal terms as the bride of Christ.
- **Julian of Norwich**. Her revelations of the experience and meaning of divine love came at the point of her death.
- **St. Catherine of Siena**. Her visions were influential, and she became an advisor to Pope Gregory XI.
- **St. Teresa of Ávila**. She described the stages of the mystical journey. She is known for her writings, including *The Way of Perfection* and *The Interior Castle*.
- **St. John of the Cross**. His famous work is the *Dark Night of the Soul*. Along with St. Teresa of Ávila, he emphasized that union with God is attainable only in the denial of self.
- **St. Margaret Mary Alacoque**. Known as the "Beloved Disciple of the Sacred Heart," she is known for her intense love and devotion to the Sacred Heart.

> **contemplation** Wordless prayer whereby a person's mind and heart rest in God's goodness and majesty.

In the fullness of time, God's Revelation became not just *a* word from God, but the definitive Word of God, Jesus, the Christ. The prologue to the Gospel of John announces that:

In the beginning was the Word,
    and the Word was with God,
    and the Word was God.
He was in the beginning with God.
    All things came to be through him,
    and without him nothing came to be.
What came to be through him was life,
    and this life was the light of the human race.

And the Word became flesh
    and made his dwelling among us,
    and we saw his glory,
    the glory as of the Father's only Son,
    full of grace and truth. (Jn 1:1–4, 14)

This passage expresses the conviction that the same Word of God that was active in creation and present in the Law and prophets has entered definitively and completely into the world. Henceforth, the expression "Word of God" meant that God's creative and saving Word is incarnate in Jesus Christ. In Jesus, God reveals and shares his very self.

Jesus Is the Fullness of God's Revelation

It's a wonderful fact about God that he chooses to reveal himself in a relationship that humans can understand and that does not cause fear and foreboding. Imagine the scene from the *Wizard of Oz* when Dorothy and her friends first creep and cower to approach the "great wizard." They then hear a bold, loud, and scary voice from on high. They all shuddered in fear. What if God had chosen to reveal his pronouncements and himself in this way?

Of course, this is very different from how God reveals himself to his people. God invites you into

♥ Picture Meditation

Like contemplation, *meditation* is a form of mental prayer. To meditate means to think deeply and continuously. Contemplation, on the other hand, calls a person to attempt to empty his or her mind of all thoughts and images and simply let God be present.

Practice a short meditation by following the steps below. In preparation, choose a piece of religious photography or a religious painting to meditate on. You may have such a piece in your home. There are several worthy photos in this textbook that can be used for meditation. You can also go to a church for this exercise. When you have found your photo or painting, quiet yourself and get ready to begin.

STEPS TO MEDITATION

1. **Observation**. Spend three to five minutes concentrating on the piece of art. What is in it? What is happening or has happened? What are the people doing? What season is it? Where is the action taking place? When? Who is in it? Why are certain actions taking place? What else to you observe?

2. **Reflection**. Spend three to five minutes discovering what the image might be telling you. Does it contain any symbols? What do they mean? What message is being communicated? If the image could talk, what would it say? Use your imagination to reflect further on the meaning of the image.

3. **Listening**. Imagine that God has a message for you in this photo or painting. Spend some time hearing what God has to say to you.

4. **Resolution**. Now that you have listened to God, write a short prayer to the Father asking him to help you to grow in your Faith.

a loving relationship with him. He reveals himself fully in the Divine Person, Jesus, who walked the earth humbly, reached out especially to the poor, and invited all into God's love. The Second Vatican Council reminded the Church that "through this revelation, therefore, the invisible God out of the abundance of his love speaks to us as friends and lives among us, so that he may invite and take us into fellowship with himself" (*Dei Verbum*).

God's Son who became man, Jesus Christ, is the completion of God's Revelation. In Jesus, everything you need to know about Salvation and sanctification is available in him. "Yet even if Revelation is already complete, it has not been made completely explicit; it remains for Christian faith gradually to grasp its full significance over the course of the centuries" (*CCC*, 66).

The preservation and transmission of this sacred memory of God's Revelation in Christ was given over to the Apostles. They fulfilled their mission by sharing the Good News both orally and in written form. In preaching the Gospel to all, they communicated that the life and message of Jesus Christ is the source of all truth and moral discipline. Under the inspiration of the Holy Spirit, this sharing of the Good News is passed on through the Sacrament of Holy Orders to the pope and bishops. This makes up the Apostolic Tradition.

SECTION ASSESSMENT

NOTE TAKING

Review the notes you took on important stages of God's Revelation and your own personal memories to help you answer the following question.

1. Why is memory necessary to maintain both personal and communal identity?

COMPREHENSION

2. How is anamnesis different from amnesia?
3. How is the sacred memory of the Church preserved?
4. What is the subject of the Church's sacred memory?

CRITICAL THINKING

5. How would the Church be incomplete without her memory?
6. Why is it necessary for all Catholics to share in the Church's sacred memory?

How the Church's Memory Is Preserved

MAIN IDEA
Through a single Deposit of Faith that is preserved, enlightened, and taught by the pope and bishops, Christ remains present in the Church and the world.

The Gospel—the Good News of Salvation preached and lived by Jesus Christ—is the source of all saving truth. God wills that everyone "be saved and come to knowledge of the truth" (1 Tm 2:4). In the Church's Apostolic Tradition, the Lord has arranged for a way for the sacred memory of this truth to be preserved and handed on to each succeeding generation.

God reveals himself in a single Deposit of Faith that is found in Sacred Scripture and Sacred Tradition. They both come together and make Christ's presence known to the Church. Jesus foretold at the commissioning of the disciples that he would be with the Church "always, until the end of the age" (see Matthew 28:16–20).

Originally, the Gospel was handed on in two ways: first, in the oral preaching of the Apostles, in their example, and in the Church Christ established; and, second, in the writings that the Apostles and others associated with them recorded. Recall that there is no further Revelation after Christ.

Sacred Scripture refers to the library of divinely inspired writings that make up the Bible. Sacred Tradition is the living transmission, or "handing on," of the Gospel message. This Sacred Tradition is contained in the Church's teaching, life, and worship. Sacred Tradition began with the Apostles, under the inspiration of the Holy Spirit. They, in turn, passed on this gift to the pope and bishops.

NOTE TAKING

Identifying Supporting Details. As you read this section, create a concept web like one of the following to record details about the meaning of Sacred Scripture and Sacred Tradition. Add more circles as needed.

inerrant — **Sacred Scripture** — inspired by the Holy Spirit

continuity with the Apostles — **Sacred Tradition** — interpreted by the Magisterium

Sacred Scripture

All of Sacred Scripture is inspired by the Holy Spirit and is free of error. This means that Scripture contains the truth God intends to be shared and that "everything asserted by the inspired authors or sacred writers must be held to be asserted by the Holy Spirit" (*Dei Verbum*, 11). The Old Testament is the inspired written testimony of the people of Israel. The New Testament preserves the memory of the Apostles and those close to them. This memory includes what Christ revealed to them about God and his plan for Salvation.

The Catholic Church teaches that Sacred Scripture must always be interpreted. Scripture is inerrant because it is the Word of God, but it is the Word of God expressed in human words and written by human authors. Like all human words and humans themselves, it is shaped by human circumstances and limitations. Scripture is valid for all times and all generations, but it was written in a particular time and for a particular group of people. In order to understand Scripture, the Church considers how Scripture was intended for its original audience.

To do this, the Church values the contributions of modern Scripture scholarship. Biblical scholars examine the context and audience of a particular writing. They also study literary forms (e.g., poetry, genealogies, parables, etc.) to understand the meanings of a passage. However, since Sacred Scripture is inspired, the Church teaches that it "must be read and interpreted in light of the same Spirit by whom it was written" (*Dei Verbum*, 3). Examining Scripture in these three ways requires:

1. *Paying attention to the Bible as a whole, not just individual passages or even books.* The entire Scripture is a unity of God's plan, and Christ is at the center of it.

2. *Reading the Bible in light of the Sacred Tradition of the Church.* The Holy Spirit inspired the authors of Scripture. It remains alive because it is interpreted by the Holy Spirit through the Church. Scripture must be read from the perspective of the Church rather than individualistically—that is, you must consider what the Church says about its meaning.

3. *Being attentive to the **analogy of faith**.* There exists an entire hierarchy of truths of Faith—of which the Scripture is a part—that must be placed in the context of the whole of God's Revelation. The Scriptures must be understood within the whole plan of God's Revelation.

Another point to remember is that there are two main ways for looking at and interpreting Scripture. These are the two main senses of Scripture—the literal and spiritual. The *literal sense* of Scripture refers to the literal meaning conveyed by the words themselves at the time, how things actually happen. The *spiritual sense* refers not to the words themselves, but rather what is signified by the words. The spiritual sense can be subdivided into the allegorical, moral, and anagogical senses.

Finally, it is important to remember that the Holy Spirit also inspired the formation of the **canon of Scripture**. In AD 367, the Church recognized the need to distinguish between sacred texts that were divinely revealed and others that did not meet the "measuring rod" or "rule" determined by the Apostles and their successors. As the Second Vatican Council defined it, "Sacred Scripture is the speech of God as it is put down in writing under the breath of the Holy Spirit" (*Dei Verbum*, 9).

---

analogy of faith The understanding that every individual statement of belief must be viewed in the context of the entire body of Faith.

canon of Scripture The official collection of inspired books of the Bible. The Catholic Bible includes forty-six Old Testament books and twenty-seven New Testament books.

Many crucifixes in Mexican culture include very visible depictions of Jesus' Blood.

Sacred Tradition

From generation to generation the Church has handed down both the written account of God's Revelation and her own understanding of that Revelation. The Church's Sacred Tradition is all of the ways in which the Church has passed on her understanding of what God has revealed to us. Some examples include creeds, doctrines, hierarchical structure, the liturgy, types of prayer, and social teaching and practice. These are things that truly make the Church apostolic. These are things that create continuity between the Apostles' understanding of Jesus and our own understanding of Jesus.

All Catholics help to pass on tradition (note the small "t"). Through Baptism, Catholics receive a supernatural appreciation of Faith (*sensus fidei*) that allows them to recognize God's Word, deepen their understanding of its meaning, and apply it more fully in their lives. This happens in many ways. For example, if you visit a Catholic church in Mexico you may notice that the crucifix looks different from a typical American Catholic church. Many crucifixes in Mexico include very visible depictions of blood, because Mexicans typically have connected Christ's suffering with their own suffering through history. The addition of blood is a small but real way Mexicans have added to the Church's understanding of Christ's suffering and to the Church's devotional tradition. The witness of ordinary believers is woven in with contributions of saints and the Church Fathers that "can be retained, modified or even abandoned under the guidance of the Church's magisterium" (*CCC*, 83).

Amid all of the contributions to the Church's tradition (with a small "t") is the authoritative teaching of the pope and bishops that protect and proclaim the apostolic teaching of the Church—that is, her Sacred Tradition. Christ commissioned the Apostles to interpret God's Word, both Scripture and Tradition. This Christ-appointed teaching authority extends to the pope and bishops in communion with Christ. The term *Magisterium* is drawn from the Latin word for "teacher." Interestingly, the Magisterium's teaching is applicable to both Sacred Tradition and tradition with a small "t." How the Magisterium teaches is the subject of the next section.

SECTION ASSESSMENT

NOTE TAKING

Use the elements you included in your concept web to assist you in answering the following questions.

1. What does Sacred Scripture refer to?
2. What is the Church's Sacred Tradition?

VOCABULARY

3. How is the canon of Scripture also inspired?

COMPREHENSION

4. What were the two ways the Gospel was originally shared?
5. What are three ways for thoroughly examining Scripture?
6. Who is responsible for protecting and proclaiming the Church's Sacred Scripture?

CRITICAL THINKING

7. Share an example of when an individual interpretation of a particular Scripture passage would be inappropriate.

APPLICATION

8. How can you personally share an element of the Church's tradition?

How the Church's Memory Is Shared

MAIN IDEA
The Magisterium teaches with Christ's own authority through creedal beliefs shared in dogma, doctrine, and Church law.

With the help of the Holy Spirit, the Magisterium teaches with the authority of Jesus Christ. This is especially true when the Magisterium defines a dogma—that is, a central truth of Revelation that Catholics are obliged through Faith to believe.

There is no universal list of Church dogma, although there are definitely dogmas that the Church recognizes as universally important.

Two primary creeds, the Apostles' Creed and the Nicene Creed, comprise the main teachings of the Church. A creed is a simple, logically ordered statement of beliefs. The basic text of the Apostles' Creed was formulated around AD 150. It highlights the essential Christian belief in the Blessed Trinity by proclaiming faith in:

- the first Divine Person—the almighty and eternal God the Father—and the work of creation;

- the second Divine Person—Jesus Christ, God the Son—and his work of Redemption;

- the third Divine Person—God the Holy Spirit—who is the origin and source of sanctification that comes to us through Christ's one, holy, catholic, and apostolic Church. (*CCC*, 190)

Your acceptance of the tenets of the Apostles' Creed and other Church dogma is essential for you to have a complete Faith and the deepest possible relationship with God. Two things to remember about Church dogma are:

1. They are infallible and irreformable.

2. They cannot change in their essence since the truth, which has been revealed by God, remains for all eternity.

This does not mean that the human language used to express dogmas cannot change. More explanation

NOTE TAKING

Summarize Information. Create a chart like the one below. As you read this section, fill in a definition of each element of Church teaching and at least one example for each.

Teaching	Definition	Example(s)
Creed		
Dogma		
Doctrine		
Canon Law		

of dogmas, other Church teachings, and the way they are expressed follows.

Dogmatic Teaching

Dogma communicates God's saving message as revealed in Scripture and Tradition. As with the creeds, the Church's dogmatic teaching includes elements of Divine Revelation, such as the divinity of Christ, the Resurrection, and Christ's Real Presence in the Eucharist.

The Church recognizes that dogmas are living teachings that can be shared in different ways in different times. Further study and theological reflection can improve the way a teaching is articulated. Though a dogma is infallible, or without error, the Church is not prohibited from finding better ways to communicate its truth. The Church may in fact over time change the way the dogma is shared, but the essential truth of the dogma itself will never be reversed. It is a basic tenet of Catholicism that every dogmatic statement protects an essential truth.

Each time the Magisterium declares that a particular statement or concept is part of the Deposit of Faith, Catholics are obliged to accept that the assertion is true. Because Catholics believe in mediated grace—that is, grace given in concrete ways and not simply through abstract concepts—dogmas must be expressed so that they can be practically understood and acted on.

What is it like for dogma to express a particular truth? Imagine that a local parish has contracted a world-renowned artist to create a sculpture of Christ the Good Shepherd. After a long wait the statue is finally unveiled for the parishioners. It is an evening ceremony and the pastor proudly turns on some specially designed floodlights that illumine the piece of art. It is unlikely that those in attendance would exclaim: "My, what impressive floodlights!" The purpose of the floodlights is not to draw attention to themselves but

to illuminate the beautiful statue. So it is with Church dogmas. Their purpose, like the floodlights, is to help you to direct your gaze on Christ, who is himself the indescribable beauty of God and the means of Salvation. The *Catechism of the Catholic Church* describes dogmas as

> Lights along the path of faith; they illuminate it and make it secure. Conversely, if our life is upright, our intellect and heart will be open to welcome the light shed by the dogmas of faith. (*CCC*, 89)

This is not to say that dogmas cannot develop over time and help to reveal even more of the truth. Turning again to the analogy, the floodlights can later be adjusted to a new angle or the bulbs changed to affect a new and brighter illumination of the statue.

Charisms of Indefectibility and Infallibility

Dogmatic teachings are taught with the charism of **infallibility** and protected with the gift of indefectibility. Both gifts ensure that the Church will never depart from teaching the truth of Faith, recalling that Jesus promised: "And behold, I am with you always until the end of the age" (Mt 28:20). The gift of indefectibility reminds us that the Church will always teach the Gospel without error, even in spite of the defects of her members, both the ordained and the laity.

Non-Catholics and Catholics alike often misunderstand the meaning of infallibility related to Church teaching. First, infallibility is not a magic wand that the pope and bishops get to wave over their teachings to make them inviolable and true. Rather, infallibility is God's promise to the Church that *when it comes to*

infallibility A gift of the Holy Spirit whereby the pope and the bishops are preserved from error when proclaiming a doctrine related to Christian Faith or morals.

THE CHURCH
and
Galileo

An interesting study of how dogmatic teaching arises and how it evolves in a new way revolves around the Church's controversial response to the scientific discoveries of Galileo Galilei, and her more recent comments on his teachings. When Galileo declared in the sixteenth century that the earth revolved around the sun, rather than the sun around the earth, many Christians were shocked. According to the thinking of the time, if the earth was not the physical center of the universe then neither the earth nor those who live on it could be central to God's plan for creation. After consultation with many theologians and scientists, the Magisterium concluded that one could not affirm the centrality of Christ to the universe without also affirming the centrality of the earth, Christ's home, within the universe. Thus, the Magisterium declared that Galileo's assertion was a heresy.

As the understanding of the difference between scientific and religious truth developed, it became clear that one could accept Galileo's teachings without rejecting Christ and the Church. Although the essence of the Church's dogma regarding the centrality of Christ and the importance of the earth as Christ's home has not changed, the way this dogma is expressed has changed completely. In 1979 St. John Paul II commissioned a group to study the Galileo case. In 1992 he announced the commission's findings acknowledging that the "birth of a new way of approaching the study of natural phenomena demands a clarification on the part of all disciplines of knowledge," and offered the Church's formal apology to Galileo, who also happened to be a devout Catholic and remained so for the rest of his life.

The pope teaches many lessons of the faith in a variety of settings that do not rise to the level of infallible.

matters pertaining to Faith and morals and Salvation, Catholics can be confident that Church teaching will be a definitive guide. This gift does not apply to other statements the pope or bishops make. The pope cannot declare, for example, that all people in Cleveland must root for the Pittsburgh Steelers and expect that Catholics would comply. Such a statement is not a matter of Faith and morals and Salvation.

The pope teaches infallibly when he teaches as a pastor of all the faithful, is proclaiming a definitive doctrine pertaining to Faith or morals, and does so intending to use his full authority in an unchangeable decision. While the teaching of the pope is the teaching of the apostolic Faith and without error, infallible *definitions* are rare. When the pope does define a doctrine of faith infallibly he does so *ex cathedra*; that is, "from the chair"—referring to the chair of St. Peter and meaning as St. Peter's successor. (The cathedra or chair of St. Peter shown on page 194 was cast and designed

for St. Peter's Basilica in the seventeenth century.) The last infallible statement declared by a pope was in 1950 by Pope Pius XII regarding the Assumption of Mary—the dogma that after her death Mary was taken into Heaven body and soul. Another infallible teaching occurred on December 8, 1854, when Pope Pius IX proclaimed the dogma of the Immaculate Conception of Mary.

You may be surprised that both of these beliefs about Mary were not official Church teachings until those relatively recent times. Regarding the Immaculate Conception, consider that from her origins the Church held a belief that Mary was always pure and perfect. From at least the sixth century, the Church celebrated Mary's birth on September 8. This was significant because the Church typically celebrated the death day of a saint—the day the saint entered Heaven and was freed from sin. By celebrating Mary's birth,

The Way God Communicates His Word

When people engage in conversation, the exchange is often imperfect. One person speaks while the other may only be thinking of what to say next. In reality, many *dialogues* turn into shared *monologues*. This is not to say that communication between two people never moves beyond the superficial level. For instance, imagine communication between two people in love: they choose their words to one another carefully and listen to each other intently because of their deep feelings for one another.

the Church was also saying that Mary was sinless from her conception, nine months before on December 8.

Scripture supported the belief. Mary was greeted by the angel Gabriel as the one who was "full of grace." Many other places in Scripture, such as the Protoevangelium in Genesis 3:15, told of the Mother of the Savior who would be victorious over evil and death.

All of these elements of Scripture and Tradition went into Pope Pius IX's decision to officially proclaim the Immaculate Conception a dogma of the Church. In addition, years before the proclamation, the pope had sent a letter to ask the bishops of the world what they, their priests, and their people believed about the Immaculate Conception. There was overwhelming support for this belief from people everywhere. This teaching about Mary was a clear reflection of the general belief of the People of God. Thus the Immaculate Conception became a dogma of Faith.

Interestingly, four years after Pope Pius IX proclaimed the dogma, the Blessed Virgin Mary appeared to a fourteen-year-old girl, Bernadette Soubirous, at Lourdes, France. In one of the apparitions, Mary told St. Bernadette, "I am the Immaculate Conception." When the young girl accounted the Lady's name to the local pastor he was amazed. There was no way she could have known that title for Mary unless it had been revealed to her. It was a stunning revelation to the Church that Mary herself had confirmed the dogma.

Catholics are always obliged to believe and uphold Church dogma, and commit heresy if they formally reject dogma. This is not to say a Catholic might not struggle with a dogma or other teaching of the Church. Some of the great saints struggled and doubted. What matters in such situations is that we remain trusting in God and pray as did the father of a son possessed by a demon: "I do believe, help my unbelief" (Mk 9:24).

Now imagine the way that God the Father communicates with human beings. God is not content to engage in idle chatter. God the Father wants to share his very life and being with you. Thus, he utters not just imperfect human words, but the Divine Word. Whereas human words fall short, the Divine Word does not. Whereas human words—even if between two lovers—always leave something unspoken or unshared, God's Word perfectly communicates his very being and his perfect love to all people. This is sometimes referred to as the Trinitarian mission of the Divine Word. God speaks himself into human history as an unsurpassable Word of love. That Word is Jesus Christ, the Second Person of the Blessed Trinity, the Eternal Word of God.

But there is more to the way that God communicates than that. When humans speak to one another their speech is made possible by their capacity to breathe. If a person is punched in the solar plexus and has the "wind knocked out" for a moment, he or she is unable to speak. You have to be able to breathe to speak. Yet in ordinary conversations no one focuses on his or her own breathing or the breathing of the other. If you heard a good lecture at school or a good homily at Mass, you don't tell your friends what a great "breather" the person was. You focus on their words, not on the breath that emits those words.

There is a connection with breath and the Trinity. In the Old Testament, the Hebrew word for spirit is *ruah* which means "wind" or "breath." Similarly, in the New Testament the Greek word for Spirit, *pneuma*, also means the same. The Holy Spirit has been described as the "holy breath of God." Thus, when the Father speaks his definitive Word of love into human history, the Word is borne by the Holy Spirit. One reason the Holy Spirit is sometimes referred to, as the "forgotten Person of the Holy Trinity" is that people do not often focus on the way the Spirit breathes God's Word. Rather, they focus on Jesus Christ who is God's Word.

This mission of the Holy Spirit is as necessary for sharing Divine Revelation as your ability to breathe is to communicating with one another in words. This is mirrored in the essential relationship between the Second Person of the Blessed Trinity and the Third Person of the Blessed Trinity. St. Paul taught: "No one can say, 'Jesus is Lord,' except by the holy Spirit" (1 Cor 12:3). And the *Catechism of the Catholic Church* reminds us that in order "to be in touch with Christ, [you] must first have been touched by the Holy Spirit" (*CCC*, 683).

Additionally, the Holy Spirit remains active within you, allowing you to receive Christ in your heart and share the Good News with others. This doctrinal teaching on the essential role of the Holy Trinity provides deep insight into not only how Divine Revelation is shared, but on the meaning of Divine Revelation itself. The Word, Jesus Christ, is the perfect expression of the Father's love for humankind. The Word is shared through the work of the Holy Spirit who also allows the Word to bear fruit in the lives of all.

The response to this communication of the Divine Word is Faith. The Second Vatican Council explained:

> To make this act of faith, the grace of God and the interior help of the Holy Spirit must precede and assist, moving the heart and turning it to God, opening the eyes and minds and giving "joy and ease to everyone in assenting to the truth and believing it." To bring about an even deeper understanding of revelation the same

The Virgin Mary reveals to St. Bernadette Soubirous that Mary is "the Immaculate Conception."

Holy Spirit constantly brings faith to completion by his gifts. (*Dei Verbum*, 5)

Divine Revelation and Faith form two parts of the sharing of God's memory with human beings: God's invitation and our response.

Doctrine

Not all of Church teaching is at the status of dogma. Doctrine refers to any belief that has the official approval of the Magisterium. All of the Church's doctrine is based upon the Revelation of God in Jesus Christ, which is expressed in dogma. In other words, doctrine helps Catholics to understand the implications of dogma.

Definitive doctrine includes teachings that are not revealed by God but are necessary for protecting and explaining Divine Revelation. Because these teachings, like dogmas, are also taught with the charism of infallibility, they are also irreversible and irreformable. One example is the Church's teaching on Purgatory, the state of purification that souls must undergo in order to enter Heaven. This teaching was not revealed directly by God, but the Scriptures support it with several examples of the faithful praying for the dead. Catholics are to firmly accept and hold as true those teachings proposed as definitive doctrines.

Authoritative doctrines are those that are not divinely revealed but which are drawn from the Church's reflection on Divine Revelation. These teachings are taught authoritatively with the assistance of the Holy Spirit but not infallibly. For example, the Church has outlined just-war principles that apply to warfare and offered clear teaching on the prohibition of artificial birth control. Each of these is in the category of authoritative doctrine. Catholics are obliged to do everything within their power to follow these teachings.

In instances when Catholics struggle with an authoritative doctrine to a point where they are considering disobeying the doctrine, it is often because they have an inadequate understanding of that teaching. They are obliged to seek out the proper understanding from a respected teacher of Faith (for example, a priest, deacon, or catechist) and to learn more about the teaching, to ensure a proper understanding. If the teaching concerns a moral matter, the person also must undergo an **examination of conscience**. This can be done under the guidance of a priest. Very often when Catholics struggle with accepting a particular doctrine, they are really afraid of changing their lives. In this case, they should pray to the Holy Spirit for strength to accept the Church's consistent teaching. Finally, they must consider the possibility that their reluctance to accept the Church's teaching comes from some resentment regarding the authority of the Church's Magisterium. It is essential for Catholics to accept the legitimacy of the Church's teaching office.

> **examination of conscience** An honest assessment of how well we have lived God's covenant of love. This examination leads us to accept responsibility for our sins and to realize our need for God's merciful forgiveness.

Canon Law

Every community and organization has to be governed by rules that guide its day-to-day life. The Church is no different. The Catholic Church is governed by a set of laws and regulations intended to identify structures, practices, and norms for Catholics to assist them on their way to holiness. This body of legislation—called *canon law*—may govern matters as diverse as how a parish is to go about purchasing land for a new church or the decision of a bishop about the number of Holy Days of Obligation to be celebrated in his diocese. The word "canon" is from the Greek word for "rule." Canon law is also called "Church law."

The Church's laws are contained in the *Code of Canon Law*. Over the centuries the *Code* has been revised several times, most recently in 1983 for the Latin Church and in 1991 for the Eastern Church. A faithful Catholic is to accept and obey canon law with humility and openness to the grace that comes with obedience even when a person may have some difficulties with a given law. To take an example from civil life, even though a person might believe the speed limit on the highway to be too low, he or she still must obey the law out of respect for law and order.

PRECEPTS of the CHURCH

Key Church laws are known as *precepts of the Church*, and include those listed in the chart. Catholics are required to keep the precepts of the Church.

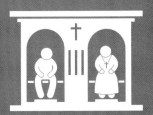

1 You shall attend Mass on Sundays and Holy Days of Obligation and rest from servile labor.

On Sundays we are obliged to attend Mass. This is rooted in the Law of the Lord and expressed in the Third Commandment. Catholics are likewise to attend Mass on Holy Days of Obligation. In the United States these are the Feast of the Immaculate Conception (December 8), Christmas (December 25), the Solemnity of Mary (January 1), the Feast of the Ascension (when celebrated on a Thursday, forty days after Easter), the Assumption of Mary (August 15), and All Saints' Day (November 1). Sunday is also a day to relax and unwind from work and to spend time with family.

2 You shall confess your sins at least once a year.

Catholics must go to confession at least once a year, and whenever they are in the state of mortal sin. The Sacrament of Penance also purifies us from venial sins. Confessing our sins to a priest assures us that we will properly be prepared to receive the Eucharist.

3 You shall receive the Sacrament of the Eucharist at least during the Easter season.

This precept is a minimal requirement for receiving the Eucharist. We should make it a habit to receive Holy Communion often, whenever we are in a state of grace.

feature continued on next page

4 You shall observe the days of fasting and abstinence established by the Church.

In the Sermon on the Mount (Mt 5–7), Jesus taught three mutually enriching paths to holiness: prayer, fasting, and almsgiving (charity to the poor). The Church has prescribed days such as Ash Wednesday and Good Friday, when we are to fast and abstain from certain types of food. Fasting requires that a person eat just one full meal and two smaller meals on that day. Abstinence laws require not eating meat. In addition, we are to observe these practices at other times throughout the year.

5 You shall help to provide for the needs of the Church.

Catholics must support the Church with the gifts of their time and talent, and their monetary gifts as well. Service to others is also a basic requirement of being Catholic.

The precepts of the Church address the moral and Christian life of all Catholics. These special Church laws are nourished by the liturgy.

SECTION ASSESSMENT

NOTE TAKING

Use the chart you completed for this section to help you answer the following questions.

1. What essential beliefs do the Apostles' and Nicene Creeds express?
2. Explain how doctrine may differ from dogma.
3. What is the intention of canon law?

VOCABULARY

4. Define the charism of infallibility.

COMPREHENSION

5. How did Mary confirm her title of "Immaculate Conception"?

ANALYSIS

6. Explain the role of the Holy Spirit in communicating God's Word.

REFLECTION

7. Share how you have been able to evolve in your articulation of a personal belief over time.

Apostolicity and Church Leadership

MAIN IDEA
The Faith that Christ first shared with the Apostles is preserved and passed on through the teaching office of the pope and bishops.

Returning to the *Catechism's* definition of the Church's apostolicity, the third quality that makes the Church apostolic is that "she continues to be taught, sanctified, and guided by the apostles until Christ's return" (*CCC*, 857). This part of the definition describes three main tasks of the pope and bishops:

- to teach
- to sanctify
- to govern

Before considering the teaching office, the particular focus of this section, note briefly the tasks of sanctification and governance.

Bishops are to be models of *sanctification*, or holiness, for the people. The First Letter of Peter directs bishops to "[T]end the flock of God in your midst, [overseeing] not by constraint but willingly, as God would have it. . . . Do not lord it over those assigned to you, but be examples to the flock" (1 Pt 5:3–4). Through the sanctifying office of the bishop, bishops (and priests) help to make the Church holy by their

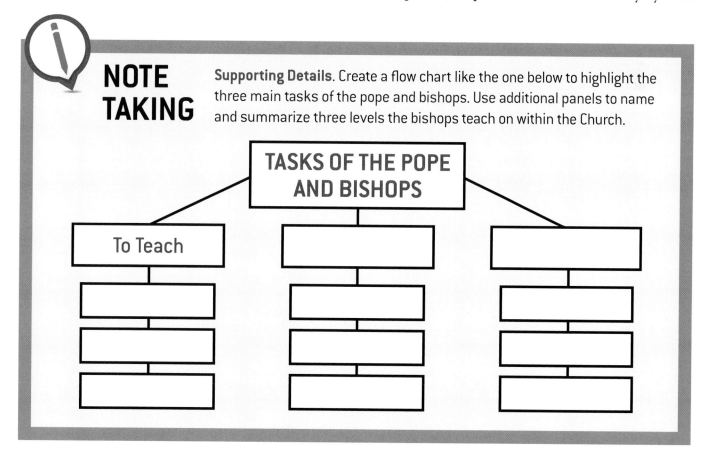

NOTE TAKING

Supporting Details. Create a flow chart like the one below to highlight the three main tasks of the pope and bishops. Use additional panels to name and summarize three levels the bishops teach on within the Church.

TASKS OF THE POPE AND BISHOPS

To Teach

1 WAY to TEACH as JESUS DID

Find or create opportunities in your everyday life to teach as Jesus did. One way you can teach the Gospel message is by volunteering to teach a lesson to younger children in a parish religious education program. You might choose to teach on Jesus' miracles or parables, or on the coming of the Holy Spirit at Pentecost. Be creative in sharing the lesson. Incorporate activities like role-plays, artwork, and discussion. Make sure your lesson is age appropriate.

In order to complete this activity, contact a parish director of religious education and explain the assignment. Volunteer to substitute for a regular classroom catechist or to teach your lesson under the regular catechist's supervision. Write a reflection summary of your lesson and teaching as your assignment for this course.

prayer, by their work, by sharing the Word of God, and by celebrating the sacraments, with special focus on the Eucharist.

As delegates of Christ, bishops also *govern* the Church. The governing office of the bishop is held in union with the pope. Bishops govern the dioceses assigned to them with their words and actions. As in his relationship with the college of bishops, a bishop interacts with the people of his diocese in dialogue and with compassion. The Second Vatican Council taught that "the faithful should be closely attached to the bishop as the Church is to Jesus Christ and Jesus Christ is to the Father" (*Lumen Gentium*, 27 § 2).

The *teaching* office of the bishop is the first pastoral task of bishops. Jesus was an exceptional teacher. He was often addressed as "rabbi," which means teacher. Christ chose Twelve Apostles and granted them the responsibility for preserving his teaching in the life of the Church. The unique authority of the Apostles as teachers is recorded throughout the New Testament, but particularly witnessed in the Acts of the Apostles. Consider Peter's transformation at Pentecost and his speech, inspired by the Holy Spirit, that moved the people of Jerusalem to accept the Lord (see Acts 2:14–42). The Apostles ordained bishops from one generation to the next, and the bishops, in union with the pope, have preserved the apostolic Faith of the Church through the teaching office.

The successors of the Apostles, the bishops, are called "heralds of faith" and "authentic teachers." Bishops have been given the power to call all people to Faith and to strengthen those who already possess a living Faith. Bishops teach the mystery of Jesus Christ in its entirety so that all people can find Salvation in him and in the Church. Their apostolic teaching ministry is undertaken in different forms and the task is also shared by priests, deacons, and all Catholics.

The Teaching Magisterium of the Bishops

Though the exercise of their teaching office, bishops "proclaim to humanity the Gospel of Christ" (*Christus Dominus*, 12). Fortified by the Holy Spirit, the teaching of the bishops calls all people to believe in Jesus Christ. For those with a living Faith, the teaching of the bishops is intended to strengthen it. For those who have not yet heard or accepted the Gospel, the bishop's teaching is a call to belief. To both audiences, the bishops teach the mystery of Christ in its entirety. They also teach the way to give glory to God, thus helping all people on the way to the reward of eternal happiness.

A bishop teaches on different levels within the Church: in his own diocese, regionally and nationally, and on a worldwide basis.

Diocesan Level

In his own diocese, the bishop teaches directly to his people and through his priests. This task is handled in

several ways. First, the bishop regularly visits parishes in his diocese. He is often present for occasions like the dedication of a new church, the installation of a pastor, a special Lenten or Advent series in which he is the featured speaker, and usually once per year as the minister of the Sacrament of Confirmation. On each of these occasions he uses the opportunity to initiate and promote dialogue with the people and offer clear teaching on matters of Faith and morals. Some of this instruction may occur in his homily at Mass.

The bishop teaches by monitoring **catechesis**, supervising the training of catechists, and setting a curriculum for religious instruction that is based on Scripture, Tradition, liturgy, and on the teaching authority and life in the Church. The bishop also has the responsibility to teach all the people of his diocese, not only Catholics. To fulfill this responsibility

> **catechesis** A process of "education in the Faith" for young people and adults with the goal of making them disciples of Christ.

he may write a **pastoral letter** or articles in the local newspaper. He may also appear in interviews done by the local media to offer the Gospel perspective on issues facing the community—perhaps the plight of local farm workers or the impending execution of a capital criminal.

Regional or National Level

Bishops also teach on a regional or national level, working with a conference of bishops from their own country to address issues that affect the entire nation. In the United States, this association of bishops is called the United States Conference of Catholic Bishops (USCCB). The group is made up of the entire body of bishops in the United States along with hundreds of support staff. It meets as a body at least twice a year. Among the issues the USCCB has recently addressed are life issues, family issues involving marriage and women in society, as well as social justice issues affecting both the United States and the world at large.

Worldwide Level

When collaborating collegially with other bishops and the pope, bishops also teach on a worldwide level. That part of the teaching office is linked with the Magisterium. Recall that it is the task of the Magisterium to preserve the truth first taught by Christ and handed down through apostolic succession. This is done through the gift of infallibility. Guided by the Holy Spirit, the college of bishops, in union with the pope, exercises the gift of infallibility when teaching about or protecting Christ's Revelation on matters of Faith or morals. As mentioned earlier, an infallible teaching may be proclaimed by an ecumenical council or by

> **pastoral letter** An open letter by the bishop to the priests and people of his diocese offering instruction, advice, or directions for behavior regarding a special circumstance.

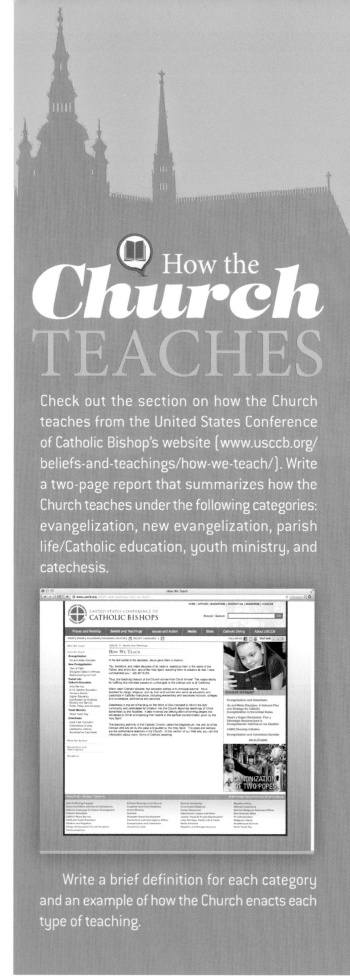

How the Church TEACHES

Check out the section on how the Church teaches from the United States Conference of Catholic Bishop's website (www.usccb.org/ beliefs-and-teachings/how-we-teach/). Write a two-page report that summarizes how the Church teaches under the following categories: evangelization, new evangelization, parish life/Catholic education, youth ministry, and catechesis.

Write a brief definition for each category and an example of how the Church enacts each type of teaching.

the bishops when they teach collectively and in union with the pope.

The goal of the Church's apostolic ministry is a significant one: to extend God's Kingdom to the ends of the earth. Then, all those that Christ has redeemed, holy and blameless, will be gathered together as one People of God. The Apostles themselves have laid the groundwork for attaining this goal. They have also established a means for the Church to remember and keep her identity, rooted in Christ. As written in the Book of Revelation:

> The wall of the city had twelve courses as its foundation, on which were inscribed the names of the twelve apostles of the Lamb. (Rv 21:14)

SECTION ASSESSMENT

NOTE TAKING

Use the flow chart you kept for this section to help you complete the True or False items below.

1. The sanctification office of the bishop is his first pastoral task.
2. Writing a letter in the diocesan newspaper is one way a bishop may practice his teaching office.
3. The first task of the Magisterium is to preserve the truth first taught by Christ and handed down through apostolic succession.

VOCABULARY

Match the term in the first column with its corresponding definition. Record the letters only as your response.

4. catechesis   A. education in the Faith
5. pastoral letter   B. a letter from the pope
6. encyclical   C. a letter from a bishop

COMPREHENSION

7. What are three main tasks of the bishops?
8. Name three ways the bishop teaches in his diocese.

APPLICATION

9. Describe an occasion when you were taught by a bishop. What was the lesson?
10. Name a Gospel passage that best represents for you Christ as teacher.

Section Summaries

Focus Question

How does the Church preserve and pass on the faith first shared by the Apostles?

Complete one of the following:

 Create a social media webpage promoting an issue of importance to teens that incorporates dialogue about God, Faith, and the Church. Some issues to consider: chastity, refraining from alcohol and drug use, protecting the sanctity of life, volunteer opportunities to help the poor.

 Read chapter 3, "On the Hierarchical Structure of the Church," of the Second Vatican Council document *Lumen Gentium*. Imagine you have been commissioned to write an abridged text of this chapter. Write a one-sentence summary for each section, 18 to 29. Write a one-paragraph summary of the entire chapter 3.

 Research and create a spreadsheet listing five popes from a particular age (e.g., the early Church or recent times) by length of time in the papacy, by chosen names, by nations of origin, by age at the time of selection, and any other category you find interesting.

INTRODUCTION (PAGES 183–184)
Preserving and Sharing

Guided by the Holy Spirit, the Church is apostolic in three ways: (1) She is founded on the Apostles, who Christ himself chose to preach the Good News; (2) She remains faithful to the teachings of the Apostles; and (3) She continues to be taught, guided, and made holy by the successors of the Apostles, the pope and bishops.

 "The Church's mark of apostolicity helps to strengthen the faith of Catholics." Comment on the truth of this statement.

SECTION 1 (PAGES 185–189)

Remembering Who We Are

The Church's sacred memory, often described as *anamnesis* or "remembrance," is essential for the Church's life and preservation. In her memory, the Church recalls God's Revelation through time and made complete in Jesus Christ, the Son of God. The Church's sacred memory is intended to be shared with all and is preserved through the Apostles and their successors, the pope and bishops.

 Share one Revelation from the Gospels that has helped you to know God's love.

SECTION 2 (PAGES 190–193)

How the Church's Memory Is Preserved

God reveals himself to the Church in a single Deposit of Faith that is found both in Sacred Scripture and Sacred Tradition. Christ commissioned the Apostles to interpret God's Word. This teaching authority extends to the pope and bishops in communion with Christ.

 Define *analogy of faith*. Describe a way you would explain this meaning to a peer who has never heard this term before.

SECTION 3 (PAGES 194–202)

How the Church's Memory Is Shared

Dogmas are infallible teachings of the Magisterium that communicate God's saving message as revealed in Scripture and Tradition. Every dogma is a doctrine, though some doctrines are not dogma nor infallible. The essential truth of dogma never changes, though the way it is articulated may change over time. Acceptance of Church dogma is essential for a complete Faith. Canon law helps to govern the Church and lead Catholics to holiness.

 Why do you think many Catholics and non-Catholics have negative associations with the term dogma? If you disagree with a Church doctrine or a regulation of canon law, what would you do?

SECTION 4 (PAGES 203–207)

Apostolicity and Church Leadership

The apostolic teaching office of the bishop is a prominent way that he helps to preserve and share the Faith of the Church. Bishops, in union with the pope, teach on different levels within their diocese, nationwide, and worldwide. The pope has a primary role as teacher.

 If you had the opportunity to tell the bishops the most effective means of communication to reach people your age, what would that be?

Chapter Assignments

Choose and complete at least one of the three assignments assessing your understanding of the material in this chapter.

1. First Person Account: The Apostles

In 2006, Pope Benedict XVI presented a series, "Catechesis on the Apostles," as part of his general audiences for the year. In his talks on the Apostles, the pope traced Scripture references to their lives while also delving much deeper into their souls to uncover their motivations for accepting Jesus' call to follow him. In some of the talks, he explored more of their stories, including what happened to them at the end of their lives. The talks can be referenced at the 2006 collection of audiences of Benedict on the Vatican website: www.vatican.va/holy_father/benedict_xvi/audiences/2006/index_en.htm.

Assignment

Choose one of the Apostles. Read about his life from the reflections of Pope Benedict and from other Catholic sources. Develop a five-minute, first person, spoken character profile of the Apostle you chose that includes background on his occupation, how he met Jesus, incidents where he is mentioned in Scripture, and how his life ended. If possible, gather clothing that resembles what the Apostles might have worn to wear for your presentation. Share your character profile on video. Play the video for your teacher or class. As a second option, perform your character profile live in class.

2. Timeline: The Spread of Christianity

The period from Constantine's *Edict of Milan* in 313 to the Eastern Schism of 1054 was a time of great growth in the Church. (See Appendix: "A Timeline of Church History, pages 255–266). The legalization of Christianity facilitated the Gospel being shared throughout Europe and the western world. The period also included the founding and spread of Islam. For this project, create a timeline of this period. To do this you must include at least twenty items, with a minimum of five from each of the following categories: (1) Events (e.g., Edict of Milan, Fall of Rome, Church councils, Charlemagne's coronation); (2) Saints (e.g., St. Augustine of Hippo, St. Anthony of Egypt, St. Monica, St. Patrick); (3) popes (e.g., Gregory the Great, Leo the Great, Zachary, Stephen III); (4) Others (e.g., Arius, Charlemagne, Charles Martel, Pepin, Mohammad).

Directions

1. Choose at least twenty items from the four categories listed above.
2. Research the items.
3. Analyze your research.

4. Make a timeline that includes equal spacing between the years 313 and 1054. Use color-coding to distinguish between the four categories above.

When you have completed your timeline, write about one item from each of the four categories. Answer the question: "Why was this event/person important to this era in Church history?"

3. Making Disciples

By virtue of our Baptism, we are all called to share our Faith. Jesus' instruction to "Go, therefore, and make disciples of all nation" (Mt 28:18) applies to everyone. The Office for Formation of the Laity of the Archdiocese of Philadelphia identified several ideas for evangelization in a short summary, "Everyday Evangelizing for Everyday Catholics." Here are some of the applications:

Before You Can Evangelize (Pre-evangelization)

- Pray daily.
- Carry a cross in your pocket.
- Read the Bible.
- Receive the sacraments.
- Communicate with those who inspire you.

Evangelizing in All Situations

- Respond "thank God" when someone shares good news with you.
- Share a story of how God works in your life.
- Ask people to pray for your intentions.
- Make the Sign of the Cross when dining out.
- Invite someone who is not Catholic to Mass.

Develop a further list of ideas for sharing the Faith with your peers, either Catholics who need a refresher in their Faith or those who have no experience of Catholicism. With these groups specifically in mind, write up an evangelization plan that focuses on what you can do

- this week,
- this month,
- this year.

For each part of the plan, include answers to the five W's and H questions:

- *Who* is to be evangelized? (Who is to do the evangelization?)
- *What* is the desired result?
- *Where* will this take place?

- *When* (during which week, month, year) will this happen?

- *Why* is this an important task?

- *How* will this take place?

For reference, note ideas from the USCCB Committee on Evangelization and Catechesis. See usccb.org/about/evangelization-and-catechesis/.

Faithful Disciple

St. Catherine of Siena

St. Catherine of Siena was the youngest of twenty-four children, born on March 25, 1347, the Feast of the Annunciation. Her twin sister died in infancy. She was a typical child who liked to frolic and play, and her home life was happy if not hectic. Her father was a wool dyer and the family home, preserved to this day, was filled with children and grandchildren.

Life changed for Catherine when she was six years old. While on the way home with her brother from a visit with a married sister, Catherine suddenly stopped and began to stare into the sky. She didn't hear her brother who was calling her from ahead. When he returned to find out what was the matter, Catherine was in a dream state. When he woke her she began to cry because the vision she had experienced of Christ seated in glory with the Apostles faded.

From that time on, Catherine sought out peace and quiet even in her noisy home. One of her favorite pastimes was to lock herself in a small room at the top of the stairs where she could pray to and meditate on Jesus. When she was about twelve years old, she refused her parents' offer to find her a husband. Instead, she cut off her hair so she would appear less desirable to a suitor and spent the next years tending her family's needs. Her parents, upset with her choice

and knowing how she liked to be alone, tried to punish her by always making sure that someone was with her. Later in her life in her famous *Dialogue*, she wrote that God had showed her how to construct an interior cell where no one or nothing could bother her. Catherine's father finally gave in to her wishes and built her a small room at the top of the house where she spent a majority of her time in prayer and reflection.

After entering a religious order of St. Dominic, Catherine began to care for lepers and those suffering from the bubonic plague. Through her spiritual counsel she also brought many people back to the Church. Some of the Dominican priests began to realize that many of the confessions they were hearing were of people who had been away from the Church for many years and who were only returning to the Church after being counseled by Catherine.

Her ability to provide wise counsel and settle disputes attracted attention beyond her region. At the end of the Middle Ages, several scandals rocked the papacy. When the French King Philip the Fair engineered the election of a Frenchman, Pope Clement VI, the French king in effect controlled the papacy. For a seventy-year period spanning the reigns of seven French popes, the home of the pope was Avignon in southern France, not Rome. Through letter writing to Pope Gregory XI, St. Catherine beseeched the pope to return to Rome. Pope Gregory wrote back to Catherine, asking her for advice.

Eventually Pope Gregory XI did return to Rome, but there were more troubles ahead for the Church. When Pope Gregory died in 1378 an Italian, Urban VI, was elected pope. The French cardinals returned home claiming that they had been pressured to vote for Urban by unruly Italian crowds. The French then elected their own pope, Clement VII. For forty years the Church was in a schism with two men claiming to be pope. Then, in an attempt to rectify the situation, a third pope was elected at the Council of Pisa. Catherine never gave up trying to help resolve the situation. She died in Rome in 1380 while attempting to reason with Pope Urban VI. Eventually the situation was resolved when Urban resigned, the other two popes were deposed, and the Council of Constantinople elected Pope Martin V.

Catherine's legacy lived on in her writings, including her letters to the popes. She wrote four treatises on the challenges of religious life, and her *Dialogue* remains a spiritual classic to this day.

St. Catherine of Siena was canonized in 1461. Her feast day is April 29. In 1970, Pope Paul VI gave her the title of Doctor of the Church. Pope Benedict XVI said of this "advisor of the popes":

> Catherine's spiritual teachings are centered on our union with Christ, the bridge between earth and Heaven. Her own virginal entrustment to Christ the Bridegroom was reflected in her celebrated visions. Catherine's life also shows us the importance of the spiritual maternity exercised by so many women in every age.

Reading Comprehension

1. How many other children did St. Catherine of Siena's mother have?
2. Who did St. Catherine see in the vision she had while returning home from a visit with a sister?
3. How did Catherine's plan for her life differ from her own plan?

Writing Task

- How might you go about constructing an "interior cell" for your own life?

Explaining the Faith

How are religious truth and scientific truth different? How are they the same?

Both religious truth and scientific truth are objective. They come from outside the human person; no one can shape them to suit him- or herself. Both religious truth and scientific truth help people to bring order to their lives. Religious truth does not deny scientific truth, but it does carry us beyond scientific truth. Observation and measurement will not contradict Revelation, because God is the source of both. Observation and measurement alone, however, will never tell you all there is to know.

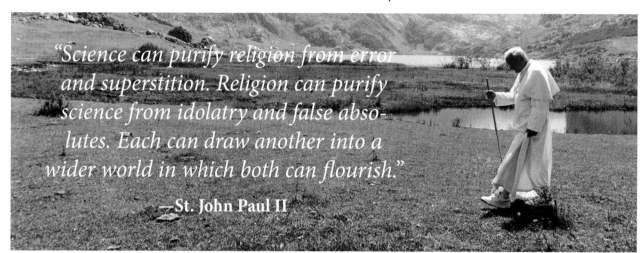

"Science can purify religion from error and superstition. Religion can purify science from idolatry and false absolutes. Each can draw another into a wider world in which both can flourish."

—St. John Paul II

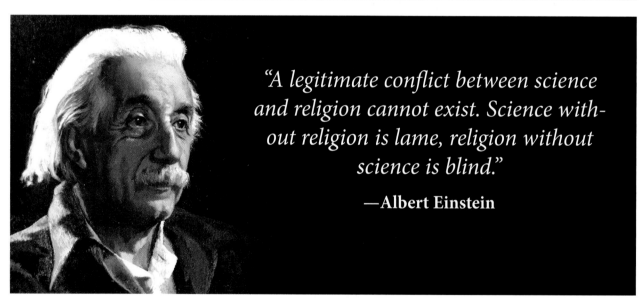

"A legitimate conflict between science and religion cannot exist. Science without religion is lame, religion without science is blind."

—Albert Einstein

Further Research

- "The scientist is being led by God, in spite of himself." How is this statement supported in the *Catechism of the Catholic Church*, 159?

Prayer

Generosity

Teach us, Lord, to serve you as you deserve;
to give and not count the cost;
to fight and not heed the wounds;
to toil and not ask for rest;
to labor and not ask for any reward,
save that of knowing that we do
your will, through Jesus Christ our Lord.
Amen.

—St. Ignatius of Loyola

THE
CHURCH
IN THE WORLD

A TRADITION OF
Catholic Health Care

The Catholic health care system in the United States—which includes more than 600 hospitals (roughly 12.5 percent of the total number of hospitals), 400 health care centers, and 1,500 specialized care facilities—originated for the non-military public in New Orleans when twelve French Ursuline sisters arrived there in 1727 and began to minister to the poor as nurses.

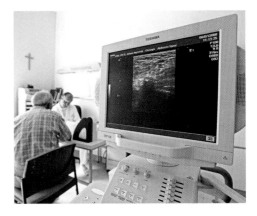

The mission of Catholic health care is rooted in the love and care that Christ had for the sick.

Catholic health care faces many challenges today. Shortly after the Supreme Court's *Roe v. Wade* decision in 1973, Congress passed a law to protect health professionals and hospitals with the right to conscientiously object to abortion. The law also declared that hospitals that take federal funding are not required to participate in abortions or sterilizations if they object based on moral or religious convictions. However, new threats against these laws arise frequently. A formidable challenge to the principles of Catholic health care arose when the US Department of Health and Human Services (HHS) first mandated, via the Affordable Care Act of 2010, that all employer health plans are to provide free contraceptives, sterilizations, and abortion-inducing drugs, without an exemption for religious institutions.

The Church continues to pursue a vigorous opposition to the mandate. If the mandate is implemented, there is a very real chance that many Catholic hospitals and care facilities would close their doors rather than offer health insurance plans that so clearly oppose Church teaching.

The Catholic health care system is worth protecting. The USCCB reminds Catholics and all citizens that "as a provider, employer, advocate, and citizen—bringing together people of diverse faiths and backgrounds—Catholic health care is rooted in the belief that every person is a treasure, every life a sacred gift, every human being a unity of body, mind, and spirit."

FOCUS QUESTION

What are my RESPONSIBILITIES AND DUTIES as a Catholic?

Chapter Overview

Introduction — Christ Has No Body but Yours

Section 1 — The Church's Divine Purpose and Mission

Section 2 — A New Evangelization

Section 3 — The Visible Witness of Faith

Conclusion — I Believe in One, Holy, Catholic, and Apostolic Church

INTRODUCTION
Christ Has No Body but Yours

MAIN IDEA
Like leavened dough, Catholics bring change to the world through the actions of their daily lives.

Catholics live a complex vocation. On one hand, they live ordinary lives. Catholics advance through school and pursue and practice careers. Most Catholic adults, like others in the general population, marry and raise children. They live in neighborhood homes and participate in community life, whether in an urban, suburban, or rural area. Catholics share in the hopes, fears, challenges, and joys of human life like anyone else.

Yet, Catholics are not only *a part* of the world, they also are *apart* from the world. Jesus said of his disciples: "They do not belong to the world any more than I belong to the world" (Jn 17:16). Similarly, the Letter to the Romans reminds Christians to "not conform themselves to this age" (Rom 12:2).

This dichotomy of understanding has sometimes led to misunderstanding. Some Christians have thought that they were called to hate the world. For them, everything of the world was to be avoided as an occasion of sin—including things like music, art, politics, and play. Some of these things were described as "works of the devil." Occasionally these kinds of beliefs have been espoused by the Catholic Church, but for the most part Catholicism has refrained from this attitude.

For example, Origen, a third-century Church Father, said that a Christian actually participates in the world by his or her participation in the Church. In *Contra Celsum* he wrote: "But we know of the existence in each city of another sort of country, created by the Logos of God." This other place is the Church. What Origen meant is that although the Church lives with

NOTE TAKING

Summarize and Expand. As you read the following section, create a chart like this one to help you list examples of the ways Catholics in the following categories "are leaven for the world"; that is, examples to others of holiness and social commitment. In each column add an additional example not found in the section.

Saints	Catholics in the News	Teenagers

one eye directed toward her final destiny in Heaven, she always lives in the world. Catholics belong to a Church that has a mission: be an instrument and human extension of God's saving love. St. Teresa of Ávila (1515–1582) described a Catholic's role as being Christ's Body on earth:

Christ has no body now on
earth but yours,
yours are the only hands with
which he can do his work.
Yours are the only feet with
which he can go about the world.
Yours are the only eyes
through which his compassion
can look upon the world.
Christ has no body on earth,
but yours.

St. Clement of Alexandria wrote: "Just as God's will is creation and is called 'the world,' so his intention is the Salvation of all, and it is called 'the Church.'" Being a Catholic makes you an instrument of God's work of Salvation. From the creation of the world, God intended you to share in divine life. In the Church this sharing becomes a reality.

Catholics Live in the World

God can be found wherever there are people seeking truth and wherever there are people bringing beauty and artistry into the world. Moreover, God is present wherever people love one another. The Letter of John explains, "Everyone who loves is begotten by God and knows God. Whoever is without love does not know God, for God is love" (1 Jn 4:7–8). For these reasons, Catholics do not reject the world as evil. To do so would be to reject God's creation and God himself.

At the same time, the world is wounded by sin. Signs of the world's sinfulness are everywhere, such as:

St. Damien De Veuster (1840–1889) was known as the "Leper Priest." He eventually contracted the disease himself.

- in the ways that humans respond to conflict with violence

- in greed and the way the human body and sex are degraded

- in the ways that many show a callous disregard for the poor

Into this graced-yet-wounded world Christ sends his disciples to both celebrate the world's goodness and to be his servants in its healing and Redemption. By bringing people back into oneness with him, St. Paul explains,

God was reconciling the world to himself in Christ, not counting their trespasses against them and entrusting to us the message of reconciliation. So we are ambassadors for Christ, as if God were appealing through us. (2 Cor 5:19–20)

In order to reconcile the world to God, Catholics must live *a part* of the world and to be willing to share in both the hopes and concerns of others. Recall the example of St. Damien De Veuster who ministered to lepers at Molokai, Hawaii, in the nineteenth century. Damien was aware that some of the leprosy was being communicated through immoral sexual activity outside of marriage, but he also knew that this wasn't the only way the disease was passed. Further, he rejected the idea that God sent this disease as a curse on the people. He saw the disease as a suffering that people should work to eliminate. Early on in his ministry, Damien was compelled to identify himself closely with the lepers. Six months after his arrival in Hawaii he wrote to his brother back home in Europe: "I make myself a leper with the lepers to gain all to Christ. That is why, in preaching, I say 'we lepers' not, 'my brethren.'"

Called to Be Leaven

St. Damien's powerful expression of solidarity with the lepers is a model for all Catholics. As the Second Vatican Council document *Gaudium et Spes* explains in its opening:

> The joys and the hopes, the griefs, and the anxieties of those of this age, especially those who are poor or in any way afflicted, these are the joys and hopes, the griefs, and anxieties of the followers of Christ. Indeed, nothing genuinely human fails to raise an echo in their hearts. (*Gaudium et Spes*, 1)

The Council calls ordinary Catholics to be "leaven" for the world, traveling "the same journey as all of humanity" and sharing "the same earthly lot with the world" (*Gaudium et Spes*, 40), not to be *apart* from the world.

Think for a minute about this image. Leaven is a substance like yeast that causes dough to rise. Leaven works by bringing about change from *within* the dough. Likewise, the Church is called to bring about the world's transformation by the way Catholics live and work within the world. In order to be leaven in the

A group of mostly Catholics rally in Detroit to protest the government's requirement that Church-sponsored health insurance plans include free contraceptives.

world and an instrument of the world's Salvation, ordinary Catholics must apply their beliefs in the Gospel of Jesus Christ to daily life. What does this mean for you? Are you to strip your clothing and give up all of your belongings as St. Francis of Assisi did? Is this the only way to live a genuine Catholic life in the modern world? The answer is "no." This is not the only way.

For example, after the HHS mandate of the Affordable Care Act of 2010 was enacted (see page 219), in 2012 Cardinal Timothy Dolan of New York called Catholics to participate visibly in the political process, not shrink from it:

> It is the duty of the laity to participate actively in political life, in a manner coherent with the teaching of the Church, bringing their

well-founded reasoning and great ideals into the democratic debate.

You can also apply the Gospel message to your life in everyday ways, such as by being honest even when your peers encourage you to do otherwise, avoiding swearing, and dressing modestly.

What is remarkable about this direction for Christian life is that you are called to imitate the way Christ lived *before* his public ministry began when he was identified as a simple woodworker (see Mk 6:3). You can be an instrument of Christ in the world when you live your unique life with dignity and pride, making sure that all your actions are shaped by your Catholic Faith. This is how you are to be "leaven for the world."

SECTION ASSESSMENT

NOTE TAKING

Use your completed chart to answer the following questions:

1. How are the risks taken by St. Damien De Veuster in ministering to the lepers and Cardinal Timothy Dolan in speaking out against the HHS mandate of the Affordable Care Act similar? How do they differ?

2. How does the image of "leaven" describe a Catholic teenager's role in the world? Your own role?

3. What do you find most difficult in living a genuine Catholic life in the modern world?

COMPREHENSION

4. According to Origen, how do Christians participate in the world?

5. How did St. Clement of Alexandria expect Catholics to participate in the divine life?

APPLICATION

6. If you were the only Christian left on earth to do the work of Christ, how would you begin?

7. How will you bring Christ to a career you imagine for yourself in the future?

SECTION 1
The Church's Divine Purpose and Mission

MAIN IDEA
Through the power of Christ, the Church is the presence of God's Kingdom on earth until he comes in fullness and glory.

If you've ever played on a team, been in the school band, or been part of a group, you know that the experience begins and ends with *objectives*. The coach or director usually begins the first practice or meeting by spelling out what he or she expects to be accomplished, both in the short and long term. The rest of the time of your participation is then spent on fulfilling the objectives, perhaps leading to a championship season or a flawless competition.

The Church has objectives too. The Church's purpose and mission for *both* now and the future is the transformation of the world; that is, to accomplish the Father's plan for Salvation and the initiation of the Kingdom of God. This is a divine task that is given to the Church by Christ. This objective is accomplished on a day-to-day basis, collectively and through the lives of individual Catholics. Think of it again as the Church's leaven expanding through every facet of the world.

NOTE TAKING

Synthesize Information. Copy this table listing primary source quotations or references included in this section. Complete the missing categories. Rephrase a summary for each quotation in your own words.

Reference	Quotation	Summary
Mk 1:15	"This is the time of fulfillment. The kingdom of God is at hand."	The Kingdom is present oriented as well as future oriented.
Mk 10:45		
	"It's better to light one candle than to curse the darkness."	
CCC, 765		
	The Church is "the initial budding forth" of God's Kingdom.	

The Kingdom of God begins with Jesus Christ as its foundation. Its growth and meaning can be traced through the course of his life:

First, in the Incarnation, the Kingdom of God broke into human history.

Next, the first words spoken by Jesus in the Gospel of Mark tell of the Kingdom: "This is the time of fulfillment. The kingdom of God is at hand. Repent and believe in the gospel" (Mk 1:15).

Finally, through his teaching and ministry, Jesus embodied the Kingdom by serving the needs of others. He showed that the Kingdom was not just future oriented. In reaching out to the blind, prisoners, the oppressed, and the poor he revealed what the world would look like when it is transformed by God's grace. He left that as an example for the Church to follow in every generation.

The Church continues to bring about God's Kingdom by imitating Jesus' example of service. Jesus "did not come to be served but to serve and to give his life as ransom for many" (Mk 10:45). At the Last Supper, Jesus demonstrated the meaning of servant leadership when he washed the feet of his disciples. And he completed a life of supreme service by freely accepting Death on the Cross.

Because of all this, service is not optional for Catholics. Preaching the Gospel in words is not enough. It is service that backs up the words with active love. Through service to others, the Body of Christ furthers and advances God's Kingdom.

> **apostolate** The ways that Catholics participate in the saving mission of Christ through different roles and functions in the Church.

Jesus Is the Source of the Church's Leaven

The work and mission of Jesus Christ is the work and mission of all the Church. All the authority, power, and responsibility of the Church comes from Jesus himself. The Church not only works toward the coming of God's Kingdom, but she is "the initial budding forth" of that Kingdom in history (*Lumen Gentium*, 5). Although the boundaries of God's Kingdom go beyond the Church, the Church is the most visible expression of the Kingdom in this world. This is a reason that the Church can be defined as sacrament.

The Church, as Sacrament, is a sign and instrument of God's offer of Salvation to all people. This sign is witnessed both in what the Church teaches through her words and how the Church responds to the world through action. When people look to the Church, they should witness Christ and his Kingdom (see St. Teresa of Ávila, page 222). The good work of the Catholic health care system in the United States is but one example.

Consider, also, how another **apostolate**, the Christophers, has made its mission to bring Christ into the workplace. Founded in 1945 by Maryknoll priest Fr. James Keller, the Christophers use the media to reach all people with the Gospel message and to encourage them to abide by the motto, "It's better to light one candle than to curse the darkness." The Christophers encourage laypeople to share the motto in their families, neighborhoods, and workplaces. The Christophers believe that everyone has a God-given mission, that everyone can make a difference, and that constructive action works miracles, which are truly gifts of grace.

Also worth noting: from the organization's beginning, the Christophers have offered programs for teens to both share with them the Good News and to facilitate ways teens can be the light of Christ to others. Some of these programs include writing and video

The Witness of the Community of SANT'EGIDIO

In 1968 it wasn't hard for high school student Andrea Riccardi to find a way to bring the Church to the world. "The periphery of Rome was like a third world city," Riccardi recalled.

The 1960s were a time of change and youthful exuberance all over the world. "Like others at my school in central Rome, I wanted to change society. I decided it was useless to change social structures without changing people, and dangerous to do so by using violence—in this I was influenced by reading the Gospel," said Riccardi.

Riccardi and a group of high school friends formed a group that eventually became dedicated to daily communal prayer and reading of Scripture, service to the poor and oppressed, peacemaking and reconciliation, and ecumenism and interreligious dialogue. They called their group the Community of Sant'Egidio.

"We had worked from places on the outskirts or places we rented in central Rome, but they were too expensive," Riccardi said. "When we heard that Carmelite nuns had abandoned a damp convent at the Sant'Egidio Church in the Trastevere district, we squatted there. Eventually, seeing the work we did, the owners—the state—allowed us to use it for peppercorn rent [a very small fee]. So we became the Sant'Egidio Community." (Sant'Egidio, or St. Giles, was a miracle-working saint in seventh-century France.)

The community quickly grew beyond its original youth membership and extended past the city limits of Rome. By the end of the 1970s Sant'Egidio communities had sprung up elsewhere in Italy. Today there are more than 50,000 members in communities in seventy-three countries around the world.

The ministries of Sant'Egidio have expanded over the years and today include ministry to the homeless, immigrants, the elderly and disabled, AIDS victims, and refugees in Africa. So great was their reputation for the work of reconciliation that in the early 1980s Sant'Egidio was asked to mediate in a religious conflict in Lebanon. The group has also been a main arbiter in peace negotiations in the Middle East, the Balkans, Latin America, Africa, and Asia.

Riccardi said that his technique is to view peacemaking not as bargaining but as an act of conversion. "We need to convince people that peace is the best situation for them and that war is madness."

In many ways the Sant'Egidio Community embodies the Second Vatican Council's teaching about the Church's mission in the world. The Council taught that the Church "has always had the duty of scrutinizing the signs of the times and of interpreting them in light of the Gospel" (*Gaudium et Spes*, 4).

This remarkable community, founded by a group of Italian high school students, began through its dedication to responding to the "signs of the times." Through prayer and reflection on Scripture, they learned that if the Church was to follow Jesus she could not turn her back on the world. Rather, the Church must be attentive to the pressing questions and needs of the day.

Friendship *with the* Poor

The Community of Sant'Egidio connects with the poor in many different ways. Browse the organization's website for a sampling of its service initiatives. Adapt and carry out one of these initiatives with the poor in your community, working together with a group of your peers. Here are some ideas.

WITH YOUNG CHILDREN

- In Italian, *rigiocattolo* means "recycled toy." In the months prior to Christmas, collect usable but soon-to-be discarded toys. When all the toys are collected, wash and repair them. Match the toys with children who might enjoy them or donate them to an agency that supports children in need.

WITH THE AGED

- Loneliness is one of the worst aspects of getting older. Yet older people typically do prefer to remain in their own homes and be as independent as possible, even without companionship. Schedule and keep to regular visits with an elderly neighbor. Use the visit to help with chores and errands, but more importantly, allow time to sit, listen, and share.

WITH FRIENDS ON THE STREET

- For safety concerns there is a legitimate tendency to keep away from people who live on the streets. On the other hand, these homeless people feel unrecognized and unloved when this occurs. If you are in a controlled situation with a group of peers or adults, acknowledge a person on the street with eye contact, a nod, or a simple "hello" as a sign of your respect.

WITH THE MENTALLY CHALLENGED

- How often do you or your peers use the "r" word to describe another person or situation? Did you ever think how this word is offensive to those with mental and emotional challenges and to those who love and care for them? Begin a campaign to eliminate use of this word among your peers.

WITH FRIENDS IN PRISON

- Jesus instructed his followers to visit those who are imprisoned. For teenagers, this is usually impossible to do unless you consider other people who may not be imprisoned behind bars, but are held captive to behaviors and habits that prohibit them from leading a good life. Consider ways to help peers who may have issues with drugs, participation in gangs, food disorders, and cutting themselves return to the mainstream of productivity at school and to participation in the life of your parish. Consult with parents, teachers, and other professionals for ideas on how you might be of help.

contests as well as internship opportunities for teens with an interest in sharing the Gospel through modern media.

Whatever vocation and career profession you eventually choose, you will be called on to share in Christ's power and mission while furthering God's Kingdom through your service of others. Living a Catholic life in this way will help to lead others to Christ, who "by all his action, prepares and builds up his Church" (*CCC*, 765).

Morning prayer to begin the school day is a powerful witness statement to the Catholic Faith.

SECTION ASSESSMENT

NOTE TAKING

Use your completed table to help you to answer the following questions.

1. Name a way that the Church is the "initial budding forth" of God's Kingdom.
2. What is the Christopher motto? What does it mean to you?

VOCABULARY

3. Define *apostolate*. Name a Church apostolate other than those named in this section.

COMPREHENSION

4. What is the Church's divine purpose and mission?
5. How did Jesus embody the Kingdom of God in his ministry?
6. What is the peacemaking technique described by Andrea Riccardi?

APPLICATION

7. Imagine your future career. Give three examples of how you might be able to bring Christ's message of God's Kingdom into your workplace.

A New Evangelization

MAIN IDEA

Catholics are called to evangelize the world through their words and actions. Pope Benedict XVI called the Church to a new evangelization.

"Preach the Gospel at all times and when necessary use words." This quotation—often attributed to St. Francis of Assisi—is apropos of the Church's mission to witness to God's Kingdom through her ministry of service. This "preaching through action" is a primary subject of this chapter. The next section ("The Visible Witness of Faith," pages 236–243) offers a synopsis of the body of Catholic social teaching that forms the core of the Church's response to the needs of the world.

In addition to preaching through action, words are also needed to share the Good News. The term **evangelization** describes the proclamation of Christ and his Gospel by testimony expressed in both action and words. Evangelization is also referred to as "Christian witness." The Apostles assigned to the bishops the duty to complete the work of evangelization, and the task remains primarily undertaken through the office of the bishop. However, Pope Paul VI emphasized that *all* Catholics are called to share their Faith with others: "We wish to confirm once more that the task of evangelizing all people constitutes the essential mission of the Church" (*Evangelii Nuntiandi*, 14).

In 2011, Pope Benedict XVI (shown here meeting with Cuban President Fidel Castro to encourage reform in the Cuban government) extended the charge for "renewed evangelization" by creating the Pontifical Council for Promoting the New Evangelization. The "new" or "renewed" evangelization addresses the

> **evangelization** The bringing of the Good News of Jesus Christ to others through words and actions.

NOTE TAKING

Definitions. Copy the chart below and write definitions for the following terms based on your reading of the text. Then add an example of how the Church puts into practice each of these definitions today.

Term	Definition	Example
Evangelization		
New Evangelization		

challenge of evangelization today, in a world that is often openly hostile to the Gospel of Jesus Christ, the Church, and even religion itself. Indeed, when nations easily choose war as the preferred means for addressing conflicts, when they ignore the plight of the poor in their midst, when they shuffle the elderly and disabled to the margins of society, and when they treat pregnancies as inconveniences easily snuffed out through abortion, it is the entire *culture* that is in need of evangelization. "In the deserts of the secularized world, man's soul thirsts for God, for the living God," Pope Benedict said in announcing the new efforts.

Renewing the Church Around the World

The efforts to reintroduce those who live in traditionally Catholic nations and cultures to the Good News of Christ was also at the heart of St. John Paul II's outreach. As pope, he made more than one hundred foreign trips and visited one hundred and twenty-nine countries. Speaking about the new evangelization to the Pontifical Commission for Latin America, the pope said: "Every project must take its point of departure in Christ and in his Gospel." Citing the words of Venerable Pope Paul VI, he added that there is no true evangelization without sharing the name, teaching, life, promises, Kingdom, and mystery of Jesus of Nazareth. In *Redemptoris Hominis*, St. John Paul II wrote, "The new evangelization is not a matter of merely passing on doctrine but rather of a personal and profound meeting with the Savior." In other words, Jesus Christ is at the center of the new evangelization.

One place where the efforts of new evangelization can bear abundant fruit is Latin America where high numbers of the population may identify themselves as Catholic, though many less actually practice the faith. Statistics from the early twenty-first century are even more disheartening. For example:

- In **Mexico**, approximately 88 percent of the population identifies itself as Catholic, a decline of 10 percent compared to the mid-twentieth century.

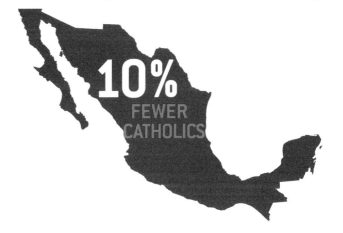

- In Brazil, a country with about 130 million Catholics out of a population of nearly 200 million, nearly a half-million Catholics have been annually leaving the Church.

- In **Colombia**, only two out of three people identify themselves as Catholic. In the 1950s nearly all of the population was Catholic.

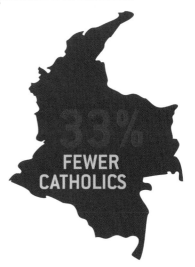

Beginning with a conference with Latin American bishops early in his papacy in 1979, St. John Paul II initiated new efforts for the Church to re-evangelize Latin America. When St. John Paul II visited Brazil in 1992 he began an anticipated celebration for the famous statue of Christ the Redeemer in Rio de Janeiro, by addressing two distinct areas of focus for the new evangelization: family and vocation. He explained that the message of the Good News is always passed on through the family. At the same time, he said, the success of re-evangelizing Latin American nations and cultures rests on being able to count on numerous and qualified evangelizers, especially priests and women and men in consecrated religious life.

In 2013, Pope Francis spoke about those leaving the Catholic Church—in Latin America and elsewhere—and how the Church can help them find their way back to the faith:

> Instead of being just a Church that welcomes and receives by keeping the doors open, let us try also to be a Church that finds new roads, that is able to step outside itself and go to those who do not attend Mass, to those who have quit or are indifferent. The ones who quit sometimes do it for reasons that, if properly understood and assessed, can lead to a return. But that takes audacity and courage.

In other words, re-evangelization requires more than a welcoming spirit; it requires action. It requires evangelizers who will go to those who have wandered away from the Church and minister to them with warmth and mercy.

The Catholic Church in the United States has not been immune to a decline among those who actively participate in the sacraments and Church life. However, recent years have brought some positive trends. For example, the influx of immigrants from Latin America has not only offset the loss of Catholics who have fallen away, but in many parts of the country their participation has reinvigorated the Church. Archdioceses and dioceses in the United States with heavy Latin American immigrant population or a significant immigrant population have focused more attention on these new Americans through initiatives such as:

- offering comprehensive social services and referrals to the proper local agencies,

- advocating politically for immigrant rights, and

- recruiting seminarians among the immigrants.

Individual parishes, too, have made special efforts to be welcoming by doing things like adding native-language Masses, celebrating ethnic festivals, and scheduling parish events later on weekday evenings to accommodate many immigrants who work late or long hours. The influx of new immigrants to the Church in the United States is not the only positive development. There has been a strong renewal led by young people in the Church through their participation in working for justice for the poor, support for the pro-life movement, and for an increased participation in the Sacrament of Penance, especially during the college years. These aspects of evangelization have contributed to a revival of the Catholic Church in the United States.

In Europe, too, there is still plenty of work to be done. Pope Benedict XVI and Pope Francis have made Europe a high priority for the New Evangelization, to counter the combination of secularism and atheism that have gained a strong hold there. Pope Benedict said that the Pontifical Council for Promoting the New Evangelization would work with bishops in every European country to promote Church teaching and to encourage active participation in the Church's life and the sacraments, use modern communication methods to share the Good News, and encourage traditional missionary activities of religious orders and new religious movements.

Dialoguing with People of All Faiths

The Church's missionary efforts springing from Jesus' charge to "make disciples of all nations" (Mt 28:19) require that the Gospel be preached to all people in all lands and in all times. This requires that evangelization also involves preaching to non-Catholics, non-Christians, and people with no religion at all. However, in some ways, "preach" is a misnomer; the Church's best efforts at evangelization of people who have not heard or have not accepted the Gospel is through *dialogue*.

Pope Paul VI explained in his first encyclical, *Ecclesiam Suam*, that "the Church must enter into dialogue with the world in which it lives. It has something to say, a message to give, a communication to make" (65). The work of evangelization does include dialogue, but, as the Congregation of the Faith noted in its 2000 declaration *Dominus Iesus,* it must at the same time recognize that "objectively speaking, they [members of other religions] are in a gravely deficient situation in comparison with those who, in the Church, have the fullness of the means of salvation" (22). This situation demands a much deeper level of dialogue, a level the Pontifical Council for Inter-Religious Dialogue explained reached deep into a person's spirit (*Dialogue and Proclamation*, 40).

In the work of evangelization, other potential dialogue partners with the Church include politicians, artists, and intellectuals from other religious faiths. The Catholic side of the dialogue represents the Church as both a human and divine institution. When the Church speaks, she speaks out for truth and against sinfulness. Dialogue is never understood as a substitute for the Church's obligation to evangelize by sharing the conviction that Salvation comes through Jesus Christ and in the Church he established.

Catholics should listen to the point of view of members of other religions in a spirit of humility, open to the possibility that prejudices and misunderstandings may be eliminated and that they might grow in a deeper understanding of their own Catholic Faith:

WORD ON FIRE
New Evangelization through Global Media

Fr. Robert Barron, from the Archdiocese of Chicago, founded Word on Fire Catholic Ministries in 1999, with the goal of drawing Catholics who have been away from the Church and non-Catholics who are just coming to the Faith into the Body of Christ. The uniqueness of Fr. Barron's ministry is that it places an emphasis on all modern forms of communication technology. Also, Fr. Barron is adept at making connections between many aspects of Catholic tradition—art, architecture, poetry, philosophy, theology, and the lives of the saints—and contemporary culture.

For example, Fr. Barron has hundreds of YouTube videos online that share theological commentary on the latest movies, television programs, and music. Among the topics Fr. Barron has commented on in his videos are:

Why people are fascinated by exorcism

Fr. Robert Barron comments on God, the Tsunami, and the Problem of Evil

God and the problem of evil

The "New Atheism"

Fr. Robert Barron comments on The Last Acceptable Prejudice

Anti-Catholicism: the last acceptable prejudice

Motion pictures like *True Grit* and *Avatar* and moral issues in the television series *The Sopranos*

In 2010, Fr. Barron became the first member of the Catholic clergy since Archbishop Fulton J. Sheen in the 1950s to host his own television program on national television. His program was called *Word on Fire with Fr. Barron*. Fr. Barron has also hosted a weekly radio show, has published a number of books and DVD programs, and reaches more than one million people a year through his Word on Fire website. In 2011, Word on Fire released Fr. Barron's ten-part television series, *Catholicism*. Catholic author and commentator George Weigel predicted: "*Catholicism* could well become one of the most significant efforts ever to advance St. John Paul II's new evangelization."

It's not just the variety of formats of media that make Fr. Barron's message appealing. His preaching is challenging, succinct, and non-combative. He shares orthodox Catholic teaching in the spirit of gracious dialogue that is able to engage many different viewpoints. In fact, Fr. Barron often addresses the online comments of his viewers and readers, dialoguing further with believers, non-believers, and critics on matters of faith.

Moreover, the fullness of truth received in Jesus Christ does not give individual Christians the guarantee that they have grasped that truth fully. In the last analysis, truth is not a thing we possess, but a person by whom we must allow ourselves to be possessed. This is an unending process (*Dialogue and Proclamation*, 49).

The Church's primary motive for sharing the Good News with non-Christians is not to prevent their damnation, but rather to invite them into the life of Christian discipleship and communion with the Blessed Trinity in Jesus Christ.

SECTION ASSESSMENT

NOTE TAKING

Use the chart you created to help you complete the following definitions. Write the definitions in your own words as if you were asked to explain the meaning of these terms to a student in a younger grade.

1. Define *evangelization*.
2. What is meant by the "new evangelization"?

COMPREHENSION

3. Who is responsible for evangelization?
4. What is the core message of evangelization?
5. What is the Church's primary motive for dialogue with non-Catholics?

REFLECTION

6. Share a profile of a former Catholic. Why do you think this person no longer practices the Faith?

APPLICATION

7. Name three ways the Church might better share her message with teenagers through technology.

PERSONAL RESPONSE

8. How can you carry out your responsibility to evangelize the world?
9. What is one thing you can do in the next month to contribute to the Church's work of evangelization?

SECTION 3
The Visible Witness of Faith

MAIN IDEA
The lived practice of Catholic social teaching embodies the Church's witness to Christ's Gospel in the world.

There have been more than fifty million abortions in the United States since the *Roe v. Wade* Supreme Court decision in 1973.

On a cold and snowy Saturday one recent winter, the taxpayer-subsidized Planned Parenthood organized a pro-abortion "Walk for Choice" protest in downtown Chicago's Daley Plaza. The organization was protesting HR 3, a House of Representatives bill that limited taxpayer funding for Planned Parenthood.

The protesters wore orange to the event. They carried signs and banners. A large orange and black banner read: "Abortion Providers Save Women's Lives." Another woman held up a homemade sign: "Abortion on Demand. No Apologies."

Only one side of the Daley Plaza was filled with protestors until the arrival of several teenagers accompanied by some adults, including two or three Catholic priests. The youth assembled inconspicuously around the plaza. Some were carrying large plastic trash bags that appeared full. And, then, suddenly music began to be blared from a speaker that had been hidden in a

NOTE TAKING

Summarize and Define. Draw a table like the one shown here. As you read the section, use short phrases to summarize and define some principles of modern Catholic social teaching, drawn from the body of Church teaching since Pope Leo XIII promulgated *Rerum Novarum* in 1891. In the third column, design a logo or symbol to help you remember each principle.

Principles of Catholic Social Teaching	Summary and Definition	Your Own Logo or Symbol
The Dignity of the Human Person	*All life is sacred; right to be born is central; "seamless garment"*	
The Common Good		
Preferential Option and Love for the Poor and Vulnerable		
Economic Justice		
Subsidiarity		
The Family Is the Model of Church		

backpack sound system. The teens emptied their bags to unveil yellow helium balloons with the word "LIFE" printed in block letters. It was a "pro-life flash mob"!

Singing, dancing, marching, and chanting words like life, spirit, and truth followed and the teens spread out a large sign that read "ORANGE YOU GLAD TO SEE US?" The teens said they had accomplished their goal of responding to the abortion message with joyful news of choosing life. Their flash mob video has been a hit on YouTube ever since.

As in the example of the pro-life flash mob, when it comes to overcoming unbelief, the visible witness of mature faith is often as valuable or even more valuable than the presentation of dogma. Evangelizing the world means, first and foremost, becoming aware of what your actions are teaching others about Christ and the Church. Throughout her history, the Church's message has been communicated in caring and often dramatic social action. And, since the nineteenth century, the Church's social action has been codified in a body of documents known as **Catholic social teaching**.

Catholic social teaching emerged in response to the social and economic conditions that left so many people in poverty in the late eighteenth and early nineteenth centuries, during the time of the Industrial Revolution. Pope Leo XIII recognized the need for identifying some basic principles to address the poverty and social inequality caused by the new industrialization. Pope Leo's 1891 encyclical *Rerum Novarum* ("The Condition of Labor") was the first of a series of papal encyclicals that would form the Church's social teaching. More recently, Pope Benedict XVI's *Caritas in Veritate* ("Charity in Truth") offered a reflection on several important economic and social issues of our time.

In considering the Church's place in the world—both in her official response and through action like that of the teenagers on a winter Saturday in Chicago—an examination of the Church's social teaching is the place to begin.

The Dignity of the Human Person

Catholic social teaching begins with the most fundamental of all beliefs; namely, that all human life is sacred. All humans have a dignity that is not based on what they do, but who they are. This is a dignity that can never be taken away. This is why even the worst criminals must be treated as humans possessing dignity as children of God. This is the basis for the Church's objection to **capital punishment**.

None of the other basic rights—including the right to food, shelter, clothing, employment, health care, and education—mean anything until a person has the right to life. If the most fundamental right—the right to be born—is not protected, then human life is under threat at every other stage. Soon the handicapped, elderly, sick—anyone who is only considered worthwhile for what they do and not who they are—can be seen as a burden to be eliminated.

Respect for the dignity of the human person does indeed translate to the other human rights. Recall that the late Cardinal Joseph Bernardin of Chicago referred to the Catholic position on life issues as a "seamless garment" (see page 167), alluding to the one worn

---

Catholic social teaching The body of Church doctrine beginning with Pope Leo XIII's 1891 encyclical *Rerum Novarum* ("The Condition of Labor") that applies Jesus' Gospel to the lives of people living in society, including its institutions and its economic and political structures.

capital punishment The infliction of the death penalty on persons convicted of serious crimes. There are few contemporary conditions that warrant the death penalty due to the state's effectiveness at keeping criminals inoffensive through secure imprisonment.

⌕READING the SOURCES

You can learn a great deal about the Church's social doctrine from papal social encyclicals. Letters of the US Catholic Bishops also address important social issues. Following is a list of the Church's social teaching documents, starting with Pope Leo XIII's 1891 *Rerum Novarum*. Research several of the documents and choose one to read in its entirety and report on. Use the reading plan that follows in developing your report.

SOCIAL DOCTRINE DOCUMENTS

1891—Leo XIII—The Condition of Labor (*Rerum Novarum*)

1931—Pius XI—The Reconstruction of the Social Order (*Quadragesimo Anno*)

1961—John XXIII—Christianity and Social Progress (*Mater et Magistra*)

1963—John XXIII—Peace on Earth (*Pacem in Terris*)

1965—Vatican Council II—The Church in the Modern World (*Gaudium et Spes*)

1971—Paul VI—A Call to Action (*Octogesima Adveniens*)

1971—Synod of Bishops—Justice in the World

1981—John Paul II—On Human Work (*Laborem Exercens*)

1986—US Catholic Bishops—Economic Justice for All

1991—John Paul II—The One Hundredth Year (*Centesimus Annus*)

1995—John Paul II—The Gospel of Life (*Evangelium Vitae*)

1998—US Catholic Bishops—Sharing Catholic Social Teaching: Challenges and Directions

1998—John Paul II—Faith and Reason (*Fides et Ratio*)

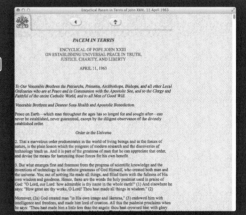

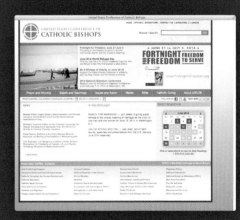

Many of the Church's documents on social teaching can be located at the following websites:

- www.vatican.va

- www.usccb.org

READING PLAN

Prepare to teach a peer about your document by doing the following:

1. *Determine the historical context*: What do you know about the author(s)? Why was it written? What was the public reaction to the doctrine at the time of the writing?

2. *Classify the source*: What kind of writing is it (e.g., pastoral letter, encyclical)? Summarize the main argument of the writing. What problems does it address? What evidence does it use? Comment on the effectiveness of the argument. List and define key words used in the source.

3. *Compare the source to other writings*: How similar is this writing to other doctrinal writings on social justice, (including non-Catholic writing)? How has history judged this writing?

4. *Offer your own understanding*: Imagine you are to explain this document to a group of your peers. Write a three- or four-paragraph summary in your own words.

by Jesus at his crucifixion (cf. Jn 19:23). This view holds that life must be respected from conception until natural death, from womb to tomb. This means that society must create economic, social, and political structures that enable all people to live with dignity. Corresponding to these rights are social duties and responsibilities—to families, local communities, and society at large.

The Common Good

The Scripture account of creation (see Genesis 1–2) not only teaches that every person is precious to God, but also that that you must live in relationship with one another. God said: "It is not good for the man to be alone. I will make a suitable partner for him" (Gn 2:18). Life together with one another is described by the principle of the **common good**. Put simply, it means that no one can make himself or herself the center of the universe. It is not enough to be concerned with how some public policy or law affects only your own interests, you must also ask: "How does it affect others, especially the most vulnerable?"

Like other principles of Catholic social teaching, speaking out for and defending the common good can lead to adversarial relationships with others. For example, when Catholic Charities near Gonzaga University in Spokane, Washington, wanted to build a forty-unit affordable-housing complex for the elderly on a dilapidated property owned by a neighborhood parish, many of the local residents protested, expressing concern over increased crime and a negative impact on real-estate values.

> **common good** The sum of the spiritual, material, and social conditions needed for a person to achieve full human dignity.

♥ AffirmAtion FLASH MOBS!

Organizing and participating in a flash mob can be fun, as long as the right place and time are chosen and the purpose is positive. For example, imagine creating a flash mob around the following themes:

- Offering congratulations to seniors recently admitted to college

- Welcoming back a victorious school team from a game (or offering consolation and support to a team that lost a tough game)

- Communicating an announcement to one or more students of reception of a honor or award

Also, a surprise flash mob might be incorporated into an school prayer service. Imagine, for example, several students "spontaneously" breaking out in songs of praise and other students standing and offering testimony to the Gospel.

PLAN Your OWN AffirmAtion FLASH MoB

To organize a flash mob, follow these suggestions:

1. Gather a core group. Invite a group of peers to help you organize the event.

2. Choose a theme. Brainstorm some ideas with your team. Also check the web for some creative ideas that have already been done. Make sure your idea is Gospel-centered and affirming.

3. Make a plan. Gather a larger group. Determine the skills of each person. Assign roles. Practice.

4. Inform the right people. If your flash mob is part of a school event, let your teacher or an administrator know about your idea to determine feasibility. At the same time, keep your flash mob plan secret from almost everyone else.

5. Execute your affirmation flash mob. Have fun!

Even though Catholic Charities president Rob McCann said that all the data showed that "for everything we've built we've seen the exact opposite," including a decrease in crime, the community continued to push the city council to deny a change in zoning regulations. McCann said some neighbors actually seemed afraid of poor people and old people: "It's disturbing to think that human beings can have such negative stereotypes and such horrifically bad views of the poor." In the meantime, the Spokane Valley Planning Commission was encouraging meetings between Catholic Charities and the neighborhood group to address concerns.

Working for the common good for example in a situation like the one described above, entails three essential elements:

1. Respect for the fundamental and inalienable rights of each human being

2. Recognizing the right of individuals and groups to develop socially, economically, politically, culturally, and spiritually

3. Peace and stability

In working and speaking out for the common good, the Church supports political and social structures that allow all people—especially the most poor and vulnerable—to live lives rooted in these three essential elements.

Preferential Option and Love for the Poor and Vulnerable

In the Parable of the Last Judgment (see Mt 25), Jesus taught that the needs of the poor and vulnerable must come first. The Church continues to make this principle a priority. Practically, it means that those with material wealth and power have a special obligation to care for those who lack material goods and the ability to care for themselves.

Individual Catholics are called to practice this preferential option for the poor and vulnerable. One way to do so is by living more simply and selflessly sharing material wealth with those who lack the basics. Further, it means recognizing that without God all of us are truly poor. In the document "Economic Justice for All," the US Catholic Bishops taught that the option for the poor calls for "for an emptying of self, both individually and corporately, that allows the Church to experience the power of God in the midst of poverty and powerlessness" (52). This option for the poor is also a practical application for the virtue of solidarity (see pages 47–49).

Economic Justice

Another related principle of Catholic social teaching involves the dignity and the rights of workers. The economy must serve the people, not the other way around. Work is an essential part of life. Work both helps people to make a living and to participate in God's creation. Work is not solely a matter of profit; it is a fulfillment of the human vocation to assist in the building of the Kingdom. The dignity of work is safeguarded when worker's rights are respected.

There are some other basic elements to Catholic teaching on the economy. For example, all workers have a right to productive work, to decent and fair wages, and to safe working conditions. Workers also have a right to organize and join unions, a consistent teaching of the Church. In recent years, the role of unions has made headlines, such as in Wisconsin in 2011, where union members protested the governor's reduction of the union's bargaining power. Milwaukee Archbishop Jerome E. Listecki commented on the situation, saying: "Hard times do not nullify the moral obligation each of us has to respect the legitimate rights of workers" while balancing his remarks adding that not "every claim made by workers or their representatives is valid" and that unions need to "make sacrifices when required" in adjusting to "new economic realities."

The Church does not support any economic system in its entirety. For example, the Church is critical of **socialism** to the extent that it suppresses the dignity of individuals while also limiting personal freedoms. Under a system of socialism, personal initiative and responsibility are often subsumed by the state. **Capitalism**, the economic system of the United States and much of the developed world, does foster individualism and a spirit of initiative. However, the Church points out that capitalism has its flaws as well. Capitalism, too, can undermine human dignity when competition and the acquisition of material goods take precedence over the care for the needs of others. In a capitalistic economy, society may be prone to equating a person's value only to what he or she can produce.

Economic justice also relates to the principle of **stewardship**. The earth must be treated with respect. God intends the goods of the earth for the benefit of everyone. Everyone has a responsibility to care for these goods as stewards and trustees, not as mere consumers and users. How people treat the environment is a measure of their respect for the Creator.

In centering on the principle of economic justice, it is wise to keep in mind the injunction in the First Letter to Timothy:

"Recourse to strike is morally legitimate when it cannot be avoided, or at least when it is necessary to obtain a proportionate benefit" (CCC, 2435).

Tell the rich in the present age not to be proud and not to rely on so uncertain a thing as wealth but rather on God, who richly provides us with all things for our enjoyment. (1 Tm 6:17)

socialism A political and economic system based on common ownership and central regulation of productive economic resources.

capitalism An economic system characterized by private investment and private ownership of goods, all operating in a free market.

stewardship The proper use of the gifts God has given to us, in particular the care for creation that will allow the earth and its resources to flourish and endure for future generations.

Subsidiarity

Subsidiarity is related to the state's or government's role in the lives of individuals and society. This principle teaches that justice and human welfare are best achieved on the most immediate level. Individuals, families, and local communities should be given the freedom and resources to address issues and challenges they face. Larger social or political structures, such as the state or federal government, should only intervene when individuals or communities are unable to help themselves. For example, in the United States the standards and operations of public schools are typically left to local communities. However, if the school system is not serving its citizens (e.g., dropout rates are high, students are not prepared for college), the state government may intervene.

> **subsidiarity** The principle of Catholic social doctrine that says that no community of higher order (such as a national or state government) should do what can be done equally well or better by a community of lower order (such as a family or local community).

The Family Is the Model of Church

The Church is present in family life. This has been true since the beginning of creation when man and woman came together as one. This was also true in the early years of the Church when the Eucharist was celebrated in family homes. Also, the vocations of those who become priests and other ministers have always been nurtured and developed through family life. Recall that the family is the *domestic church* and the "original cell of social life" (*CCC*, 2207). Today, the Christian family remains the first place for education in prayer and the practice of prayer. Many of the Church's social teachings stress the importance and the sacred nature of the family. St. John Paul II wrote:

> The family is indeed sacred: it is the place in which life—the gift of God—can be properly welcomed and protected against the many attacks to which it is exposed, and can develop in accordance with what constitutes authentic human growth. In the face of the so-called

culture of death, the family is the heart of the culture of life. ("On the Hundredth Anniversary of *Rerum Novarum*," § 39)

Care of families must be at the heart of any social program. This is because care for families respects both the unique dignity of each person and the social nature of each person. Family members accept the basic responsibility for the development and well-being of one another.

All of Catholic social teaching reflects basic moral truths and is an extension of the **natural law**. Quoting St. Thomas Aquinas, in his encyclical *Veritas Splendor*, St. John Paul II defined the natural law as the "the light of understanding infused in us by God, whereby we understand what must be done and what must be avoided. God gave this light and this law to human beings at creation" (§ 12). The reason that much of the Church's social teaching makes sense to many non-Catholics is because it is drawn from natural law. When Catholics live out the main Catholic social teachings in their daily lives they participate in the mission of the Church to be leaven for the world. They become servants of the Kingdom of God.

> **natural law** The moral sense God gave people to know through their intellect and reason what is good and what is evil. The natural law is written in the human heart and in all of God's creation.

SECTION ASSESSMENT

NOTE TAKING

Use your completed chart to help you to answer the following questions.

1. Define Catholic social teaching.
2. Name the six Catholic social teachings listed in this section and explain the meaning of each with a word or phrase.

COMPREHENSION

3. How did Catholic social teaching emerge?
4. Why is the most fundamental right associated with the dignity of the human person the right to life?
5. What are the three essential elements of the common good?
6. What position does the Church take on particular economic systems?

REFLECTION

7. Imagine you were a witness to the Chicago teenagers' flash mob event at the Planned Parenthood demonstration. Describe some of the feelings you might have as you watch the events unfold.

APPLICATION

8. How does the Parable of the Last Judgment (Mt 25) embody your understanding of the preferential option for the poor and vulnerable?
9. Based on the principle of subsidiarity, why is the family essential?

I Believe in One, Holy, Catholic, and Apostolic Church

"I believe in one, holy, catholic, and apostolic Church." These words—expressing the marks of the Church—became an official part of the Nicene Creed at the First Council of Constantinople in 381. The marks of the Church express the nature of the Church, the subject of this course. This nature and these marks are unchangeable—that is, they cannot be changed to suit the whims and wishes of different people at different times. The nature of the Church is an expression of the nature of God.

One

- The Church is one because the Trinity is one. The true Church cannot be divided any more than the Father, Son, and Holy Spirit can be separated. Unity is part of the nature of God, and restoration of the unity between God and humankind was part of Christ's mission on Earth.

Holy

- The Church is holy because she is the Body of Christ. The Church is also holy because the Holy Spirit dwells within her. All holiness has its root in God who alone is truly holy. God is the only one who is completely apart from the rest of creation, because God is the only one who is uncreated. The Church is holy—set apart from the rest of creation—because of her intimate connection with God.

Catholic

- To say that the Church is catholic is to say that the totality of the Body of Christ is present in the Church. There is nothing of God that is lacking in Christ's Body, the Church. The Church has a role everywhere and in every situation. Church teaching is based upon the whole of God's Revelation from all time and places.

Apostolic

- *Apostolic* means "having been sent." The Church is apostolic because Christ has sent her into the world. The Church remains faithful to her apostolic nature by recognizing that she is built on the foundation of the Apostles, adhering to Scripture and the teachings of the Apostles, and continuing to accept the guidance of the Apostles through their successors, the pope and bishops.

Christ remains active in the Church through the Holy Spirit, constantly shaping the Church by making these four marks present through how she lives her mission in the world. Understanding the four marks can help you to understand how the Church is the Sacrament of Christ on earth and all the ways Christ remains present and visible in the Church and the world today.

Section Summaries

Focus Question

What are my responsibilities and duties as a Catholic?

Complete one of the following:

 Read the May 20, 2009 "USCCB Health Care Statement to Congress" (www.usccb.org/issues-and-action/human-life-and-dignity/health-care/). Name the essential elements the U.S. Catholic Bishops requested in a comprehensive health care reform.

 Summarize the Church's protest of the HHS Mandate first proposed in 2012 by President Barack Obama. See: www.usccb.org/issues-and-action/religious-liberty/conscience-protection/. Answer the following question: Why is this primarily an issue of religious liberty?

 List one corresponding right and one corresponding responsibility for each of the six principles of Catholic social teaching mentioned in "The Visible Witness of Faith" section (pages 236–243).

INTRODUCTION (PAGES 221–224)

Christ Has No Body but Yours

Catholics are to live not only as *a part* of the world, but also *apart* from the world. This means that although Christ himself said that his followers "do not belong to the world" (Jn 15:19), Catholics, through their participation in the Church, must be Christ's Body on Earth to serve the needs of all and draw all to him.

 The Second Vatican Council taught that "Christians should rejoice that, following the example of Christ who worked as an artisan, they are free to give proper exercise to all their earthly activities and to their humane, domestic, professional, social, and technical enterprises by gathering them into one vital synthesis with religious values, under whose supreme direction all things are harmonized into God's glory" (*Gaudium et Spes*, 43). How does this statement apply to your own life goals?

SECTION 1 (PAGES 225–229)

The Church's Divine Purpose and Mission

The Church's divine purpose and mission is the transformation of the world. Whenever you imitate Christ by serving others, you participate in the transformation of the world and the Kingdom of God is initiated.

 Research and summarize some of the ways the Christophers encourage teens to participate in their apostolate.

SECTION 2 (PAGES 230–235)

A New Evangelization

Along with the witness of their actions, all Catholics are called to evangelize through words. Evangelization is the proclamation of Christ and his Gospel. St. John Paul II called for a "new evangelization"—that is, a recommitment to share the Good News with Catholics who have fallen away from the Faith.

 Think of some family members, friends, and peers who are in need of the Church's efforts at a new evangelization. Name some effective strategies for reaching these groups with the truth of the Gospel of Jesus Christ.

SECTION 3 (PAGES 236–243)

The Visible Witness of Faith

The Church's presence in the world is visibly witnessed in the statement of her Catholic social teaching and the subsequent practice of this teaching. The modern body of the Church's teaching on social justice began with Pope Leo XIII's encyclical *Rerum Novarum*. The foundation of Catholic social teaching is the belief that all life is sacred and that dignity is not based not on what we do, but who we are.

 Explain in your own words the meaning of the image of the "seamless garment" to define Church teaching on life issues.

Chapter Assignments

Choose and complete at least one of the following three assignments to assess your understanding of the material in this chapter.

1. The Importance of Christian Names

In January 2011 after baptizing twenty-one infants at the Sistine Chapel, Pope Benedict XVI reminded Catholic parents of the importance of choosing Christian names for their children. Choosing Christian names is a practice that dates back to the fourth century and perhaps earlier, with girls often named for the Blessed Mother and boys named the Apostles. A Christian name, Pope Benedict said, signifies that in Baptism "every baptized person" has acquired a new character and an "unmistakable sign that the Holy Spirit gives birth anew." Complete the following exercises:

1. Research a list of the five most popular names for boys and girls for at least five concurrent decades, including the present one. Create a chart or graph that compares and contrasts the popularity of Christian names with non-Christian names over your chosen time period.

2. Detail some information about your own name. What does your name mean? How did your parents choose your name?

3. If you were named for a saint (either your first name or middle name), write a short profile of the saint. Tell about some qualities of the saint that you admire and how the saint is a model for your life. (If you were not named for a saint, choose a favorite saint to write about.)

2. Promoting Universal Health Care

The United States Conference of Catholic Bishops has consistently spoken out for universal health care for US citizens. In the 1993 document *A Framework for Comprehensive Health Care Reform: Protecting Human Life, Promoting Human Dignity, Pursuing the Common*, the US bishops highlighted this position with these four points:

1. Universal health care must be a truly universal health policy with respect for human life and dignity.

2. Universal health care must be accessible for all with a special concern for the poor and inclusion of immigrants.

3. Universal health care must respect the common good and preserve pluralism, including freedom of conscience and variety of options.

4. Universal health care must restrain costs and apply them equitably across the spectrum of payers.

Use the document (http://usccb.org/sdwp/national/comphealth.shtml) and other resources at the USCCB site (http://usccb.org/healthcare/index.shtml) to develop a ten- to fifteen-minute presentation that provides a basic overview of the four points above. Also cite current news events that help to explain each issue. For example, related to the access to health care of the poor and inclusion of immigrants, anecdotally share a recent news story where this issue came to the forefront because an individual or family was denied care. Organize your coverage of each of the points around the following structure:

1. A synopsis of the point including the teaching of the Bishops

2. A current news story that illustrates the importance of the issue

    Plan to share your presentation with your classmates.

    Optional: Choose one of the four issues above and develop a more substantial presentation that addresses the issue in more detail.

3. Oral Presentation: New Evangelization

All Catholics share in the aspect of the Church's apostolic mission of being sent out in the world to share the Good News in various ways. It is the task of all Catholics to share the Good News of Jesus Christ to the ends of the earth. Outline a plan for participating in the new evangelization by doing the following:

1. Read St. John Paul II's Apostolic Letter *Novo Millennio Ineute* at the Vatican website.

2. Create a reading model to outline one of the pastoral priorities named in Part III, "Starting Afresh in Christ." Begin by selecting one of the priorities.

3. Set up an organizer like the one below that (1) lists the priority you have chosen; (2) summarizes St. John Paul II's teaching on the priority; (3) shares how the priority is being enacted in your local parish or community today; and (4) tells how you can personally enact the priority in your life. The organizer should look like this:

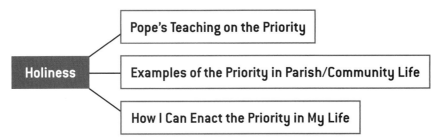

(For more information on the new evangelization, read Joseph Cardinal Ratzinger's (Pope Benedict XVI) address to catechists titled "The New Evangelization: Building the Civilization of Love" (December 12, 2000). Also watch Fr. Robert Barron's November 2010 video presentation on the new evangelization.)

Faithful Disciple

Dorothy Day

Dorothy Day is a modern example of living out the Church's social teaching. Like many other holy people in the Church, before her conversion Dorothy lived a rather wild life.

Dorothy Day was born in Brooklyn in 1897, and was raised in Chicago. Once while in the home of a young Catholic friend she happened to see her friend's mother on her knees in prayer through the bedroom doorway. That image stayed with Dorothy for a lifetime.

Dorothy began her career as a journalist, but she always had an eye for social issues and ways to help those in need. She belonged to the communist party at one point.

Dorothy's personal life was filled with wandering and regret. She lived at different times with several different men out of wedlock. She ended one pregnancy with an abortion. Later, after the birth of her daughter, Tamar, she began to be attracted to the Catholic Church. Soon after, in 1927, she and her daughter were both baptized and she broke off the relationship with her common-law husband.

When writing for the Catholic magazine *Commonweal* Dorothy met a former Christian Brother and social activist named Peter Maurin. With his encouragement, Dorothy started her own newspaper called *The Catholic Worker*. The newspaper, which sold then (and now) for one cent, addressed the contemporary social problems in light of Catholic social teaching.

People who read the newspaper began to come to Dorothy and Peter for further support. Dorothy opened her home to those in need, first women and later men. She eventually established Catholic Worker homes, places where those "down on their luck" or suffering from alcoholism or other emotional ailments could find support and refuge. By 1936 there were thirty-three houses across the country. Those who staffed the houses were given room and board but little else. Unlike other halfway houses, there was no time limit for guests of a Catholic Worker house. The homeless were treated as family.

The Catholic Worker movement continued to spread, preaching nonviolence and pacifism as the core of social change. Dorothy Day spoke out against every war from World War II through Vietnam. Her views made her unpopular in many circles. The newspaper lost readers and many Catholic Worker houses closed because the volunteers did not agree with her views.

Dorothy once wrote, "The mystery of poverty is that by sharing in it, making ourselves poor in giving to others, we increase our knowledge of and belief in love." She continued her ministry through Catholic Worker until her death in 1980. In 2000 the Vatican opened Dorothy Day's "cause," the first step to beatification and canonization.

Reading Comprehension

1. What was an image from Dorothy's childhood that became a catalyst for Faith?

2. Who was Peter Maurin?

3. What led to many of the Catholic Worker houses closing for a time?

4. When did the Vatican begin Dorothy's cause for beatification and canonization?

Writing Task

- Write a three-sentence description of Dorothy Day's life that uses these three words: *conversion*, *pacifism*, and *justice*.

Explaining the Faith
What is the best way for a teenager to spread the Catholic Faith?

The Catechism of the Catholic Church teaches that evangelization is simply "the proclamation of Christ by word and the testimony of life" (*CCC*, 905). Certainly a teenager and any Catholic should be willing to share in words the importance of their Faith in Jesus Christ for your life. But perhaps the best way for a teenager to evangelize is through the testimony or good example of his or her life. This entails living a life of virtue, justice, and love toward everyone.

Jesus said in the Sermon on the Mount that his followers were to be salt of the earth and light of the world. Just like salt preserves meat or adds flavor to food, a Catholic's acts of love help Jesus' saving deeds tough lives and change the world for the better. Just as light illuminates the way in the dark, the Catholic who lets Christ shine through him or her is like a beacon pointing to Heaven. Jesus is the Way, the Truth, and the Life. Non-believers learn about Jesus from those who live Christ-like lives and who can point to Jesus, the Savior.

Further Research

- Read Matthew 5: 14–16 with an accompanying commentary. How do Jesus' words "A city set on a mountain cannot be hidden" connect with the imperative to spread the Faith?

Prayer

For Justice and Peace

Almighty and eternal God,

may your grace enkindle in all of us

a love for the many unfortunate people whom poverty

   and misery reduce to a condition of life unworthy of human beings.

Arouse in the hearts of those who call you Father

a hunger and thirst for justice and peace, and for fraternal charity

   in deeds and truth.

Grant, O Lord, peace in our days,

peace to souls, peace to families, peace to our country,

and peace among nations.

Amen.

—Pope Pius XII

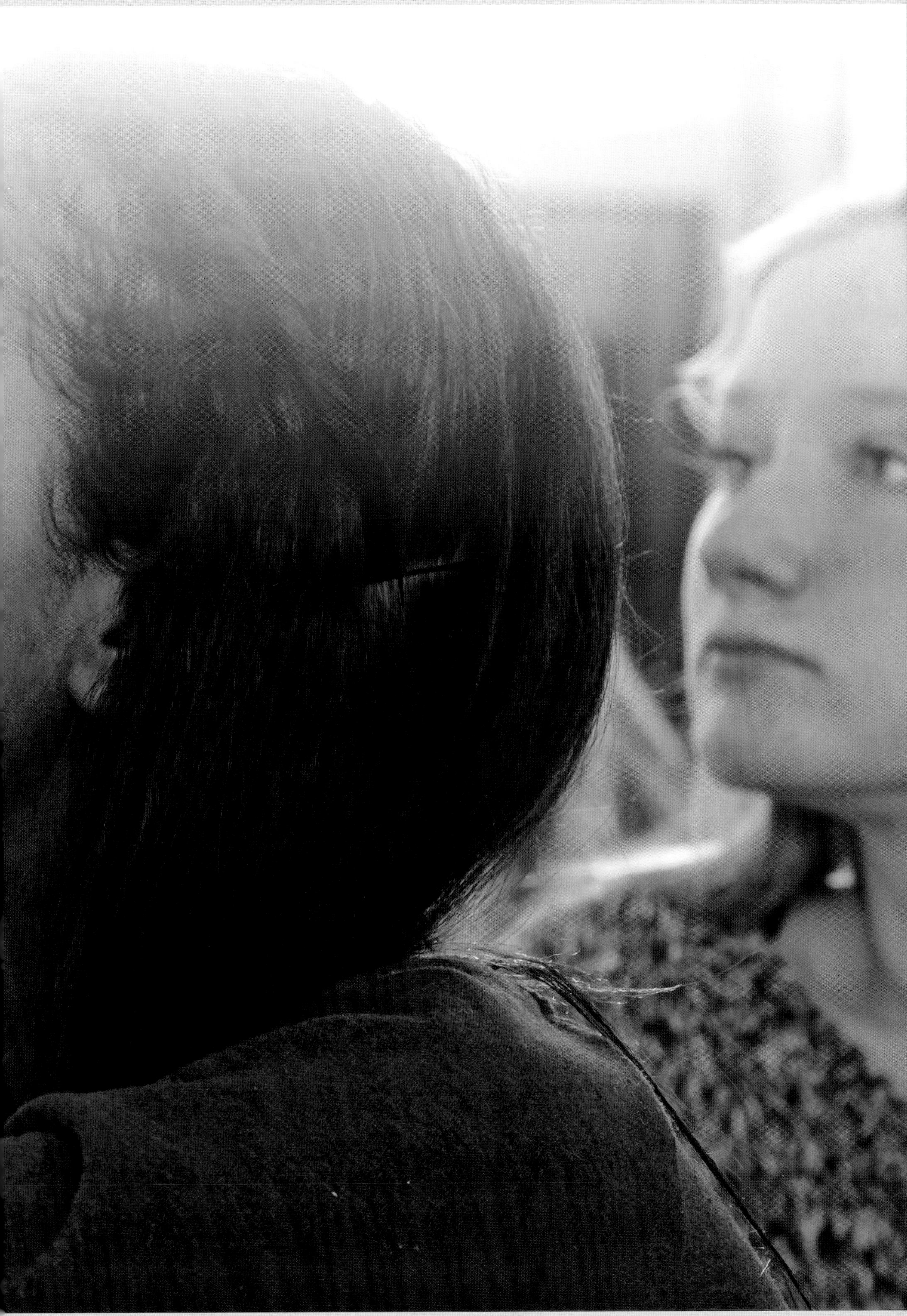

The Nicene Creed

I believe in one God, the Father almighty,
   maker of heaven and earth,
   of all things visible and invisible.

I believe in one Lord Jesus Christ,
      the Only Begotten Son of God,
      born of the Father before all ages.
   God from God, Light from Light,
      true God from true God,
   begotten, not made, consubstantial
      with the Father;
      Through him all things were made.
   For us men and for our salvation
      he came down from heaven,
      and by the Holy Spirit was incarnate
      of the Virgin Mary,
      and became man.
   For our sake he was crucified
      under Pontius Pilate,
      he suffered death and was buried,
      and rose again on the third day
      in accordance with the Scriptures.
   He ascended into heaven
      and is seated at the right hand of the Father.
   He will come again in glory
      to judge the living and the dead
      and his kingdom will have no end.

I believe in the Holy Spirit,
      the Lord, the giver of life,
   who proceeds from the Father and the Son,
   who with the Father and the Son
   is adored and glorified,
      who has spoken through the prophets.

I believe in one, holy, catholic,
      and apostolic Church.
   I confess one baptism for the forgiveness of sins
         and I look forward to the resurrection
         of the dead and the life of the world to come.
Amen.

The Apostles' Creed

I believe in God,
the Father almighty,
Creator of heaven and earth,
and in Jesus Christ, his only Son, our Lord,
who was conceived by the Holy Spirit,
born of the Virgin Mary,
suffered under Pontius Pilate,
was crucified, died and was buried;
he descended into hell;
on the third day he rose again from the dead;
he ascended into heaven,
and is seated at the right hand of God the Father
   almighty;
from there he will come to judge the living and the dead.

I believe in the Holy Spirit,
the holy catholic Church,
the communion of saints,
the forgiveness of sins,
the resurrection of the body,
and life everlasting. Amen.

A Timeline of Church History

"The world was created for the sake of the Church."
—attributed to Christians of the first century

The Early Church (AD 33–early fourth century)

Following the events of the Paschal Mystery, the Life, suffering, Death, Resurrection and Ascension of Christ, the Apostles awaited the fulfillment of his promise to send them an Advocate. That promise was fulfilled on Pentecost. From that day forward, the Apostles took up Jesus' command to "go and make disciples of all nations" (Mt 28:19). Thus began the development and growth of the young Church in the Roman Empire.

Pentecost, 33

During the Feast of Weeks, the Apostles and Mary were gathered in a small upper room of a house in Jerusalem. The Holy Spirit came down upon them, giving the Apostles the grace to begin their preaching ministry.

Martyrdom of Stephen, 34

Stephen, a deacon, was stoned to death by an angry mob that included Saul, later to become St. Paul.

Conversion of St. Paul, 35

Paul, previously known as Saul, was a persecutor of Christians. After his conversion, following an encounter with Christ, he became one of the early Church's greatest missionaries, traveling throughout the Roman Empire to establish and provide support to church communities.

The Council of Jerusalem, 49

At this meeting, the leaders of the Church decreed that Gentiles can be baptized into the Church, and are not subject to Jewish regulations regarding circumcision and dietary laws. This decision contributed to the rapid growth of Christianity throughout the Roman Empire.

St. Peter emerges as the bishop of Rome, ca. 55

Because the Church of Rome had primacy among the other centers of Christianity, St. Peter had primacy over the other bishops. Rome became the see (from the Latin *sedes*, or "seat") of Peter, and therefore the seat of the Church.

The Gospels are written, 62–100

Mark's Gospel is believed to be the first written, between 65 and 70. John's Gospel is believed to be the last written, around 90–100. A number of Paul's letters are believed to have been written before the Gospels, around 50–60.

Persecution of Christians begins under Emperor Nero, 64

When a fire destroyed Rome, Nero, who is believed to have set the fire himself, blamed Christians, inciting mass persecutions. Both Sts. Peter and Paul were martyred during this time (Peter in 64 and Paul in 67).

Destruction of the Temple in Jerusalem, 70

In AD 70, the Roman army conquered Jerusalem and destroyed the Temple.

The Didache is written, ca. 100

Written anonymously, the *Didache* was a pastoral manual of teachings and practices. Lost in the early centuries of the Church, this document was rediscovered in 1873.

The canon of the New Testament is established, early second century

Under the guidance of the Holy Spirit, the leaders of the early Church discerned the official canon of the New Testament, recognizing that the authors of the sacred books were inspired by the Holy Spirit and that the writings were apostolic—that is, based on the teaching of the Apostles or their closest disciples. The Councils of Hippo (393) and the Council of Carthage (397) were instrumental in forming the canon of Sacred Scripture for both the Old and New Testaments.

The Gnostic heresy emerges, early second century

Gnostics denied the goodness of the created world and claimed that only a select few can have the knowledge needed for Salvation, St. Irenaeus (ca. 130–200), bishop of Lyons, responded with his *Against Heresies*, a treatise comprised of five books.

Tertullian (ca. 160–220) and other apologists explain the faith, second–early third centuries

The early apologists were writers who defended and explained Christianity to non-believers. Tertullian was the first of the apologists to write in Latin. He defended Christianity against charges of immorality and subversion. St. Justin Martyr (ca. 100–165) also made a great contribution. His writings include his *First Apology* and *Second Apology*. He also wrote extensively about the Eucharist.

Waves of persecution of Christians continue in the Empire, through the third century

Persecutions were carried out under various emperors, including Domitian (AD 91–96), Hadrian (117–138), and Marcus Aurelius (161–180). Christianity was often punishable by death. Perhaps the most severe persecutions took place under the Emperor Diocletian (284–305), whose aim was to uproot Christianity from the Empire.

The monastic movement is established, third century

The founding of Christian monasticism is traditionally attributed to St. Anthony of the Desert (251–356). Around age twenty, Anthony withdrew from society and went to live as a hermit in the desert. His way of life attracted many followers. Around 320, Pachomius, one of Anthony's contemporaries, organized the first monastery.

Edict of Milan establishes toleration for Christianity, 313

In 312, Constantine became Roman emperor, following a battle victory that also led to his conversion. In 313, shortly after assuming power, Constantine and his eastern counterpart, Licinius, issued the *Edict of Milan*, a decree that proclaimed religious toleration in the empire and legalized Christianity. As a result, Christian worship became public, and Christian missionaries could preach the Faith without fear of retribution.

The Arian controversy begins, 315

Arianism, a teaching promoted by Bishop Arius of Alexandria (ca. 250–336), denied Christ's divine nature, and therefore his power to redeem us. This heresy posed one of the first major threats to the Church's doctrine.

Emperor Constantine commissions the construction of the Basilica of St. Peter in Rome, ca. 318

Pope Sylvester I consecrated the basilica in 326.

Emperor Constantine defeats Emperor Licinius and becomes the sole Roman Emperor, 324

Constantine moved the seat of government from Rome to Byzantium, in what is today Istanbul, Turkey, renaming it Constantinople. The empire now had two centers of power, Rome and Constantinople. Different styles of celebrating the sacraments and the liturgy, as well as different styles of church architecture, emerged in each.

Age of the Fathers (early fourth century–sixth century)

With the Edict of Milan, *Christianity could be practiced and witnessed too publicly. The Church continued to grow and thrive in this new environment, it also faced new threats from within: heresies promulgated by bishops and other leaders. Church Fathers, such as St. Jerome and St. Augustine, and ecumenical councils played an essential role in defending the Church's doctrine.*

Constantine convenes the Council of Nicaea, 325

To respond to the teachings of Arius, Constantine convened the Church's first ecumenical council in Nicaea. The bishops developed the Nicene Creed in response to the Arian heresy.

Council of Constantinople, 381

Because the Council of Nicaea had not clarified the nature of the Holy Spirit, this became a new source of division within the Church. This council firmly affirmed the divinity of the Holy Spirit.

Conversion of St. Augustine, 387

Before his conversion, Augustine lived a life of dissipation. Following his conversion, he became one of the most important Church Fathers. He was the bishop of Hippo, in modern-day Algeria. His writings, which include *City of God* and *Confessions*, continue to influence Christian thought.

Publication of St. Jerome's Latin translation of the Bible, 400

In 382, Pope Damasus I commissioned St. Jerome to begin a Latin translation of Scripture from its original Hebrew and Greek. His translation became known as the Vulgate, the Church's official version of Scripture.

Council of Ephesus, 431

This third ecumenical council was convened by the emperor Theodosius II. The council reaffirmed that Jesus is both God and man and that Mary is *Theotokos*, that is, "God bearer" or the Mother of God.

Council of Chalcedon, 451

In response to the heresy of Monophysitim, which said that Jesus' human nature was lost in his divine nature, this council declared Christ's two natures as undivided, unchangeable, and inseparable.

Pope St. Leo the Great halts the attack of Attila the Hun, 452

Pope Leo took the title *Pontifex Maximus*, meaning "chief bishop." In 452, at the request of the Roman emperor, Pope Leo intervened to make peace with Attila the Hun, who was threatening to invade Rome.

Fall of the Roman Empire in the West, 476

After decades of continuing invasions and decline, the Western Roman Empire collapsed in 476, when the emperor was deposed by a barbarian chieftain. In the leadership void that resulted, popes began to fill leadership roles in the civil sphere, and the Church often provided for citizens' basic needs.

Early Middle Ages (Dark Ages) (476–1000)

With the fall of the Roman Empire in the West, Europe faced an authority vacuum, weakened civil rulers, and an absence of services to meet the needs of citizens. The Church stepped in to fill the void, and frequently brought order to the chaos.

St. Benedict of Nursia establishes monastery at Monte Cassino, 528

St. Benedict (480–550), who has come to be known as the Father of Western Monasticism,  established a monastery at Monte Cassino and developed a rule for monasticism that emphasized prayer and work ("*ora et labora*"). Eventually a group of women, led by St. Scholastica (Benedict's twin sister), also formed a monastic community not far from Monte Cassino.

Pope St. Gregory the Great introduces key reforms and sponsors missions to Great Britain, 590–604

St. Gregory, a Doctor of the Church, developed a system for providing charitable aid to the poor, oversaw the development of seminaries, and introduced liturgical reforms that still influence the Church's liturgical celebrations. He is also remembered for sponsoring missions to Great Britain, as well as for the development of an unaccompanied style of liturgical singing, known Gregorian chant.

St. Augustine of Canterbury evangelizes Great Britain, 596–604

Sent by St. Gregory the Great to evangelize the Anglos and Saxons, this Benedictine monk is credited with the Christianization of England. His missionary work resulted in the baptism of thousands. He became the first Archbishop of Canterbury.

The development of Islam and Islamic conquests of Christian lands, seventh century

Early in the seventh century Islam was founded by Mohammed and established as the religion of the Arabian Peninsula. A Muslim army was established and marched eastward and westward, conquering many previously Christian areas. The first major cities to fall were Damascus and Antioch (636 and 637) in Syria, followed by Jerusalem (638) and Alexandria (642). In 711, Muslim armies invaded the Iberian Peninsula.

St. Boniface evangelizes the Germans, 716–718

Known as the Apostle of the Germans, St. Boniface is credited with bringing Christianity to the Frankish Empire, in present-day Germany.

Iconoclasm Controversy begins, 730

When Byzantine Emperor Leo III gave orders to remove an image of Christ at the Palace of Constantinople, the removal of all holy images in Eastern Church ensued. This conflict between those who venerated holy images, or icons, and those who opposed them was resolved by the Second Council of Nicaea in 787.

The Battle of Tours, 732

In this key battle Charles Martel, the king of the Franks, defeated Muslim invaders, halting their expansion in Europe. Although most of the Iberian Peninsula was by then under Muslim control, the Christian identity of lands north of the Pyrenees Mountains was preserved.

Venerable Bede writes *Ecclesiastical History of the English People*, 731

In the *Ecclesiastical History of the English People*, Bede demonstrated the growth and history of the Catholic Church in Great Britain.

Founding of the Papal States, 756

In 751, Pepin, son of Charles Martel, became king of the Franks, beginning the Carolingian Dynasty. In 756, in the Donation of Pepin, he gave Pope Stephen II control over the middle regions of Italy, establishing the Papal States, which existed until 1870.

Charlemagne is crowned Holy Roman Emperor, 800

Charlemagne, Pepin's son, became king in 771. He engaged in military campaigns throughout Europe and created a vast empire. On Christmas Day in 800, Pope Leo III crowned him Holy Roman Emperor, cementing the alliance between the crown and the Church. Charlemagne believed he ruled by divine right and actively involved himself in Church affairs. His crowning as Holy Roman Emperor increased tensions between East and West.

Sts. Cyril and Methodius begin evangelizing the Slavic peoples, 862

Cyril and Methodius developed the Glagolitic alphabet, a predecessor of the Cyrillic alphabet still used today, and translated the Bible into Slavonic. Known as the "Apostles to the Slavs," they successfully evangelized the Slavic people.

The monastery at Cluny is founded, 909

This monastery in Cluny, France, became a fountainhead for monastic and eventually Church reform. It was free of corrupt control of lords and bishops. It had free elections of abbots and was answerable only to the pope. The Cluniac reform spread throughout France, Italy, Spain, and England.

High Middle Ages (1000–1300)

The High Middles Ages, beginning around AD 1000, was a period of intense activity in European society and in the Church. Key developments for the Church include the founding of the university system, the development of Gothic architecture, and the birth of new religious orders.

Muslims destroy the Church of the Holy Sepulchre in Jerusalem, 1009

The Holy Sepulchre, long believed to have been built over Jesus' burial place, was destroyed. This act of vengeance and desecration fueled the call for a crusade to retake the Holy Land.

The Great Schism, 1054

Following centuries of growing differences and tensions over doctrine, liturgical practices, and politics, the Churches of East and West issued a mutual excommunication. In 1976, Pope Paul VI and Patriarch Athenagorus I lifted the excommunication. Ecumenical efforts continue, in the hope that one day the two Churches will be united.

The University of Bologna is founded, 1088

This was followed by the University of Paris (1150) and the University of Oxford (1167). By the start of the fourteenth century more than eighty universities had been established in Europe.

The First Crusade, 1096–1099

In 1073, Seljuk Turks had conquered Palestine and began a campaign of persecution of Christian pilgrims to the Holy Land. In 1095, Pope Urban II called for a crusade to reclaim the Holy Land from Muslims. A series of major and minor crusades followed. Militarily, the Crusades were of limited success. Jerusalem and Asia Minor ultimately remained under Muslim control. A positive consequence of the Crusades was the exchange of ideas, scholarship, and scientific advances between East and West.

Concordat of Worms, 1122

Especially beginning in the eleventh century, some bishops had become subservient to secular leaders, leading to the practice of lay investiture, in which secular leaders appointed bishops throughout their domains. The Concordat of Worms established the pope's authority to appoint bishop and abbot and invest them with spiritual authority. The emperor, in turn, was responsible for temporal rule.

Murder of St. Thomas Beckett, 1170

For refusing to cooperate with England's King Henry II's attempts to gain control of the Church courts, St. Thomas was murdered in Canterbury Cathedral.

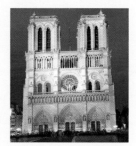

Development of Gothic architecture, beginning in eleventh century

Magnificent cathedrals and abbey churches built between 1000 and 1400 symbolize the spirit and grandeur of the medieval Church. Each cathedral contained the bishop's *cathedra* (chair), symbolizing his teaching authority and power. Notre Dame Cathedral in Paris, constructed in the Gothic style, was constructed over two centuries, from 1163 to 1345.

Fourth Lateran Council, 1215

Among other decrees, this ecumenical council defined *transubstantiation*, the transformation of the bread and wine into the Body and Blood of Christ during the consecration at Mass.

Founding of mendicant orders, early thirteenth century

With the decline of feudalism, mendicant or "begging," orders emerged to serve the Church by witnessing to simple Gospel values. The Carmelites and Augustinians began at this time, but the two most important new orders were the Dominicans, founded by St. Dominic (1170–1221), and the Franciscans, founded by St. Francis of Assisi (1181–1226). St. Clare of Assisi (1194–1253), a friend of St. Francis, left her rich family to found an order of religious women known as the Poor Clares.

The Medieval Inquisition begins, 1231

In response to the development of several heretical groups, Pope Gregory IX established this inquisition (also known as the Papal Inquisition). Inquisitors served as investigators and judges. Some found guilty of heresy were condemned to death. Most sentences were "canonical" penances, such as fasting and making pilgrimages.

St. Thomas Aquinas writes the *Summa Theologiae*, 1265–1274

In this treatise, St. Thomas Aquinas makes an argument for the existence of God, and clarifies how we can know God through human reason. The *Summa*, a twenty-one-volume work, remains one of the greatest works of theology and philosophy.

Late Middle Ages (1300–1450)

Although this was a period of continued growth and developments, the period was also marked by strife and suffering, most notably resulting from the Black Death.

The Avignon Papacy, 1309–1377

In 1309, Pope Clement moved the Church's headquarters from Rome to Avignon, in France, where it remained for nearly seventy years. Seven popes lived there, until Gregory XI returned to Rome.

The Black Death strikes Europe, 1348

This epidemic of bubonic plague is estimated to have killed more than a third of Europe's population. The plague permeated the medieval mindset. Because of the constant presence of death, the Sacrament of Penance came to dominate a great deal of the Catholic experience.

The Western Schism, 1378–1418

When Pope Gregory XI died in 1378, French cardinals deposed the newly elected Pope Urban VI. They elected a new pope, known as an antipope, to replace him. Named Clement VII, the antipope reestablished the papal court at Avignon. The conflict continued for nearly forty years, with two or rival claimants to the papacy at times. The conflict was resolved at the Council of Constance (1414–1418).

St. Joan of Arc is burned at the stake, 1431

A peasant girl from France, Joan had visions of God telling her to lead her nation to reclaim their land in a victory over England. She led her troops to a number of victories, but at age nineteen she was captured by the English and burned at the stake as a heretic. Twenty-five years later, Pope Callixtus III declared her a martyr.

Invention of the printing press, 1440

Johanne Gutenberg's invention of a printing press that used moveable type revolutionized the way information was disseminated, and its availability to the masses.

Renaissance and Reformation (1450–1650)

During the Middle Ages, society was ordered around religion and the Church. In the fifteenth century, focus began to turn to human achievement, often expressed through art.

The Spanish Inquisition is established, 1478

Queen Isabella and King Ferdinand established an inquisition to ensure conformity to Catholicism. In 1492 a decree was passed requiring all Jews and Muslims to convert or leave Spain.

Construction begins on a new Basilica of St. Peter, 1506

Begun under the direction of Pope Julius II, St. Peter's is built over the next two centuries. In 1508, Michelangelo  starts painting the ceiling of the Sistine Chapel.

Spanish colonizers arrive in South America and Mexico, early fifteenth century

As Spanish explorers arrived in the New World, they set out to conquer the natives—Aztecs in Mexico and Incas in South America. The explorers often brought Catholic missionaries with them. Along with working to convert and baptize the native peoples, the missionaries often also became their advocates and defenders. In the Americas, Bishop Bartolomé de las Casas (1474–1566), a Dominican friar, worked for the rights of native people of the West Indies and other conquered territories. St. Peter Claver (1581–1654) ministered to the slaves in Colombia and the West Indies. St. Martin de Porres (1579–1639) did the same in Peru.

Martin Luther posts his Ninety-Five Theses on a church door in Wittenberg, Germany, 1517

Although Luther had not intended to start a movement, the posting of the ninety-five theses became the spark that ignited the Protestant Reformation. One of Luther's chief complaints was against the practice of selling indulgences. Initially, he intended to engage Church leaders in examining the issues. When the Church was slow to respond, Luther broke with the Church. Luther advocated Scripture over Tradition, the priesthood of the laity, and the doctrine of justification by faith alone. He criticized the papacy and taught that there were only two valid sacraments: Baptism and Eucharist. Luther was excommunicated.

Christianity in Europe further splits into different branches, sixteenth century

After Lutheranism is formally established (1530), other protestors followed Luther. Ulrich Zwingli (1484–1531) established Protestantism in Switzerland, where he encouraged a church with democratic rule. John Calvin (1509–1564), known for the doctrine of *predestination*, developed his own version of Protestantism, known as Calvinism. John Knox (1514–1572) brought Presbyterianism, a brand of Calvinism, to England.

King Henry VIII breaks with the Church, 1534

The Protestant Reformation came to England not over a doctrinal dispute but because the pope would not allow King Henry VIII to divorce his wife, Catherine of Aragon. In response, Henry declared himself head of the church in England, through Parliament's Act of Supremacy. He dissolved all monasteries in England and seized all Church property. He also required an oath of allegiance to himself. A few Catholics refused this oath, most notably St. John Fisher and St. Thomas More, both of whom were beheaded for the offense, in 1535.

Society of Jesus (the Jesuits) is founded, 1534

St. Ignatius of Loyola (1491–1556) founded the Society of Jesus. Along with the traditional religious vows of poverty, chastity, and obedience, the Jesuits took a fourth vow: obedience to the pope.

Our Lady of Guadalupe appears to Juan Diego, 1531

The Blessed Mother appeared to an Aztec peasant in Mexico. As a miraculous sign, Mary's image was imprinted on his cloak. A church was built in her honor. As word of the apparitions and miracle spread, millions of Mexicans were baptized.

The Council of Trent, 1545–1563

This council was the Church's response to the Protestant reformers. The council reaffirmed Church teaching on papal supremacy, the doctrine of transubstantiation, the sacrifice of the Mass, the Sacrament of Penance as the normal means of forgiveness for sin committed after Baptism, the number of sacraments, and the necessity of both faith and good works for Salvation.

Missionaries arrive in the Far East, sixteenth–seventeenth centuries

The greatest missionary to the Far East was Jesuit St. Francis Xavier (1506–1552), who brought Christianity to India and Japan. Another Jesuit, Matteo Ricci S.J. (1552–1610), is credited with helping the Gospel take root in China.

St. Teresa of Ávila writes her spiritual masterpiece, *The Interior Castle*, 1577

St. Teresa of Ávila also undertook important reforms of her religious order, the Carmelites.

St. Isaac Jogues and his companions are martyred, 1646

Eight Jesuit missionaries to the native populations of North America are killed by Mohawk Indians in what is now upstate New York.

The Age of Reason (seventeenth and eighteenth centuries)

Also known as the Enlightenment, this period saw the rise of philosophers and scholars who denounced religion and the Church and encouraged a view that only human reason, separated from religious belief, can provide truth.

The rise of rationalism and empiricism, 1700s

Empiricist and rationalist philosophers posited that all knowledge could come from science and human experience, and rejected beliefs based on faith.

Junípero Serra establishes the first California missions, 1769

Franciscan missionary Serra established the first nine of California's thirty-one missions.

John Carroll becomes America's first bishop, 1789

Among Carroll's achievements were the establishment of the first seminary in America and the founding of Georgetown University.

The French Revolution, 1789

Along with anger at the monarchy, revolutionary leaders called for sweeping changes for the Church in France. Church property was nationalized, religious men and women were forced out of their convents, and laws were passed prohibiting the taking of religious vows. Nearly forty thousand priests were forced into exile, and many were killed.

The Modern Era (nineteenth century through present)

In society, this period is marked by dramatic social and economic changes, as well as two world wars. These events in turn resulted in changes in the way the Church interacts with the world.

The Church in America grows through immigration, nineteenth and twentieth centuries

The first wave of Irish immigrants to the United States took place between 1830 and 1860, increasing the Catholic population in America by 800 percent. The Irish wave was followed by an influx of German Catholics (1860–1890), and Italian and eastern Europeans (1890–1920). Over two million Catholics immigrated to the United States in the first decade of the twentieth century. In the nineteenth century, Catholic immigrants in America faced prejudice. The Know-Nothing party questioned the patriotism of Catholics. The Ku Klux Klan, a nativist group, targeted African Americans and also Catholics.

Dogma of the Immaculate Conception, 1854

Pope Pius IX declared dogmatically that Mary was conceived without sin and remained free of sin all her life.

Lourdes apparitions, 1858

The Blessed Mother appeared to St. Bernadette Soubirous (1844–1879) in Lourdes, France, under the title of the Immaculate Conception.

Loss of Papal States, 1870

When Italy was unified in 1861, most of the Papal States were seized from the Church. The last Church territory was claimed by Italy in 1870.

First Vatican Council, 1869–1870

Pope Pius IX convened Vatican I, the twentieth ecumenical council, to affirm papal authority in spiritual matters. The Council defined the doctrine of papal infallibility, which says that the pope is preserved from error when teaching *ex cathedra* on matters of Faith and morals.

Pope Leo XIII releases *Rerum Novarum* ("On the Condition of Workers"), 1891

In response to the labor conditions and economic inequality caused by the Industrial Revolution, Pope Leo XIII issued the first modern social encyclical. *Rerum Novarum* formed the early framework for Catholic social teaching.

Our Lady of Fatima apparitions, 1917

From May to October, Our Lady appeared to three peasant children in Fatima, Portugal.

St. Pius X permits First Communion at the age of reason, rather than at age twelve, 1910

The pope also encouraged frequent reception of Holy Communion and the Sacrament of Penance.

Codification of canon law, 1917

St. Pius X commissioned the revision and codification of canon law, or Church law. The work was completed under his successor, Pope Benedict XV. For the first time, Church law was gathered in a single volume.

Lateran Treaty establishes Vatican City, 1929

A treaty signed by Benito Mussolini and Cardinal Gasparri established the independent state of Vatican City. Vatican City is the smallest sovereign state in the world.

The Church Responds to World War II (1939–1945)

In response to the suffering, death, and mass atrocities carried out by the Nazis during the Second World War, Pope Pius XII (1939–1958) worked, often behind the scenes, to save the lives of thousands of Jews. The Vatican also used diplomacy to encourage an end to the global conflict.

Second Vatican Council, 1962–1965

St. John XXIII (1958–1963) convened the Church's twenty-first ecumenical council. The council enacted many changes, including the change of the celebration of the liturgy from Latin to the vernacular, or local languages. The council issued sixteen documents, mainly treating the Church, her inner workings, and her relationship to the world. St. Pope John XXIII died before the end of the Council, which was closed by Pope Paul VI (1963–1978).

St. John Paul II elected pope, 1978

Karol Józef Wojtyła became the first Polish pope and the first non-Italian pope in 450 years. Not long after his election he was the victim of an assassination attempt. He played an important part in the fall of Communism in Eastern Europe, especially in his native Poland, where he encouraged workers to stand up for their rights and supported a worker's movement known as Solidarity. On his death in April 2005, millions of pilgrims traveled to Rome to pray and pay their respects. He was declared a saint by Pope Francis in April 2014.

First World Youth Day is held, 1986

St. John Paul II instituted World Youth Day. Since 1986, World Youth Day has been held every two to three years in countries around the world, with attendance in the millions.

Publication of the *Catechism of the Catholic Church*, 1992

Commissioned by St. John Paul II, the *Catechism* became the official Catechism of the universal Church.

Bl. Mother Teresa dies, 1997

Mother Teresa began her work of service to the poor and dying in the streets of Calcutta, India. She founded the Missionaries of Charity. The religious order now numbers in the thousands and serves in all part of the world. Mother Teresa was declared blessed by St. John Paul II in 2003.

US Bishops issue the *Charter for the Protection of Children and Young People*, 2001

After years of investigation, the full body of Catholic bishops of the United States approved the charter as a response to cases of sex abuse committed by members of Church leadership against minors.

Luminous Mysteries to the Rosary, 2002

St. John Paul II added the Luminous Mysteries, or the Mysteries of Light, to the Rosary, bringing the total of mysteries to twenty.

Election of Pope Benedict XVI, 2005

Cardinal Joseph Ratzinger of Germany elected to the Chair of Peter following the death of St. John Paul II. He called for a new evangelization, to bring the Gospel to those who have lost their faith in the increasing secularization of the modern world.

Kateri Tekakwitha canonized, 2012

St. Kateri (1656–1680), known as the "Lily of the Mohawks," became the first Native American saint.

Resignation of Pope Benedict XVI, February 28, 2013

Pope Benedict became the first pope to resign his office since Pope Gregory XII in 1415.

Pope Francis is elected, March 13, 2013

Cardinal Jorge Mario Bergoglio of Buenos Aires, Argentina, became the first pope from the Americas. He is also the first Jesuit pope.

The thirteenth World Youth Day is held in Rio de Janiero, Brazil, August 2013

The 2013 World Youth Day marked the first missionary trip of Pope Francis since being elected pope. More than three million pilgrims attended.

The Sacraments: Witness through Words and Deeds

Catholics encounter Christ in the Church in a real way through the Seven Sacraments. In the thirteenth century, St. Thomas Aquinas pointed out that it was reasonable for Christ to institute exactly Seven Sacraments because human development is likewise marked by a similar seven stages. Consider these profiles of contemporary Catholics at different stages of life.

We Are Born (Baptism)

Kristen and Mike Morin's four children all attended St. Joseph Grade School in South Bend, Indiana—just as their mother, grandparents, and great-grandmother, who graduated in 1924, had done.

In 2007, while watching the *American Idol* special "Idol Gives Back" that highlighted dire conditions in Africa, the Morins were both grateful for their own blessings and also moved to give back themselves to make life better for others. In 2009 with all four of their children in tow, Kristen and Mike traveled to Ethiopia to pick up two new siblings, six-year-old Geta and two-year-old Tamene.

Geta and Tamene were baptized at St. Joseph's Church in August 2009. The older Morin children wore clothes from Ethiopia to honor their new sister and brother's heritage. The Morins, with their large and diverse family, are easy to spot each Sunday morning at the St. Joe family Mass.

We Grow (Confirmation)

Ryan Markiewitz is the first member of his family to enter the Catholic Church. "I grew up in another denomination, drifted away, but always felt something was missing in my life. I realized it was religion." While in college at Elon University in North Carolina, Markiewitz "explored the Catholic Faith and fell in love with it." In April 2011 Markiewitz and twenty-one other college students from the Diocese of Raleigh's six college campus ministry programs were confirmed by Bishop Michael Burbidge at Sacred Heart Cathedral in Raleigh.

The bishop urged the newly confirmed to live out their Faith on campus and in society. He reminded them that Faith is often contradictory to popular culture. "You see the materialistic messages on your campuses that we can find happiness in the things we can accumulate. Not true," the bishop said in his homily. "Our lasting joy is found in only one way: saying 'yes' to the Lord, to God's way, to God's will."

We Are Fed (Eucharist)

Sonia, a junior at a Catholic high school in Miami, Florida, recently submitted a question in her third-period theology teacher's "question and answer" box. When the teacher, Mr. Hamman, opened it, this is what he found: "Why do Catholics put so much emphasis on the Mass?" Since Sonia signed her name, her teacher took some time to personally pen a response. It went like this:

Dear Sonia,

Great question. You could spend every minute of the rest of your life trying to learn about the meaning of the Mass and never know it all. May I suggest that you begin by examining words like *sacrifice, meal,* and *community* in connection with the Mass? Further, look at each of these issues in light of another idea: *God's presence* and *our presence* at Mass.

Take the difficult and seemingly two ways of understanding Jesus' sacrifice. What did Jesus "give up" by accepting the Cross? As he ate this last meal with his disciples, the awareness of the sacrifice must have been overwhelming for Jesus: within a few hours he would give up being physically present to his friends. I remember a couple of years ago when I moved 2,000 miles away from my parents and friends. The depth of what I was giving up by making this move really hit me as I spent my last night with my family. I was really going to miss being with them: seeing them, doing things with them–not to mention my mom's fried chicken. I was going to miss the experience of being involved in their lives in the next months and years. Jesus' sacrifice of giving up his life for us was contained at the Last Supper and is at every Mass since. (By the way, the *Catechism of the Catholic Church* offers a clear explanation of the sacrifice of the Eucharist. See paragraphs numbered 1362 to 1372.)

What could Jesus do to solve this longing to remain present to his friends—both those first disciples and all in future generations whom he would befriend? He could make sure that everyone had the same chance to share a meal with him. Hence the words: "Take and eat. Take and drink. This is my Body. This is my Blood." If you surveyed the general population about "what Catholics believe about the Mass" some would no doubt answer: *Catholics believe that Jesus is truly present there.* How so? Jesus is present in the priest who acts in his name, in the community you speak of, in the Gospel readings shared at Mass, and most especially in Eucharistic species which are his Body and Blood. I am always reminded of this after the Holy Thursday Mass as the altar is stripped and the Eucharistic species are moved to a place of repose. Everyone joins the procession. Why? To follow a plate of ordinary bread and a flask of ordinary wine symbols? Hardly. Jesus is with us. And we are with Jesus. I offer that this is a good starting point for you to not only study the importance of the Eucharist in your life and the lives of all Catholics, but to pray on the question as well.

Finally, one last thing: If you want another reason why the Mass is so important, how about Heaven? Take your cue from St. Pius X who said:

> The Mass is the shortest and safest way to heaven. There are others: innocence, but that is for little children; penance, but we are afraid of it; generous endurance of life, but when they come we weep and ask to be spared. The surest, easiest, and shortest way is the Eucharist.

All the best,
Mr. Hamman

We Are Healed (Penance)

Project Rachel is the name of the Church's healing ministry for those who have been involved in abortion. Its name is derived from Scripture:

> In Ramah is heard the sound of moaning,
>> Of bitter weeping!
>
> Rachel mourns her children,
>> She refuses to be consoled
>>
>> Because her children are no more.
>>
>> Thus says the Lord:
>
> Cease your cries of mourning,
>> Wipe the tears from your eyes.
>
> The sorrow you have shown shall have its reward . . .
>
> There is hope for your future. (Jer 31:15–16)

Project Rachel was founded in 1984 in the Archdiocese of Milwaukee by Vicki Thorn after a friend confided in her the pain she experienced following an abortion. "People always ask me if I get depressed hearing all the painful stories that I hear," Thorn shared. "I never do because I *know* that God will heal anyone who asks. No one has ever called me and said that healing didn't happen, if they opened their heart to the Lord."

There are now Project Rachel ministries in every corner of the world, helping women and men to find healing, forgiveness, and reconciliation after an abortion. St. John Paul II echoed: "The Father of mercies is ready to give you his forgiveness and his peace in the Sacrament of Reconciliation."

We Comfort and Care
(Anointing of the Sick)

Around the world the Catholic Church provides care for one out of every four people living with HIV. Through the AIDS Relief Project, the Catholic Relief Service helps provide lifesaving antiretroviral therapy to more than 130,000 people living with HIV in nine countries, more than 100,000 of whom are children. The project also provides care for an additional 216,000 people who do not yet require medication.

A particular example of how the Church offered care for those living with HIV occurred in Kenya where about ten percent of the nation's 33 million people are HIV positive. Only 25,000 of these have access to medication.

Sr. Florence, an Assumption Sister of Nairobi, was in the United States studying at Loyola University Chicago when she learned that Kenya had finally publicly recognized the presence of AIDS. She knew she had to be more involved. "I did not want to sit on the other side of the fence," she said.

Sr. Florence, a nominee for the Nobel Peace Prize, has since organized a staff of six and a group of twenty trained volunteers to provide temporary shelter, basic health care, community education, voluntary testing, and counseling and support for her agency, Upendo Village. In the rural area of Naivasha, people are coming out now. "There is hope. They have someone to hold with love. There's a feeling of support," said St. Florence.

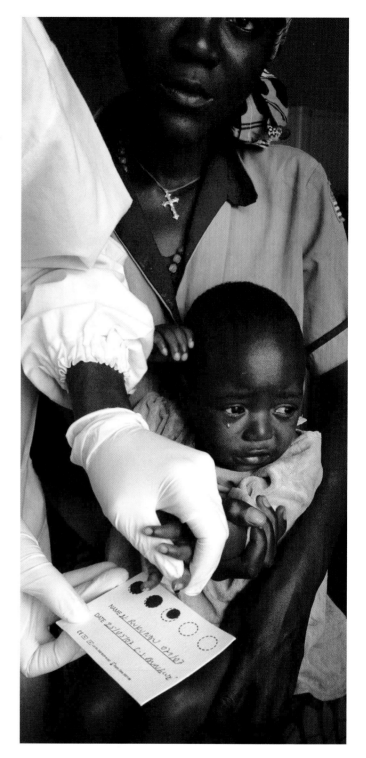

We Join Together (Matrimony)

Among several statistics on marriage in the United States compiled by the United States Catholic Conference of Bishops, one has remained constant over the past thirty years: roughly two-thirds of both married men and married women rate their marriages as "very happy." Other statistics related to marriage are not all positive; for example, the projected divorce rate still stands at around 50 percent. Catholics are less likely than Protestants to get divorced (25 percent to 39 percent). All studies point to couples who share a common religious affiliation having a better chance of making their marriages work.

Many single Catholics are opting to meet potential spouses through specifically Catholic online dating services. At one site, both men and women users are asked to answer single words or short phrases with one of two options: "Yes, I accept the Church's teaching" or "No, I do not." The seven topics are in the areas of the Eucharist, contraception, the sanctity of life, papal infallibility, premarital sex, the Immaculate Conception, and Holy Orders.

"The questions are a good part of the vetting process," said Brian Barcaro, one of the founders of a Catholic online dating site. "They help people find those who are like-minded in their Faith and in interest in their Faith."

Matthew Richards, who met his wife through an online dating service, appreciated the seven pointed questions. "It made the religious aspect a no brainer," he said. "It made the question, 'Do you want to go to church sometime?' much easier."

We Need and Respond to Others (Holy Orders)

Fr. Gregory Boyle, S.J., is the director of Jobs for a Future and Homeboy Industries, an employment referral center for at-risk youth and economic development programs in East Los Angeles. The area has the highest concentration of gang violence in Los Angeles. Within sixteen square miles, fifty gangs claim 16,000 members, both Hispanic and black.

"I've buried a lot of kids who were killed by kids I loved," Fr. Boyle said. "That's always hard to do. But I take what Jesus said seriously, which is that we should stand with those on the margins, with those whose dignity has been denied and with those whose burdens are more than they can bear."

The motto for Homeboy Industries, founded in 1992, is "nothing stops a bullet like a job." Homeboy Industries sponsors business enterprises, such as bakeries, silk screening and embroidery, and merchandising, where former gang members work side-by-side baking bread, imprinting designs on clothing, and providing cleaning services for movie locations.

Fr. Boyle has been criticized for officiating at funerals of slain gang members. He maintains that all people need to be treated with respect and dignity. "What I try to do is hold up the mirror to these kids and show them that they really have been created in God's image. As soon as they understand that they are exactly what God had in mind when he made them, then they begin to become that reality. And then their lives begin to change."

Fr. Gregory Boyle, S.J.

Epilogue: Why You Need the Church

Chapter 1 began with a description of those who describe themselves as "spiritual but not religious." This approach to faith is a missed opportunity to know Jesus, God-in-the-Flesh, and his Revelation of God the Father. The missed opportunity comes from not participating in the Catholic Church, especially in the Eucharist and other sacraments where Jesus remains present, bringing about Redemption through the saving actions of the Paschal Mystery.

Participating in the Paschal Mystery

Through every celebration of the Mass Catholics sacramentally participate in the Paschal Mystery of Christ:

> The Paschal mystery of Christ . . . cannot remain only in the past, because by his death

he destroyed death, and all that Christ is—all that he did and suffered for all men—participates in the divine eternity, and so transcends all times while being made present in them all. (*CCC*, 1085)

It is participation in the Paschal Mystery that Catholics discover the truth that life comes only through death. What transpired in Jesus' last days on earth was but a dramatic manifestation of an overall pattern of life, characterized simply as one of life—death—life. Jesus taught: "Unless a grain of wheat falls into the ground and dies, it remains only a single grain; but if it dies it yields a rich harvest." (Jn 12:24) The central challenge for a Christian disciple is to internalize and make this spiritual rhythm your own.

Through Christ's Paschal Mystery—present in the sacraments—Catholics are introduced to the peculiar pattern for Christian discipleship: If you want to be happy, work for the happiness of others. If you would be fulfilled, abandon the quest for fulfillment. In order to delight in the gifts of creation, you must learn to periodically abstain from them. To know the joy of the feast, you must embrace the longing that arises from the fast. This is the mystery that you participate in at each Eucharist.

Participation in the Mass is a bit like participation in a dance class. Think about how in a dance class the person at first may be likely to stumble. The steps and rhythms of the dance initially seem foreign. But over time the person learns how to internalize the moves; eventually their body just "knows" what to do.

Through the Mass you enter sacramentally into the rhythm of the Paschal Mystery. Participation in the Church though her liturgy is the way Catholics are drawn into the rhythms of Christian living and are formed, day by day, more deeply into relationship with Jesus.

Why do you need the Catholic Church? You need the Church to help you shape your life according to the Life, Passion, Death, Resurrection, and Glorification of Jesus.

analogy of faith: The understanding that every individual statement of belief must be viewed in the context of the entire body of Faith.

Annunciation: The visit by the angel Gabriel to the Virgin Mary to announce that she would be the Mother of the Savior. After giving her consent, Mary became Mother of Jesus by the power of the Holy Spirit. The Feast of the Annunciation is on March 25.

apologist: "Defender of the faith." A Catholic who works hard to dispel the false rumors about Catholicism and Christianity and who makes the faith appear both more reasonable and acceptable to non-Christians.

apostasy: The denial of Christ and the repudiation of the Christian Faith by a baptized Christian.

Apostles: Originally, the term referred to the Twelve whom Jesus chose to help him in his earthly ministry. The successors of the Twelve Apostles are the bishops. In the widest sense, the term refers to all of Christ's disciples whose mission is to preach his Gospel in word and deed. Apostles are those sent to be Christ's ambassadors to continue his work.

apostolate: The ways that Catholics participate in the saving mission of Christ through different roles and functions in the Church.

apostolic: One of the marks of the Church, this term comes from *apostle*, which means literally "having been sent."

Assumption: The Church dogma that teaches that the Blessed Mother, because of her unique role as the Mother of God, was taken directly to Heaven when her earthly life was over. The Feast of the Assumption is on August 15 and is a Holy Day of Obligation.

beatific vision: Seeing God "face-to-face" in Heaven, the source of our eternal happiness; the final union with the Triune God for all eternity.

begotten: A term that means "to bring about"; Jesus is begotten because he was not generated by God the Father as human fathers generate their children. He has always existed.

Blessed Trinity: The central mystery of the Christian Faith. It teaches that there are Three Divine Persons in one God: Father, Son, and Holy Spirit.

canon of Scripture: The official list of inspired books of the Bible. Catholics list forty-six Old Testament books and twenty-seven New Testament books in their canon.

capital punishment: The infliction of the death penalty on persons convicted of serious crimes. There are few contemporary conditions that warrant the death penalty due to the state's effectiveness at keeping criminals inoffensive through secure imprisonment.

capitalism: An economic system characterized by private investment and private ownership of goods, all operating in a free market.

catechesis: A process of "education in the faith" for young people and adults with the goal of making them disciples of Christ.

Catholic social teaching: The body of Church doctrine beginning with Pope Leo XIII's 1891 encyclical *Rerum Novarum* ("The Condition of Labor") that applies Jesus' Gospel to the lives of people living in society, including its institutions and its economic and political structures.

Church Fathers: A traditional designation given to theologians of the first eight centuries whose teachings made a lasting mark on the Church. Also called Fathers of the Church.

common good: The sum of the spiritual, material, and social conditions needed for a person to achieve full human dignity.

common priesthood of the faithful: The priesthood of all the baptized in which we share in Christ's work of Salvation.

contemplation: Wordless prayer whereby a person's mind and heart rest in God's goodness and majesty.

Covenant: The open-ended contract of love between God and human beings. Jesus' Death and Resurrection sealed God's New Covenant of love for all time.

Crusaders: The name for participants in one of the nine armed expeditions by Christians beginning in 1095 and ending in 1291 that were intended to drive the Muslims out of the Holy Land and in the process, reunite Christians of the East and West.

Crusades: The nine armed expeditions by Christians beginning in 1095 and ending in 1291 that were intended to drive the Muslims out of the Holy Land and in the process reunite Christians of the East and West.

Day of Atonement: Known as Yom Kippur, this is the holiest day of the year for the Jewish people. It is a day when Jews ask forgiveness for both communal and personal sins.

Deposit of Faith: "The heritage of faith contained in Sacred Scripture and Sacred Tradition, handed down in the Church from the time of the Apostles, from which the Magisterium draws all that it proposes for belief as being divinely revealed" (*Catechism of the Catholic Church*, Glossary).

disciples: Followers of Christ. A disciple is someone who learns from and follows Jesus and who accepts a share of his ministry in the world.

Doctor of the Church: A Church writer of great learning and holiness whose works the Church has highly recommended for studying and living the Faith.

dogmas: Central truths of Revelation that Catholics are obliged to believe.

domestic church: A name for the Christian family. In the family, parents and children exercise their priesthood of the baptized by worshiping God, receiving the sacraments, and witnessing to Christ and the Church by living as faithful disciples.

ecumenical councils: Gatherings of all the Catholic bishops of the world. The word *ecumenical* pertains to a theological recognition of and willingness to learn from those different faith traditions. Ecumenical councils determine those things that all the local churches (dioceses) will hold in common.

ecumenism: The movement, inspired and led by the Holy Spirit, that seeks the union of all Christian religions and eventually the unity of all peoples throughout the world within the Catholic Church.

episcopal collegiality: All the bishops of the Church with the pope as their head. This college together, but never without the pope, has supreme and full authority over the universal Church.

episcopal synod: A representative body of bishops assembled periodically by the pope to advise him on important Church concerns. It is not a legislative body.

evangelical counsels: Vows of personal poverty, chastity understood as lifelong celibacy, and obedience to a bishop or to the superior of a religious community.

evangelization: The bringing of the Good News of Jesus Christ to others through words and actions.

examination of conscience: An honest assessment of how well we have lived God's covenant of love. This examination leads us to accept responsibility for our sins and to realize our need for God's merciful forgiveness.

Great Commissioning: The instruction given by Jesus in Matthew 28:16–20 to spread the Gospel to the world and to baptize all nations in the name of the Father, and of the Son, and of the Holy Spirit.

heresy: An obstinate denial after Baptism to believe a truth that must be believed with divine and Catholic Faith, or an obstinate doubt about such truth.

hypocrisy: The condition of a person pretending to be something that he or she is not, especially in the case of morals or religion.

hypostatic union: A Greek term employed to describe the union of the human and divine natures of Jesus Christ, the Son of God, in the one divine person (*hypostasis*). The First Council of Ephesus used and affirmed this teaching.

idolatry: Worshiping something or someone other than the true God.

Immaculate Conception: The belief that Mary was conceived without Original Sin. The Feast of the Immaculate Conception is on December 8 and is a Holy Day of Obligation.

infallibility: A gift of the Holy Spirit whereby the pope and the bishops are preserved from error when proclaiming a doctrine related to Christian Faith or morals.

Inquisition: A Church tribunal established in the thirteenth century that was designed to curb heretical teachings and beliefs. In collaboration with secular authorities, papal representatives employed the Inquisition to judge the guilt of suspected heretics with the aim of getting them to repent. Unfortunately, before long, many abuses crept into the process.

intercession: A prayer of petition for the sake of others.

Kingdom of God: The reign or rule of God. The Kingdom of God has begun with the coming of Jesus Christ. It will exist in its perfect form at the end of time.

Liturgy of the Hours: The prayer of the Church; it is also known as the Divine Office. The Liturgy of the Hours utilizes the Scriptures, particularly the Psalms, for specific times of the day from early morning to late evening.

Magisterium: The official teaching authority of the Church. Jesus bestowed the right and power to teach in his name on Peter and the Apostles and their successors. The Magisterium is the bishops in communion with the successor of Peter, the bishop of Rome (pope).

marks of the Church: The four traditional marks of the Church are one, holy, catholic, and apostolic.

martyr: Someone who has been killed because of his or her faith. To be martyred is to be killed for one's faith.

mortal sin: A serious violation of God's law of love that results in the loss of sanctifying grace (God's life) in the soul of the sinner. To commit a mortal sin, there must be grave matter, full knowledge of the evil done, and full consent of the will.

motu propio: A Latin term that means "of his own accord." It signifies words in papal documents that were decided by the pope personally.

natural law: The moral sense God gave people to know through their intellect and reason what is good and what is evil. The natural law is written in the human heart and in all of God's creation.

New Covenant: The climax of Salvation History, the coming of Jesus Christ, the fullness of God's Revelation.

novena: A nine-day prayer for a certain intention.

Original Sin: The sin of disobedience committed by Adam and Eve that resulted in their loss of original holiness and justice and their becoming subject to sin and death. Original Sin also describes the fallen state of human nature into which all generations of people are born. Jesus Christ came to save all people from Original Sin (and all sin).

pantheism: The belief, in opposition to Christian doctrine, that God and nature are one and the same.

Papal States: Territories on the peninsula of Italy that were under control of the papacy from the sixth century until 1870.

Paschal Mystery: Christ's work of redemption, accomplished principally by his Passion Death, Resurrection, and glorious Ascension. This mystery is commemorated and made present through the sacraments, especially the Eucharist.

pastoral letter: An open letter by the bishop to the priests and people of his diocese offering instruction, advice, or directions for behavior regarding a special circumstance.

Pentecost: The day when the Holy Spirit descended on the Apostles and gave them the power to preach with conviction the message that Jesus is risen and is Lord of the universe.

Pharisee: A person who belonged to a religious party or sect in Jesus' day. *Pharisee* means "separated." The Pharisees thought of themselves as separated from others in Judaism because they strictly observed the Law to distinguish themselves from lukewarm religious practice and Gentile influence.

pontiff: A term that literally means "bridge-builder." It refers to the bishop of Rome, or pope.

predestination: A false doctrine taught by John Calvin that God determines people for Salvation or damnation before they are born and that no human effort can merit Salvation or entrance into the elect.

Protestant Reformation: An effort to reform the Catholic Church in the sixteenth century which led to the separation of large numbers of Christians from communion with Rome and with each other.

Protoevangelium: A term that means "the first gospel," which is found in Genesis 3:15, when God revealed he would send a Savior to redeem the world.

Purgatory: The state of purification that takes place after death for those who need to be made clean and holy before meeting the all-holy God in Heaven.

Real Presence: The unique and true presence of Christ in the Eucharist under the species or appearance of bread and wine.

sacramental graces: The grace of the Holy Spirit, given by Christ, that is proper to each sacrament.

sacramental: A sacred sign (e.g., an object, a place, or an action) that resembles the sacraments. Through the prayers of the Church, spiritual effects are signified and obtained.

Sacred Tradition: The living transmission of the Church's Gospel message found in the Church's teaching, life, and worship. It is faithfully preserved, handed on, and interpreted by the Church's Magisterium.

schism: A break in Christian unity that takes place when a group of Christians separates itself from the Church. This happens historically when the group breaks in union with the pope.

Second Coming: The final judgment of all humanity when Christ returns to earth. It is also known by its Greek name, *Parousia*, which means "arrival."

secularization: A process of drawing society away from religious orientation in order to make it more worldly and less influenced by religion.

socialism: A political and economic system based on common ownership and central regulation of productive economic resources.

solidarity: A Christian virtue of charity and friendship whereby members of the human family share material and spiritual goods.

stewardship: The proper use of the gifts God has given to us, in particular the care for creation that will allow the earth and its resources to flourish and be long lasting.

subsidiarity: The principle of Catholic social doctrine that says that no community of higher order (such as a national or state government) should do what can be done equally well or better by a community of lower order (such as a family or local community).

transcendence: A trait of God that refers to his total otherness and being infinitely beyond and independent of creation. While God is immanent to humanity with a deep and loving relationship with man and woman that resembles that of a parent for a child, God is neither male nor female. He is pure spirit. He is God.

vocation: The calling or destiny we have in this life and in the hereafter.

Subject Index

A

Abortion, 236–237

Abraham, 9–10, 186

Adam and Eve, 9, 186

Affordable Care Act, 219, 224

Agape, 51, 116

Alexander VII, Pope, 70

Ambrose, St., 54, 127

American Blesseds, 138

American Servants of God, 139

American Venerables, 138–139

Analogy of Faith, 191

André Bessette, St., 138

Anne-Thérèse Guérin, St., 138

Annunciation, 128

Anointing of the Sick, Sacrament of, 109
    sacramental graces of, 109

Apollinarianism, 59

Apologist, 76

Apostasy, 55–56

Apostles
    conversion of St. Peter, 164
    Council of Jerusalem, 29–30, 164
    defined, 20
    Gentiles and early Church, 28–30

Great Commissioning, 25–26
    growth of early Church and, 26–27
    Jesus appearing to, 20–21
    Pentecost and, 21–22, 163
    persecution and, 28
    Peter's role in early Church, 26
    Philip and Ethiopian, 163
    preaching to Samaritans, 163

Apostles' Creed
    Blessed Trinity, 194
    Church dogma, 194
    historical perspective on, 54
    as source of unity, 54

Apostolate, 226

Apostolic, defined, 183

Apostolicity of Church
    canon law, 201–202
    Church dogma, 194–200
    Deposit of Faith and, 190
    doctrine of Church, 200
    God's Revelation, 186–189
    leadership of Church and, 203–207
    as mark of Church, 48, 244
    precepts of the Church, 201–202
    preserving Church's memory, 190–193
    sacred memory of Church, 185–188
    Sacred Scripture and, 191
    Sacred Tradition and, 192–193
    sharing Church's memory, 194–202

teaching Magisterium of bishops, 205–207

ways Church remains apostolic, 184

Apostolic societies, 115

Apostolic succession, 74–82

  bishops and, 74, 76–78

  deacons and, 78

  early Church and, 76–77

  importance of papacy, 78–82

  priest and, 78

  role in unity of Church, 74–76

Arianism, 58

Assumption of Mary, 130, 197

Athenagoras I, Patriarch, 60

Augustine, St., 16, 51–52, 166

  on Holy Spirit's role, in Church, 22, 23

  mixed body of saints and sinners, 105, 124

Authoritative doctrine, 200

B

Babylonian Exile, 10–11

Badin, Stephen, 175

Baptism, Sacrament of, 110–112

  Apostles' Creed and, 54

  common priesthood of the faithful, 110–111

  early Church, 27

  as foundation of unity with all Christians, 159–160

  sacramental graces of, 108

Baraga, Frederic, 174

Barron, Robert, 234

Beatification, of saint, 120

Beatific vision, 121

Beatitudes, as moral guide, 110

Begotten, defined, 150

Benedictines, 115

Benedict XVI, Pope, 31–32, 48, 64, 70, 155, 237

  new evangelization, 230, 231

Bernadette, St., 198

Bernardin, Joseph, Cardinal, 167, 237, 239

Bernard of Clairvaux, St., 187

Bible, Protestant Reformation and *sola scriptura*, 60

Bishop of Rome, 30

Bishops, 30

  college of, 78

  in early Church, 76–78

  episcopal synods and, 76–77

  governing office of, 204

  local church and unity with diversity, 154–155

  pastoral letter of, 206

  roles of, 113

  sanctification office of, 203–204

  selection of, 74

  teaching office of, 204–207

Blesseds, American, 138

Blessed (Holy) Trinity

  Apostles' Creed and, 54, 194

  defined, 48

Constantine, 176

Constantinople, Church of, 57

Constantinople, sacking of, 60

Consumerism

    religion and, 5–6

    upgrading mentality, 5–6

Contemplation, 187

Cope, Marianne, Bl., 175

Council of Chalcedon, 59

Council of Ephesus, 59

Council of Jerusalem, 29–30, 164

Council of Nicaea, 58, 77

Council of Trent, 61, 62–63, 77

    Tridentine Mass, 70

Covenant

    with Chosen People, 102

    defined, 10

    with Israelites, 10–12

    New Covenant, 12

Creation, diversity of, 149–150

Cross, Church born on, 14–15

Crusaders, 60

Crusades, 103

Culture, Catholicity and, 165–169

Cunningham, Lawrence, 120

Cyprian, St., 51

Cyril, St., 176–177

D

Damien De Veuster, St., 138, 175, 222, 223

Day, Dorothy, 249–250

Day of Atonement, 102

Deacons, 27, 74

    apostolic succession and, 78

    roles of, 114

Decius, 55

Definitive doctrine, 200

de Monthceuil, Yves, 17

Deposit of Faith, 61, 184

    apostolicity and, 190

de Smet, Pierre, 175

Dignity of human person, 237, 239

Diocese, 75

    bishop's teaching office at diocesan level, 205–206

Disciples, defined, 13

Diversity

    of creation, 149–150

    as strength for unity of Church, 48–49

    unity with diversity, 152, 154

Divine Office, 97

Divine Revelation

    doctrine and, 200

    Holy Spirit and, 199–200

Divine Word, Trinitarian mission of, 199

P

Pantheism, 150

Papacy. *See also* Pope

apostolic succession and, 79–82

defending primacy of, 79–82

importance of, 79

roles of, 80, 82

Paschal Mystery

Church born from, 14–15

defined, 12

living graces of Baptism and, 110, 111

Pastoral letter, 206

Paul, St., 6–7, 17

Christ and Church, 52–53

early life of, 28–29

marks of the Church, 33

missionary journeys of, 26, 29

Paul VI, Pope, 60, 131, 215, 230, 231, 233

Penance

renewal to holiness and, 124, 126

sacramental graces of, 108

Pentecost

as birthday of Church, 22

events of, 21–22

missionary work of Apostles after, 163–164

Peter's speech at, 21–22

Perfection, in living a holy life, 109–110

Perpetual virginity, 129

Persecution, early Church and, 28

Peter, St.

conversion of, 164

Gentiles and, 29–30

primacy passed on to bishop of Rome, 30

role in early Church, 26

speech at Pentecost, 21–22

Peyton, Patrick, Servant of God, 139

Pharisee, 28

Philip, St., 163

Pius IX, Pope, 252

Immaculate Conception of Mary, 197, 198

Pius XI, Pope, 63

Pius XII, Pope, 63, 78, 129–130

Assumption of Mary, 197

Pontifex Maximus, 79

Pontiff, 80

Poor

concern for, and Israelites, 10

friendship with, and Community of Sant'Egidio, 227–228

Mary as mother who care for, 131

preferential option and love for poor and vulnerable, 240

Pope. *See also* Papacy; *specific popes*

as bishop of Rome, 30

infallibility of, 195, 197

Peter's primacy passed on to, 30

tasks of, 203

S

Sacramental, 125

Sacramental graces

of Anointing of the Sick, 109

of Baptism, 108

of Confirmation, 108

defined, 107

of Eucharist, 108

of Holy Orders, 109

of Matrimony, 109

of Penance, 108

Sacraments, unity with one another, 68–69

Sacred Scripture

apostolicity and, 191

canon of Scripture, 191

defined, 190

interpreting Scripture, 191

literal and spiritual sense of, 191

Sacred Tradition

apostolicity and, 192–193

defined, 58, 190

Deposit of Faith, 61

Magisterium and, 193

response to Gnosticism, 58

Sacrifice, in Old Testament, 110–111

Saints. *See also specific saints*

American, 138

beatification and canonization process, 120, 137

beatific vision and, 121

intercession of, 121

list of American saints, 138–139

mark of holiness calling to, 99

Mary, Queen of all saints, 127–128

miracles associated with, 119

as models of holiness, 119–120

praying to, 120–121

private revelations and, 187

relics of, 119

religious medals of, 125

unity with, 72–73

veneration of, 119–120

Salvation

Church necessary for, 160–161

grace alone, 61

predestination, 61

Sanctification office of bishops, 203–204

Sant'Egidio Community, 227

Schism, 56–60

Eastern Schism, 57, 60

main issues that led to, 57

Seamless garment image, 167, 237, 239

Second Vatican Council, 9

bishop's role and, 77

culture and, 169

Decree on Ecumenism, 63–64

ecumenical dialogue with Orthodox Church, 60

Mass and, 70–71

papal primacy, 80

Primary Source Index

Scripture Index

Jesus and the Church

Catechism of the Catholic Church Index

PHOTO CREDITS

AP

p. 30 © 2006 AP Photo/Alessandra Tarantino

p. 140 © 2010 AP Photo/The Green Bay Press-Gazette, Jim Matthews

p. 197 © 2013 AP Photo/L'Osservatore Romano

p. 219 © 2008 AP Photo/Jens Meyer

p. 274 © 2004 AP Photo/Kevork Djansezian

Art Resource

p. 29 Scala/Art Resource, NY

p. 33 Gianni Dagli Orti/The Art Archive at Art Resource, NY

Bill Wittman

pp. 15, 41, 108, 116, 117, 203, 204, 210, 251, 252–253, 268, 270, cover

Corbis

p. 28 © SHABELE MEDIA/X02084/Reuters/Corbis

p. 31 © DAVID GRAY/Reuters/Corbis

p. 32 © BOBBY YIP/Reuters/Corbis

p. 56 © MOHAMMED AMEEN/Reuters/Corbis

pp. 67, 85 © Robin Alam/Icon SMI/Corbis

p. 80 © Gregorio Borgia/ /AP/Corbis

p. 95 © HO/Reuters/Corbis

p. 103 © Andrea Cova/Splash News/Corbis

p. 104 © Reuters/CORBIS

pp. 119, 134 © Andres Pardo/Demotix/Corbis

p. 145 © Alex Brandon/ /AP/Corbis

p. 145 © Janet Mayer/Splash News/Corbis

pp. 147, 170 © Steve Raymer/National Geographic Society/Corbis

p. 157 © M. Spencer Green/ /AP/Corbis

pp. 159, 171 © RONALD KABUUBI/epa/Corbis

p. 167 © Les Stone/Sygma/Corbis

p. 168 © Alex Masi/Corbis

p. 181 © Sebastien Desarmaux/Godong/Corbis

p. 219 © NIR ELIAS/Reuters/Corbis

p. 227 © Stefano Montesi/Demotix/Corbis

p. 228 © Philippe Lissac/Godong/Corbis

p. 228 © Fred de Noyelle/Godong/Corbis

p. 228 © Alessandro Serranò / Demotix/Demotix/Demotix/Corbis

p. 228 © TONY GENTILE/Reuters/Corbis

p. 229 © Keeler, Scott/ZUMA Press/Corbis

p. 230 & 246 © OSSERVATORE ROMANO/Reuters/Corbis

p. 233 © Pascal Deloche/Godong/Corbis

p. 244 © Sebastien Desarmaux/Godong/Corbis

p. 261 © Corbis

p. 265 © Vittoriano Rastelli/Corbis

p. 266 © Marco Campagna/Demotix/Corbis

p. 272 © Rick D'Elia/Corbis

John Kennington Photography

p. 136

GoodSalt

pp. 190, 209 © GoodSalt Inc./Providence Collection

p. 255 © GoodSalt Inc./Bill Osborne

p. 255 © GoodSalt Inc./Lars Justinen

HappySaints.com

p. 99 © 2014 Victor Teh, happysaints.com

Holy Cross Vocations—the United States Province of Priests and Brothers

pp. 74, 85 © Matt Cashore/University of Notre Dame

NET Ministries, Inc. (www.netusa.org)

p. 162, 165, 172, 179, cover

Pro-Life Action League

p. 236, 246

SuperStock

p. 72 DeAgostini / DeAgostini

p. 192 Ray Laskowitz / Ray Laskowitz

p. 263 Richard Cummins / Richard Cummins

pp. 47, 84 age fotostock / age fotostock

p. 103 Richard Levine / age fotostock

p. 55 Lucas Vallecillos / age fotostock

pp. 154, 171 Bruce Bi / age fotostock

p. 259 Ivan Vdovin / age fotostock

p. 120 age fotostock / age fotostock

pp. 223, 241 Jim West / age fotostock

pp. 221, 245 Walter Zerla / age fotostock

pp. 183, 208 GeoStock / Exactostock

pp. 3, 6, 35, 109, 111, 160, 161 Photononstop / Photononstop

pp. 27, 178 Corbis / Corbis

pp. 108, 114, 259 Image Asset Management Ltd. / Image Asset Management Ltd.

pp. 28, 33, 57, 88, 121, 163, 214, 258, 262, 264 DeAgostini / DeAgostini

p. 205 imageBROKER / imageBROKER

p. 258 Raimund Kutter/imageb / imageBROKER

pp. 50, 84 Florian Kopp/imagebro / imageBROKER

p. 176 Lydie Gigerichova/ima / imageBROKER

p. 266 Eye Ubiquitous / Eye Ubiquitous

pp. 21, 143 Design Pics / Design Pics

p. 131 Keith Levit / Design Pics

pp. 70, 78 Robert Harding Picture Library / Robert Harding Picture Library

pp. 81, 124, 216 Universal Images Group / Universal Images Group

p. 163 Hanan Isachar / Hanan Isachar

p. 216 Prisma VWPics / Prisma VWPics

p. 227 vito arcomano / Marka

p. 142 Art Archive, The / Art Archive, The

pp. 194, 209 Tino Soriano / National Geographic

p. 18 Elena Elisseeva / Elena Elisseeva

p. 199 Pantheon / Pantheon

pp. 39, 52, 87, 164 Fine Art Images / Fine Art Images

p. 264 Album / Oronoz / Album